SOCIALIST HERITAGE

NEW ANTHROPOLOGIES OF EUROPE

Michael Herzfeld, Melissa L. Caldwell, and
Deborah Reed-Danahay, *editors*

SOCIALIST HERITAGE

The Politics of Past and Place in Romania

Emanuela Grama

INDIANA UNIVERSITY PRESS

This book is a publication of

Indiana University Press
Office of Scholarly Publishing
Herman B Wells Library 350
1320 East 10th Street
Bloomington, Indiana 47405 USA

iupress.indiana.edu

Manufactured in the United States of America

Cataloging information is available from the Library of Congress.

ISBN 978-0-253-04479-2 (hdbk.)
ISBN 978-0-253-04480-8 (pbk.)
ISBN 978-0-253-04483-9 (web PDF)

1 2 3 4 5   23 22 21 20 19

To Geoff
and in loving memory of my grandparents

CONTENTS

ACKNOWLEDGMENTS

Bᴏᴏᴋꜱ ʜᴀᴠᴇ ꜱᴛᴀʀᴛᴇᴅ ᴀꜱ ᴘᴀʟɪᴍᴘꜱᴇꜱᴛꜱ: ʟᴀʏᴇʀꜱ ᴏɴ ʟᴀʏᴇʀꜱ of meaning, forming a map of connections and influences that go back in time. This book is a palimpsest as well. It began as two chapters of my dissertation, written while in the anthropology and history doctoral program at the University of Michigan. I am grateful for the mentorship I received from my doctoral committee. Katherine Verdery sent me notes of encouragement while I was doing fieldwork, read and commented on several drafts of my dissertation, and most importantly taught me that one should always aim high and never settle for less. Her outstanding scholarship has been exemplary. My gratitude also goes to Gillian Feeley-Harnik, for showing me that the key to almost everything is first to wonder and then to take thousands of notes. Ever since grad school, I have not ceased to be inspired and humbled by Gillian's originality, astuteness, and kindness. The late Fernando Coronil asked me, "Why heritage?"—making me pause and seek to understand what is my own "Romania." His keen intellect, warmth, and politically engaged scholarship is sorely missed. Brian Porter, Krisztina Fehérváry, Alaina Lemon, Stuart Kirsch, David Cohen, Kathleen Canning, and Michelle Mitchell offered me advice and encouragement at different stages of my graduate studies.

Ann Arbor was truly a home for me in so many ways. I enjoyed the vibrant intellectual atmosphere of graduate school and the sense of shared fellowship, especially with friends and colleagues like Ania Cichopek, Kim Strozewski, Britt Halvorson, Henrike Floruschbosch, Oana Mateescu, Daniel Lățea, Luciana Aenășoaie, Laura Brown, Chandra Bhimull, Maria Perez, Doug Rogers, Genese Sodikoff, Josh Reno, Laura Heinemann and Chris Weber, Sara and Josh First, Emil Kerenji, Edin Hajdarpasic, Alice Weinreb, Yasmeen Hanoosh, and Susanne Unger.

Part of the research for this book was carried out with the generous support of the following institutions: the International Research and Exchanges Board (IREX), through a 2005–6 IARO fellowship funded by the US Department of State's Title VIII Program; the Wenner-Gren Foundation, through a 2006 Individual Doctoral Research Grant; and the Institute for Advanced Studies "New Europe College" (Bucharest, Romania), through a 2007–8 "Europe" research fellowship funded by the Volkswagen Foundation. In addition, I benefited from research grants from the Center for Russian and Eastern European Studies,

Center for European Studies, Rackham Graduate School, Eisenberg Institute for Historical Studies, and Doctoral Program in Anthropology and History, all at the University of Michigan. A 2008–9 Fellowship for East European Studies from the American Council of Learned Societies provided support for dissertation writing. During the summers of 2015 and 2016, I conducted additional fieldwork and archival research in Bucharest with the support of a Falk research grant and a Berkman grant, both from Carnegie Mellon University. These grants also enabled me to spend some time at the Library of Congress in Washington, DC, where I consulted the collection of two major Romanian dailies between 1990 and 2015, in both microfilm and paper. I thank especially Arlene Balkansky, reference specialist of the periodicals section, for her help.

I am especially grateful to the people I met in the buildings and streets of the Old Town in summer 2016, who were willing to share their stories and woes with me (and whose names I changed for purposes of anonymity). I also greatly benefited from the insights and expertise of other interlocutors I met in Bucharest, especially (in alphabetical order) Ştefan Bâlciu, Alexandru Beldiman, Maria Berza, Şerban Cantacuzino, Mariana Celac, Liviu Chelcea, Peter Derer, Nicolae Lascu, Mioara Lujanschi, Vera Marin, Dan Mohanu, Anca Oroveanu, Andrei Pippidi, Andrei Pleşu, Corina Popa, Irina Popescu-Criveanu, Şerban Popescu-Criveanu, Cătălina Preda, Irina Prodan, Gabriel Simion, Teresa Sinigalia, Bogdan Suditu, and Aurelian Trişcu. I am also thankful for the professionalism and kind help of many archivists at the National Archives in Bucharest (ANIC), as well as of archivist Iuliu Şerban of the National Institute for Patrimony. As a Europa fellow between October 2007 and June 2008, I relished being part of the community of New Europe College (NEC), the institution that Andrei Pleşu, Anca Oroveanu, and Marina Hasnaş have transformed into an intellectual and human oasis in the midst of a turbulent Bucharest. I also thank Carmen Popescu and my peers of the 2007–8 Europa fellowship cohort for their warm collegiality and critical comments on my work in progress.

The chance of being one of the 2011–12 Max Weber postdoctoral fellows at the European University Institute in Florence, Italy, was a multilayered gift. I thank Pavel Kolar for his mentorship; Ramon Marimon, the then director of the program, for his support and flexibility; and especially those friends who made a world of difference to me: Sheila Neder Cezeretti, Karin de Vries, and Dan Lee. As a visiting assistant professor in the history department at Oberlin College, I received strategic advice from my colleagues, especially Len Smith, Annemarie Samartino, Steven Volk, and Emer O'Dwyer, as well as Erika Hoffman-Dilloway and Crystal Biruk in anthropology. Starting with 2013, being part of the history department at Carnegie Mellon University has been a privilege. My colleagues Paul Eiss, Lisa Tetrault, Michal Friedman, and Wendy

Goldman read different parts of this manuscript and gave critical comments. Other colleagues such as Caroline Acker, Judith Schachter and Albrecht Funk, Kate Lynch, Don Sutton, John Soluri, Joe Trotter, Noah Theriault, and Chris Phillips offered encouragement and listened to arguments in progress. Donna Harsch, my department head, relieved me of teaching responsibilities for one semester so that I could focus exclusively on revisions.

In summer 2018, when health reasons prevented me from traveling, I benefited from Narcis Tulbure's unique generosity. He went to the archives in Bucharest several times to request files and sent me digital copies. Archaeologist Florin Curta of the University of Florida shared his wide expertise and resources, especially invaluable information about the first excavations at the Old Court. Nick Falk of Urbed, London, sent me key materials about the British team's proposal for the Old Town.

At different stages of this book, Irina Livezeanu, Ania Cichopek-Gajraj, and Josh Reno read and offered feedback on three separate chapters. Britt Halvorson generously shared her insights by reading and commenting on this manuscript. Paul Sager copyedited some of the chapter drafts, and Amberle Sherman copyedited a draft of chapter 5. Alex Iacob, Norihiro Haruta, and Alexandru Stoicescu kindly allowed me to use some of their photographs of the Old Town. Daniella Collins created four beautiful maps. At the last minute, Răzvan Voinea, Sarah Andrews, and, indirectly, Miriam Putnam-Perez helped me retrieve three important images. Maria Mănescu, editor in chief of *Arhitectura* journal, and Ileana Tureanu, president of the Romanian Union of Architects, granted me permission to use some of the visual material published in the journal. Ştefan Bâlciu, manager of Institutul Naţional al Patrimoniului, and Adrian Majuru, manager of the Bucharest Municipality Museum, allowed me to use photos from the archives and journals of these institutions. My deepest thanks!

At Indiana University Press, I am grateful to Jennika Baines for her kind and constant support of this project, as well as to Allison Chaplin, Rachel Rosolina, and Leigh McLennon for guiding this book through the production process. I would also like to thank the two anonymous readers for their invaluable suggestions on an earlier draft of this book, as well as Joyce Li, who copyedited the final manuscript.

Throughout the years, I was lucky to enjoy the friendship of an extraordinary group of people. Since my arrival in Pittsburgh in 2013, I have valued the wonderful company of friends such as Michal Friedman, Paul Eiss, Lisa Tetrault, Andreea Ritivoi, Katja Wezel, Laura Brown, Heath Cabot, Anna Phillips, Laura Gotkowitz, and Lillian Chong. Over the years and across the ocean, Marlene Ionescu and her family have been dear and loyal friends. Jane and Dan Hinshaw have been extraordinary friends during extraordinary circumstances. I will always be grateful for their amazing support and kindness, especially for their hospitality and generosity when I found myself at a crossroad. Laura Mihai has been a wonderful presence in my life, and I am thankful for her friendship, honesty, and ability to see beauty in almost anything. From the time we met on the Diag in Ann Arbor on a September day so long ago, Ania Cichopek-Gajraj has been a great friend and a constant source of encouragement. I cherish her sense of humor, her keen intellect, and her warmth. Britt Halvorson is one of the most extraordinary people I have met. Her unbounded creativity, brilliance, and tenacity have inspired me in more ways than I can count. I am truly grateful for her sharp and creative comments on my work and for her generous friendship.

I also thank my family. My mother, Veronica Paraschiv, has shown me how to stay strong and positive no matter what life throws at you. My sister-in-law, Heather Hutchison, and my parents-in-law, Janet and John Hutchison, have shared their warmth and great humor. My wonderful stepkids, Bella and Danny, introduced me to the world of Harry Potter and especially to the magic of their innocence. My partner, husband, and best friend, Geoff Hutchison, has been a constant source of fun, love, optimism, kindness, and wisdom. This book is also a late token of love to the memory of my grandparents, Nedelea and Niculae Paraschiv, who partially raised me, who taught me the alphabet, and who always believed in me. Their infinite love has made me who I am.

A NOTE ON SOURCES

SECONDARY SOURCES ARE REFERENCED IN THE TEXT USING parenthetical citations. To make it easier for the reader to identify and locate a wide range of primary sources, from archival references to interviews, online content, and newspapers, I have chosen to cite primary sources using endnotes. In the case of archival sources, the citation includes the name of the archive, the name of the documentary fond, the number of the file, and the specific page numbers in the file. In some archives (e.g., those of the National Institute of Patrimony), some files were not included in an archival fond; sometimes, these files were also composed of a series of disparate documents that did not have continuous page numbers. In those cases, I identify the source by the archive, the file number, the title of the document, and the specific pages within the document. Excerpts from interviews or fieldwork conversations are cited by the date, the place, and the pseudonym I gave the interviewee. Newspaper articles retrieved from printed newspapers are cited by the name of the newspaper, the date, the original title of the article, and (if identifiable) the journalists' names.

Newspapers and Periodicals Cited as Primary Sources

Arhitectura (1952–89)
România Liberă (1990–2015)
Adevărul (1990–2015)
Revista 22 (1990–98, 2000–2015)

LIST OF ABBREVIATIONS AND SHORT NAMES

ANIC: Arhivele Naţionale Istorice Centrale, National Central Historical
Archives, Bucharest
Fond Cabinetul Consiliului de Miniştri
Fond: CC al PCR-Cancelarie

AINIM: Arhiva Institutului Naţional al Monumentelor Istorice, Archives
of the National Institute of Historic Monuments (currently Institutul
Naţional al Patrimoniului, National Institute of Patrimony), Bucharest

City Museum: Muzeul de Istorie a Oraşului Bucureşti, the Museum of History
of the City of Bucharest

DHM: Direcţia Monumentelor Istorice, the Department of Historic
Monuments (1947–77), Bucharest

Project Bucharest: Institutul "Proiect Bucureşti," Bucharest

city council: Sfatul Popular al Municipiului Bucureşti, the city people's
council (1947–89)

city hall: Primăria municipiului Bucureşti, Bucharest's city hall (1990–)

State Committee for Architecture: Comitetul de Stat pentru Construcţii,
Arhitectură şi Sistematizare, the State Committee for Building,
Architecture, and Urban Planning, Bucharest

UNESCO archives: Fond Romania, Paris

SOCIALIST HERITAGE

INTRODUCTION

"Everyone wants to come see the historic center, but I am disgusted and bored with it. I am sick of it! This house is like a deserted mansion. . . . At night, drug users come into the courtyard to do shots and piss. A house collapsed right across the street; all of the rats from there came here. You sit in the courtyard and see them running across the pavement."[1] This is what Carmen, a woman in her midtwenties, told me when I asked how long she had been living in this three-story building in Bucharest's Old Town. It was the only home she had ever known. Born right before Romania's communist regime collapsed in 1989, she had grown up in this building. A few years before we spoke in May 2016, her parents moved to the countryside and left the single room that they used to share to Carmen and her partner. The young couple then built a small addition in the courtyard, where they put in a kitchen. When I met her, Carmen was sitting outside her kitchen, drinking coffee from a plastic cup and smoking a cigarette.

At the time I visited, forty-three other families lived in this now dangerously decrepit building, which in the late nineteenth century and throughout the interwar period used to be a middle-class hotel. The utilities the building provided during that time (running water in each room and a common bathroom at the end of the corridor) did not change much after 1948, when the hotel became nationalized and the rooms and apartments were rented to poorer people as state tenants. Only the apartments facing the street were more spacious and had their own bathrooms. When I spoke with Carmen, her building was still government-owned housing, but city authorities had stopped investing in it. Carmen told me that she did not remember the last time any repairs had been done, because "the state [was] at war with the [former] owner," a "war," she said, that had started more than six years before our conversation. The building was officially considered a historic monument, but no one seemed to care about its semidecrepit look—and its fate is shared by many other houses that currently form the compact urban tissue of this neighborhood in the center of Bucharest.

Although relatively abandoned by state authorities during the late communist period and throughout the 1990s, the district came back to life, so to speak, when the local officials suddenly viewed its eclectic architecture and its narrow cobblestone streets as material proof of Bucharest's European history. In the mid-2000s, with funds from the European Union, local authorities launched a refurbishment of the area meant to attract tourists, consumers, and investors. The revitalization project entailed not only a thorough overhaul of the underground infrastructure and new pavement for the streets but also a change of name. In different historical periods, the district was known among Bucharest's residents as the Old Town, or Lipscani, from the name of the main commercial street that runs through its core. Starting in the mid-2000s, the authorities branded the district as the "historic center," a name intended to make it more appealing to Western tourists. It is not surprising that such a privatization of history enabled the authorities to further disavow their responsibility to the city and its people. City hall used the uncertain legal status of many of the historic buildings in the district to justify their lack of intervention in the buildings' preservation, while pointing to state tenants, many of them living in semidecrepit buildings, as being the only ones responsible for the dire state of their homes.

In this book, I draw on archival and ethnographic research on Bucharest's Old Town to argue that heritage making (and unmaking) functions as a form of governance. The process through which a regime or a group places objects and people in and outside the category of "heritage" with an eye to creating its own legacy is not just an attempt to stylize, essentialize, or create a distinct aesthetic representation for a historical narrative. It also signals and tangibly reifies subtle hierarchies and criteria of political and social belonging. An analysis of how a place moves in and out of the category of "heritage" offers a unique window into the broader process of state making; this includes how a new state comes into being by creating its own history in order to define the criteria of belonging to the body politic.

Heritage is implicitly political. By appealing to a rhetoric of heritage that promoted sanitized histories and idealized notions of community, power structures from states to corporations have attempted to influence individuals to develop new loyalties and behave in ways that served elite political and economic interests (Breglia 2006; Collins 2015; Smith 2006).[2] However, in comparison to nineteenth- and early twentieth-century instances in which defining heritage was often the exclusive right of the nation-state (Swenson 2013), what has distinguished the processes of heritage reification emerging at the end of the twentieth century has been their intensely rhizome-like quality, their embeddedness in an increasingly diffused web of contradicting loyalties and relations.[3] Starting especially with the 1970s and the emergence of identity politics, various groups, from indigenous communities to states and international organizations, have negotiated their role in promoting the right to heritage as a human right (Coombe and Weiss 2015; Hodder 2010; Jokilehto 2012; Meskell 2010, 2015; Silberman 2012; Silverman and Ruggles 2007). Previously marginalized groups, such as indigenous communities, have increasingly mobilized the rhetoric of heritage to pursue political visibility, to claim stewardship over territory (such as archaeological sites), and to insist on their property rights over unique forms of knowledge, ranging from biodiversity to customary law (Coombe 2016; Coombe and Weiss 2015; Geismar 2013). By engaging with heritage as a system of knowledge that (re)defines and orders social relations, such groups have managed to upend practices that previously had been the exclusive right of the powerful. Heritage appears thus not just as a "hegemonic idiom," as anthropologist Jaume Franquesa (2013, 346) put it, or a trope and method of interpellation for people to adopt norms and behaviors that they would otherwise reject but also as a strategy of political empowerment.

This book shows how such empowerment does not happen, however, only through valuing unique knowledge or objects as "heritage." In fact, defiant political action may emerge as an active *antiheritage* stand. State officials may embrace such a stance to sever links to a problematic communist past and to promote themselves as fervent proponents of Europeanization, innovation, privatization, and capitalism. At the same time, an active rejection of heritage could signal the disenchantment of particular groups with state institutions. The poor residents living in the Old Town's dilapidated buildings have adopted a sarcastic tone when they talk about heritage. Carmen's bitter comments about how "disgusted and bored" she felt conveyed her adverse reaction to empty rhetoric meant to cover up the reality of the Old Town as she knew it: a place the local authorities advertised as a "historic district" that "everyone wanted to see" when in fact they did not bother to renovate the houses. But there was more to her criticism: she pointed to the emptiness of the very meaning of *heritage*, seeing herself as stripped of dignity while her own home became a public restroom for consumers looking for distraction in the Old Town. To her, "heritage" was a mockery, a byword for state corruption and the city officials' blatant disregard for the old buildings and their people.

I examine how, at different political junctures, from the early 1950s to 2016, politicians, urban planners, historic preservation experts, and state tenants have negotiated power by imbuing old buildings and their remnants with cultural and historical value—or, on the contrary, denying those buildings and their people a place in history. At different political moments, state officials in communist and postcommunist Romania have mediated their relationship with their subjects and asserted control over them through objects, ranging from archaeological artifacts to ruined walls and redecorated house facades. The authorities' care or lack thereof for old buildings and their decision to assign these buildings a heritage status or not signaled whom they viewed as "proper" citizens and whom they regarded as unworthy of social rights and political visibility.

Such an analysis is particularly relevant in contexts that have undergone profound political and social transformations, such as the postwar communist bloc and the subsequent postcommunist regime. With a focus on Romania after 1945 to the early 2010s, *Socialist Heritage* analyzes the specific expertise, urban visions, aesthetic choices, and material forms that state officials have used to construct a narrative about the past with an eye to gaining legitimacy in the present. Specifically, it pays attention to what objects and aesthetic categories were invested with political meaning, by whom, and under what circumstances. Moreover, it shows how state officials employed such objects to maneuver their relation with their citizens—that is, to create social and ethnic distinctions and new categories of belonging.

Romania is a country in Eastern Europe, a region that has been a major laboratory for radical political experiments during the last two centuries. During the first half of the twentieth century, Romania's political scene was dominated by an intense nationalism that aimed to silence the country's German, Hungarian, Jewish, and Roma minorities. After the Communist Party came to power at the end of World War II, the new regime initially made their mandatory bows to Stalinist USSR, but soon after Stalin's death, state officials turned to nationalism. They did so with an eye to making themselves more appealing to the population and to gaining relative autonomy from the Soviet Union. Despite the alleged internationalism promoted by communist ideology, the Romanian postwar state fully embraced nationalism. Party and state leaders not only commissioned historians to rewrite a narrative about the national past but also turned to archaeologists and architects to redefine Romanian cultural heritage through the remodeling of urban space.

I suggest the production of a socialist modernity in 1950s Romania—a common theme in studies about the emergence of the communist regimes in the Soviet bloc—must be analyzed in tandem with the production of a national history.[4] This book explores how Romanian state authorities translated these two interconnected projects in material terms. It argues that the state aimed to transform Bucharest into a city of the future and of the past—a modern capital whose urban nucleus represented a national history ideologically compatible with a socialist future. The communist state officials collaborated first with archaeologists and then with architects to make the Old Town into a symbol of the city's Romanian past. These experts reconstructed a ruined sixteenth-century palace in the middle of the district and promoted it as a national historic site signaling the Romanians' fight for independence against the Ottoman

Empire. After the palace was open to the public in 1972, the local officials sought to redecorate the old houses of the Old Town and thus transform the entire district into an architectural site allegedly showcasing a Romanian architectural style. The Old Town's new political function was twofold. First, the district was to function as a point of contrast with the modern socialist architecture being built in other areas of the city and, thus, to highlight rapid urbanization. Second, this transformation was intended to Romanianize the urban space. The planned remodeling of the old houses was to be the final stage of the economic and ethnic nationalization of the Old Town after 1945, with the communist state whitewashing its multiethnic history as the houses and shops became state property and most of their Jewish residents left the country.

The book thus joins a body of work (Berdahl 1999; Berdahl, Bunzl, and Lampland 2000; Burawoy and Verdery 1999; Fehérváry 2013; Rogers 2004; Stan 2013; Stark and Bruszt 1998; Verdery 2003) that has challenged an approach to socialism as a radical social and cultural break with the past. My study shows how the communist state in Romania sought to exploit the past for its own benefit, using history in the form of historic buildings and archaeological artifacts as yet another instrument in its effort to consolidate its power in Romania's postwar society. Neither the goal of creating a past to support the future nor the complex negotiations about how to define and reach that goal disappeared with socialism's collapse. The postcommunist elites parlayed the meanings attached to the urban environment into financial and political resources that allowed them, depending on their situation, to consolidate or to challenge state power. In the 1990s, using the pretext that the Old Town had no historic or economic value, state officials opposed proposals to restore the historic buildings in the district. In fact, their strategy was to retain control of the real estate value of a highly central location. The houses and commercial venues of the Old Town played a key role in these politicians' consolidation of economic power and their ability to become the first millionaires of the postsocialist transition. In the 2000s, however, when Romania sought to be included in the European Union, state officials suddenly acknowledged the value of the Old Town's eclectic architecture, presenting it as a material proof of Romania's historical links to Europe. The Old Town thus has proved to be an ambiguous location, absorbing and reflecting multiple moments of change. The constant negotiations around the district, its people, and its buildings form a thick history that refutes a clear distinction between the socialist and postsocialist periods.

Ultimately, this is a book about the fraught attempt to create symbolic and physical spaces of belonging whose aura and aesthetics convey a link to the past and enable distinct groups to feel at home in history—or, better put, to entice such groups to recognize those distinct spaces as their "home," and to make exclusive claim on these spaces' history. Obviously, such processes of learning and recognition are accompanied by multiple exclusions: of histories that are no longer accepted as being part of "history," the all-encompassing narrative produced and promoted by official institutions; of people whose ethnic or economic background make them inconsequential and thus invisible in the eyes of these institutions; and of things such as semidecrepit nineteenth-century houses whose aesthetic and functional value has been erased not only by time but also by the same institutions' strategic disregard. This is also a book about the challenges, temptations, and perils accompanying the pursuit of making history into a home. It explores the new forms of political action emerging as defiant responses to the state-sponsored pursuit of taming multiple histories and molding them into a narrative about an allegedly harmonious past.

The Old Town Betwixt and Between: A Sign of the Nation or a Place of the Other?

The Old Town has never been a neutral part of the city of Bucharest; on the contrary, throughout the centuries, starting with the late eighteenth century up to the present (2010s), the district has been a site of contention among different political factions, between the elites and the poor, between politicians and different groups of professionals, such as archaeologists, historians, and architects. These tense debates signaled broader negotiations about the meaning of class, urbanity, political participation, ethnic and economic belonging, and the ways in which these categories have continued to shape one another.

The mid-2000s promotion of the Old Town as a symbol of cosmopolitan history was fundamentally ahistorical. Local officials' upholding of the Old Town as the historic center of a formerly European city (interwar Bucharest), and their promise that they would bring back that cosmopolitanism with funds from the European Union, ignored another history—that of the blatant nationalism of the interwar years. This is when a famous historian and politician decried the "denationalization" of Bucharest's population, which he saw as an effect of the "invasion of the Galician Jews," who allegedly made the Romanians poorer and poorer and emptied the Romanian churches (Iorga 1939, 332). If local officials of twenty-first-century Bucharest had truly wished to revive the nineteenth-century atmosphere on the streets of the Old Town, they would have talked about a highly heterogeneous town, a transit zone for so many people but also a place in which so many others chose to settle and make it a home. And a home it became for Hungarian and Romanian bakers, Serbian pastry makers, Hungarian and Czech musicians, Venetian and Jewish jewelers, German clockmakers, Austrian, Greek, and Bulgarian teachers, and especially traders. In Bucharest of 1804, there were eighty-six traders of Bulgarian, Albanian, Armenian, Serbian, Italian, Greek, Austrian, Dalmatian, and Transylvanian descent, in addition to fifty Jewish merchants (Iorga 1939, 206).

The district that later came to be known as the Old Town emerged from the buzzing economic life that developed around the first princely palace of Bucharest. Established in the fifteenth century, when the principality of Wallachia fell under the suzerainty of the Ottoman Empire, what later became known as the Old Court had functioned as the new residence of the rulers of Wallachia (who, at the Ottomans' request, abandoned the historical residence in Târgoviște and moved to Bucharest) (Ionescu-Gion 1899, 28–29). Starting with the end of seventeenth century, the court became further extended and embellished under the reign of Constantin Brâncoveanu, a Romanian prince who sought relative political autonomy from the Ottoman Empire. However, his intent to launch a local cultural Renaissance made him suspicious to the Ottomans, who convicted him of treason and imprisoned and killed him together with his family.[5] By the mid-eighteenth century, the princely palace that impressed foreign visitors with its large halls decorated with marble stairs and colonnades, surrounded by lush gardens, was destroyed in a fire and eventually abandoned (Iorga 1939, 116).[6] Around that time, the Ottoman Empire decided to forgo appointing local rulers from among the Romanian boyars and brought instead a series of rich Greek merchants from Constantinople (the Phanariotes) to stand in as their political proxies. The abandonment of the Old Court after the fire and the construction of a new princely palace up the hill might have also been politically motivated: an attempt of the new rulers to create symbolic and spatial distance from their predecessors and thus signal their unwavering loyalty to the Ottoman Empire.

The mid-eighteenth to the early nineteenth century was a time of acute political upheaval, as the Ottoman, Russian, and Habsburg empires were vying for control of the principalities of Wallachia and Moldovia. The new rulers, the Greek Phanariotes of the Ottoman Empire, sought to maintain control by increasing taxes, which triggered further discontent among the local population. As the capital of Wallachia, Bucharest was caught in the middle of this political storm, becoming an uncertain territory, prone to attacks from the Habsburgs, the Ottomans, the Russians, and even from the rebels who fought against them. In May 1802, in the midst of one of these attacks, the Phanariote prince appointed by the Ottomans fled Bucharest together with his court and army (Iorga 1939, 195). Part of the city's population took flight as well, leaving the town totally abandoned. This is when the beggars who had occupied the ruined site of the Old Court (Ionescu-Gion 1899, 128) chose to become temporary kings of the city. Led by a former mercenary, the vagabonds entered the

new court, took away the symbols of power—the princely hat and the Ottoman tughs and flags—and began marching in the streets wearing these and
mimicking a coronation ceremony (Iorga 1939, 195). The beggars' "rule" lasted
only two days. Alerted by the fleeing prince, the Ottoman troops came into
the city to put an end to the revolt by hanging all of the beggars (Ionescu-Gion
1899, 125; Iorga 1939, 196). The prince and his court returned, followed by the
population. On his return to the city, a merchant could not contain his surprise:
"Bucharest escaped from a terrifying menace. It must have been the will of God
[that protected the city]. It stayed for so many days without a ruler and people,
[occupied] only by thieves, 'kings,' and the desperate, and it still remained in
one piece, with no house or shop being destroyed!" (Iorga 1939, 196). However,
none of these historians who mentioned the revolt (e.g., Iorga and Ionescu-
Gion) chose to notice the broader implication of that merchant's testimony that
no house or store had been damaged. This short-lived revolt of the poor and the
marginal was not a collective act of plunder but rather a fundamentally social
and political one—an impromptu carnival, a street performance mocking the
political institutions of the time.

The episode of the vagabonds becoming temporary "kings" of Bucharest
entered the local lore as a symbol of widespread disorder, culminating with
the radical reversal of power—the ragged ones turning themselves into the rulers.[7] To erase the memory of the revolt and to restore order, the prince then
in power, one of many Phanariotes who came and left in rapid succession,
ordered that the ruins be leveled and the land of the Old Court be auctioned
to merchants (Ionescu-Gion 1899, 129). Throughout the eighteenth and early
nineteenth centuries, Greek, Armenian, Polish, German, Turkish, and Jewish
merchants settled in this district, with new inns opening and commercial venues and shops trading goods brought from as far away as Leipzig (hence the
name of the main commercial street, Lipscani), Padua, or Paris.[8] Inevitably,
by becoming the city's economic nucleus, the area turned into a social magnet
as well, attracting people from all social and economic strata. The site became
renowned not only for the luxurious goods displayed in the shops aligned on
Lipscani Street or the money absorbed by the new banks but also for the black
market and prostitution flourishing on the same streets.

This underworld, combined with the ethnic heterogeneity of the place
and its commercial, and thus allegedly immoral, character reinforced the Old
Town's ill-famed reputation in the symbolic geography of the city. The district came to be perceived as a place of deep moral morass but one that still
exuded a fatal magnetism, enticing and ensnaring its visitors. The legend of
the kings of the Old Court was kept alive not only by rumors and legends
but also by literary accounts. The writer Mateiu Caragiale drafted the novel

with the same title at the turn of the twentieth century, but he published it almost twenty years later in 1929. *Craii de la Curtea Veche* (The kings of the Old Court, 2001) became a much-circulated epic of a "Levantine" Bucharest at the end of the nineteenth century, "where nothing is ever too severe."[9] Echoing modernization debates between "traditionalists" and "Europeanists" that dominated Romania's interwar scene, the book revolved around the adventures of two local aristocrats (boyars) who straddled two seemingly antagonistic worlds—the purportedly modern and civilized West and the morally lax Levant. Forced to make a choice, they disavowed their Western manners and immersed themselves in the debauchery and depravation thriving in the Old Town's "cramped lanes, with houses stuck one to another" (64). In the novel, the district is depicted as a symbol of fin de siècle decadence in a city undergoing a rapid economic expansion as well as an increasing social polarization. Mateiu Caragiale described the Old Town's depravation as originating in its own place of birth, the ground onto which the pubs and shops had been built and from where the commercial site had sprouted: the site of the Old Court. He presented the Old Court as being an ugly decor, matching "the wickedness of a ruling clique made of all foreign scumbags, with much Gypsy blood running through their veins" (64).

This overtly xenophobic description of the Old Town echoed other negative perceptions of the place as a seat of dangerous transactions and transgressions. It is not surprising that the urban elites of the early twentieth century sought to "tame down" the place and to alter its aesthetics so that it would better fit the urban development occurring in the northern part of the city. In fact, by the 1920s, the expansion of the city into the north and the modern buildings along the larger boulevards made the elites begin associating the city center with the modernist constructions and dismiss the Old Town as obsolete and marginal, both socially and economically. If we examine a map of Bucharest from 1934, we notice that the area of the Old Town was located at the periphery of what was then considered the city center.

In 1931, Martha Bibescu, a famous writer and socialite, decried the "ugly and unsanitary market houses" that abutted the southern side of the Old Town.[10] By the early twentieth century, the Central Market had been established on the southern periphery of the district. It was the largest market in the city, emerging from the eighteenth-century fair by the northern side of the Dâmbovița River.[11] Bibescu saw the market as emblematic of "the lack of respect and of common-sense" that accompanied "the conquest of Bucharest by the triumphant vulgarity," and made "Romanians lose their sentiments for their own history."[12] Otherwise, she asked, alluding to the historic significance of the disappeared Old Court, how could they have allowed for a market to be

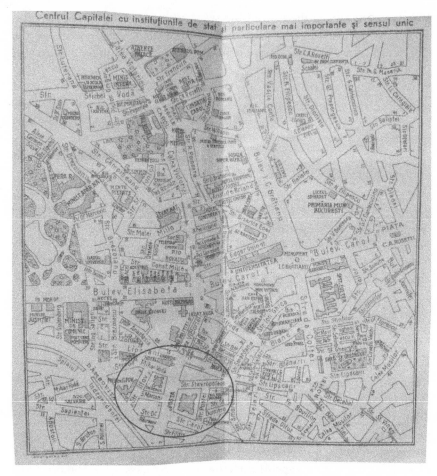

Fig. 0.1. The circle marks the Old Town on the map of the city center in 1934. Source: *Bucureşti. Ghid Oficial* (1934). Public domain.

built on the site of "the palace of the Romanian princes"? To restore urban order and revive that national sentiment, she proposed the removal of the Central Market. She also suggested that all of the houses in the Old Town be painted in similar pastel colors and that the district's narrow streets be expanded and aligned with colonnades and arches.

Local authorities paid attention to such proposals but tried to find less radical solutions. Architect Cincinat Sfinţescu (1932, 30, 150–55), then head of the urban planning division of Bucharest's city hall, pointed out that the Central Market represented "tradition" and therefore should not be "liquidated" but rather preserved and improved. However, he agreed with Bibescu that the commercial center, which included the Old Town, had to be given a more "hygienic form"—that is, be "cleansed" of the small industry producing noise and smoke (45–46). Even though he also disliked the narrow streets of the Old Town, Sfințescu viewed the expansion and realignment of the streets as impractical. Instead, he proposed having the Old Town's main commercial venues, such as Lipscani, refurbished with closed colonnades and have that new policy imposed on the shop owners. In his view, this was a much more economical solution for the state, as city hall would not have to pay compensation for the expropriated land, but the merchants would have to cover the costs of the reconstruction (162).

None of these proposals ever achieved a material form, but they were significant as both aesthetic and social critiques. Bibescu's opposition of the "unsanitary" market and comments about Romanian national sentiment were a veiled critique of the ethnic and social heterogeneity of the district.[13] Sfințescu's (1932, 163) suggestion to add arches and colonnades to the shops on Lipscani signaled an intention to impose a relative uniformity to an urban space that he himself acknowledged as being "so heteroclite." Their tone reflected an increasing irritation with the presence of an unnamed Other, a presence that other writers, however, had no qualms identifying and especially vilifying.

Here is how Nicolae Iorga (1939, 334), the most important Romanian historian of the interwar era, described Bucharest's economic and social life in the late 1930s: "The Romanian trade . . . has been polluted by foreign elements to such extent that, as a newspaper noted recently, during the holidays in September [the Jewish celebrations of Rosh Hashanah and Yom Kippur] most of the shops on Lipscani are closed. Once, the [Romanian] population had led their own traditional life around their churches. The abandonment of the religious traditions and the invasion of the Jews have altered its solid moral essence." Iorga's depiction of Lipscani, the major commercial street of the Old Town, as the epicenter of Bucharest's Jewishness reflected both a state-promoted ethnic nationalism as well as an economic fact.

In 1938, the capital had the largest number of Jewish-owned businesses and industrial enterprises, representing a third of the total.[14] The Old Town was a thriving commercial location, displaying a large range of shops, workshops, and small businesses, from tailors, shoemakers, and hatmakers to bicycle workshops, florists, delis, bookshops, pharmacies, rug stores, and doctors' and lawyers' offices. In 1937, as a close perusal of that year's phone book shows, the majority of the business owners on Lipscani were Jewish—a characteristic that made the Old Town become known as the "Jewish quarter" of the city.[15] At the same time, the district remained highly heterogeneous, attracting a large crowd of visitors both day and night, as well as socially and ethnically diverse residents. Derek Patmore (1939, 27–28), a British journalist who visited Bucharest in summer 1938, noted this diversity:

> Further down-town, near the river, is . . . Lipscani. This is the Jewish shops quarter of the city, and even at night this famous street is alight with shops displaying cheap merchandise. It is full of color, this section of the town, very Eastern in atmosphere with washing and rolls of material hanging in its narrow streets. At night these streets are full of people. There are cheap cafes clanging with garish music.
>
> Although this is pre-eminently the Jewish section of the city, it is also the working quarter, and here live the many peasants who have come to the city in search for work. On Sundays, the large rural population forgets the city for a while. The peasants from the various [regions] put on their national costumes and hold reunions amongst themselves. They . . . rarely mix.

This depiction captured the vibrant commercial atmosphere of the Old Town as well as the clear boundaries and cautious distance among different social and ethnic groups living there.

Despite the district's heterogeneity and its intense commercial attractions, the reputation of the Old Town as a place of the Other had only intensified in the 1930s—as attested by its negative portrayal in Nicolae Iorga's (1939) otherwise erudite and source-based *History of Bucharest*. Iorga's depiction of the Old Town as a quintessentially Jewish place was meant to justify his further call for action, addressed to his (presumably ethnic Romanian) readers to "cleanse the capital . . . of all of the worthless elements that we have received [in the country], from the beggar who came from some shabby villages in Bessarabia to the representatives of foreign businesses, with their work methods foreign from ours" (14).

The increasing criticism around the Old Town as a symbol of a foreign Other—and more specifically of a Jewish Other—must be placed within the increasingly illiberal political context of the 1930s, which only intensified the ethnonationalism pervasive after World War I. At the end of Great War, with the annexation of the regions of Bukovina, Transylvania, and Bessarabia in 1918, Romania's territory and population more than doubled. The formation of Greater Romania prompted its political elites to seek to instill a "national consciousness" into all of the regions and ethnicities in the country—a strategy of Romanianization that informed the economic and cultural policies of the interwar years (Livezeanu 1995). As historian Maria Bucur (2003, 60) put it, "what stood in a centrist position in the Romanian political landscape of the interwar years would easily qualify as a rightist position in the larger European context." The Depression only accentuated the frustrations of various social groups with the political elites' internal struggles for power and the spreading corruption.

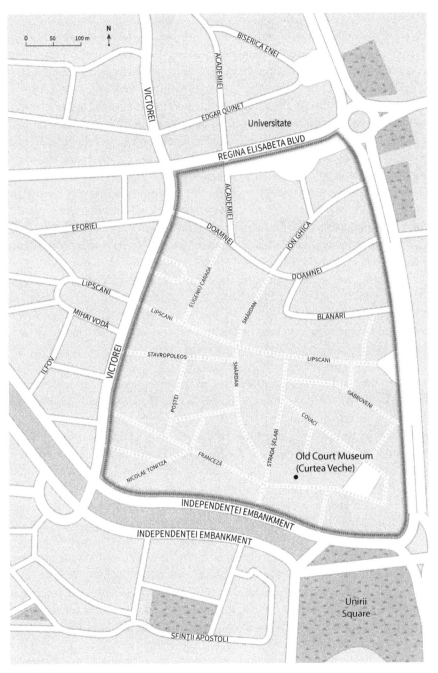

Map 0.1. Map of the Old Town district (2018). Map by Daniella Collins.

Many people began finding the extreme Right and its violent xenophobia increasingly appealing and embraced their radical agenda: a total eradication of the state institutions and parliamentary politics, and the social, political, and economic exclusion of all non-Romanian and non-Orthodox groups (Clark 2015; Heinen 1999; Livezeanu 1995). By the early 1930s, the violently antisemitic movement of the Iron Guard became highly popular among the urban youth as well as peasants and urban clergy—a popularity revealed by their electoral success in 1937, when they won 16 percent of the votes and became the third largest party in parliament (Hitchins 1994, 405, 419). The rise of the extreme right and its direct attack on the state enabled King Carol II to launch his own authoritarian regime. In February 1938, he abolished the constitution that granted parliament the decisive political role and replaced it with a new one that concentrated the power in the hands of the king. He also took drastic action against the Iron Guard, which he regarded as his chief enemy, by imprisoning most of its members and killing some of the leaders (Hitchins 1994, 416–20).

However, a few years later, the Iron Guard took its revenge. Once World War II began in September 1939, Carol II chose at first a neutral position for Romania, but he paid dearly for this neutrality. Romania's large territorial losses following the 1939 nonaggression pact between the Soviet Union and Germany triggered massive discontent among the population, leading to the king's abdication in 1940 and the coming to power of a military dictatorship. Carol's nineteen-year-old son became the de jure monarch of a country effectively controlled by Marshal Ion Antonescu, Romania's chief of state and Hitler's closest ally in the region. Antonescu's dictatorship brought the antisemitic policies launched by the previous governments to a new level. Initially, Antonescu and the Iron Guard shared power, but the Iron Guard's extreme violence and their dismissal of the rule of law made Antonescu turn against the movement.[16] If the earlier economic measures had aimed to curtail the economic activity of the Romanian Jews, the Antonescu-led Romanian state launched a full-fledged expropriation of all assets owned by the Jewish population.[17] What came to be officially named the Romanianization of labor and property triggered a chain reaction of resistance, further corruption, and a legal and bureaucratic war between the Jews and the state—a process that intensified the tensions in a society already torn apart by the war and eventually eroded any legitimacy that Antonescu managed to build by playing the nationalist card (Ionescu 2015, 190).

This short foray into the tense political context of the interwar years and the rising antisemitism allows us to better understand the changing meaning of the Old Town in Bucharest's symbolic and social geography during the interwar period. While the district retained its commercial function throughout the nineteenth and early twentieth century, its social and ethnic heterogeneity became increasingly invisible, being instead associated exclusively with a Jewish middle class (Iorga 1939). Even though the Jewish merchants had been there for generations, the district became a symbol of an unwanted foreignness—an eyesore for the Romanian elites who sought various ways to "regain" the place and, by extension, the city and the country. The city's Jewish history, part and parcel of Bucharest's history and deeply interwoven with its social, cultural, and economic development, was excised from the official historical narrative.

The irony is that while state-sponsored attempts at the Romanianization of the Old Town had solidified and expanded during the interwar period, culminating with the confiscation of Jewish property under the pro-Nazi regime between 1940 and 1944 (Ionescu 2015), it was eventually the postwar communist state that succeeded in that pursuit. While the new state officially spurned the "bourgeois" social order, it recognized the continuous appeal of the nationalist rhetoric and tried to revive it with an eye to gaining public consent. The communists' particular strategies and the role that a Romanianized Old Town would play in strengthening nationalist ideology under socialism are discussed in the first part of the book.

Place, Materialities, and State Making

The transformation of fragmented postwar landscapes into socialist modernist cities entailed a reordering not only of urban spaces but also of their history. In contrast to other works that have emphasized the significance of modernist architecture to socialist regimes (LeNormand 2014; Molnár 2013; Rubin 2016; Zarecor 2011), I focus on the urban planning policies that were not just meant to turn Romania's cities solely into modern urban habitats. These policies also aimed to highlight the Romanian past of these cities and thus erase their ethnically diverse histories. In communist Romania, the official historical narrative was not only produced through state-sponsored publications, novels, and textbooks (Iacob 2011; Verdery 1991) but also through urban space. A focus on these spatial interventions—the specific actors who imagined, sponsored, and promoted them; the strategies they used; and the materials they employed—allows us to better understand how a new state was literally building itself.

Far from assuming the state as a given, I examine the ways various actors—from top politicians to professionals such as archaeologists, architects, and planners—produce the state through continuous negotiations. I unpack the abstract category of "the state" and identify its particular sources of power: specific individuals and institutions that functioned as cultural brokers or the final decision makers. By tracing the materials and aesthetic styles that characterized a particular heritage regime, I ask why a state privileged them over others. For instance, to understand the process of state making under communism, I look at how archaeological artifacts could become more valuable than written archival documents. I also explore why state officials agreed to have the Old Town be transformed into a national architectural reserve, with house facades redesigned in an allegedly Romanian style despite elementary principles of historic preservation. For the postcommunist period, I look beyond institutions per se, trying to find "the state" in less expected places. I analyze the ways people of the Old Town talk about feeling unsafe in the semidecrepit buildings that they currently inhabit as state tenants. I examine the relatively recent policies for traffic regulation in the district, implemented by Bucharest's city hall, and the social and economic changes such policies triggered. I also pay attention to the silences that accompany the local institutions' strategic lack of action and use them to unravel broader strategies of consolidation of power and capital, especially among the postcommunist elites.

My approach obviously draws on Michel Foucault's concepts of governmentality and micropolitics, which have inspired so many anthropologists who have attempted to "read" the state.[18] Gail Kligman and Katherine Verdery (2011, 454) proposed a view of the state as "a contradictory ensemble of institutions, projects, and practices rather than an organized actor, and as a cultural and relational (rather than largely institutional) phenomenon in which subjectivities are a central element." Michel-Rolph Trouillot (2001, 133) emphasized that the state is an inherently processual, always-in-the-making entity, whose power emerges not just from actions pursued by official institutions but also from interstitial spaces occupied by the seemingly banal, the everyday. In my analysis of the Old Town in the postcommunist period, I critically examine this everydayness by looking at the political implications of unusual situations. Such cases include postponed plans to change the utilities infrastructure, leading to streets left unpaved and disheveled for years; buildings strategically abandoned to accumulate value paradoxically through their degradation; and documents attesting to high-level corruption that were left to rot in the basement of an abandoned bank for more than a decade.

The book thus joins a burgeoning field of ethnographies of the state through a critical inquiry into several processes: how a state makes itself into a tangible entity, how it captures power through material possessions, and how it imbues distinct materials with political significance in order to reify and expand its power. Other scholars have already highlighted the political potential of materiality and its role in constituting the state as a concept and a presence (Ferguson and Gupta 2002). Focusing on Pakistan's bureaucracy and its documentary practices, Matthew Hull (2012) has argued that a bureaucratic file could display its own political agency. He highlighted the files' multilayered ability to convey secret messages among various bureaucrats and thus constitute the state, as well as to function as instruments of political dissent by mobilizing coalitions fighting the same state and its expropriation of land.

Drawing on Hull's arguments, I approach the file of correspondence around the Old Court palace in the Old Town as a political actor. The file was formed around a letter of denunciation that a group of archaeologists sent to the communist government in December 1962. During the 1950s, archaeologists had conducted research in different locations of the Old Town, hoping that they would find the vestiges of the Old Court, abandoned centuries ago. While they did unearth some ruined walls that they identified as being part of the Old Court palace, they wanted to continue their research. However, a group of architects commissioned by Bucharest's city council proposed an expansion of a central square abutting the Old Town. This intervention would have solved the traffic problems in the area, but it would have entailed the modernization of a part of the district, including the areas where archaeologists had hoped to continue their digs. Appalled by this imminent scenario, the archaeologists tried to thwart the architects' plans by portraying them as an attempt to erase the city's history. The letter of denunciation triggered a long chain of back-and-forth written responses between Bucharest's city council, central government, and various archaeologists and architects and the institutions with which they were affiliated. By tracking the correspondence among these institutions, I re-create a network of political alliances and conflicts that reflected diverging priorities and contrasting urban visions. These letters make the file into a political palimpsest that carried different meanings as the political significance of the Old Court grew during the state's turn to nationalism in the 1960s and 1970s. I analyze how the first exchanges of letters created the Old Court as a political case. By appealing to the nationalist agenda increasingly embraced by the communist state during de-Stalinization, archaeologists eventually persuaded state authorities that the walls of the Old Court, abandoned centuries ago and found during the archaeological digs in the early 1950s, were vestiges of national importance. They thus managed to silence the otherwise highly powerful architects who considered the ruined Old Town only cumbersome rubble. Instead of channeling funds into expanding and modernizing a central square, the state authorities eventually decided to support the rebuilding of a site whose historic value was controversial and to transform it into an open-air museum.

To understand how the state took form in the midst of these multiple contestations and negotiations, I examine how different professionals and politicians created and naturalized links among disparate things by imbuing them with similar meaning—and how those links changed at different political moments. For instance, how did ruined walls, archaeological artifacts found on the site of the Old Court, and the nineteenth-century houses of the Old Town all came to stand as symbols of the nation? To answer this question, I draw on Krisztina Fehérváry's (2013) poignant analysis of the making and unmaking of a socialist aesthetics in Hungary. Looking at transformations of meaning and aesthetics of "the home" in socialist and postsocialist Hungary, Fehérváry (2013, 9) has argued that "we need to look at how radical changes to people's material environments become implicated in transformations of value that can reconfigure sociopolitical cosmologies." To understand how political change could be induced, indirectly, by what she called the "affective powers of the material" (9), she has adopted an ethnographic perspective on aesthetics. As she noted, "perceptual qualities can form the basis for a unifying 'aesthetic' by linking materialities to one another through common associations" (8). It is these common associations, she argued, that, if they are shattered or redefined, could generate profound sentiments that may precipitate political action. Such associations could take the form of an aesthetic instability that may generate a sentiment of political insecurity; it could also emerge as a new appreciation for a place meant to instill strong national allegiances or patriotic sentiments. This process is also illustrated by the transformation of the Old Court into a heritage site in Bucharest's "historic center." The link between the ruined walls of the palace, the archaeological artifacts unearthed from the site, and the surrounding houses that architects planned to redecorate in an allegedly national architectural style was not just that of a common location—the Old Town district. What brought them together was also an attempt by the communist regime to endorse a concentrated version of the national past in the center of a socialist city—a vision directly informed by the centralized political and economic system of the new state.

I bring Fehérváry's ethnographic approach to aesthetics to bear on Katherine Verdery's (1996, 20–22) argument that the socialist state drew its power from hoarding assets and means of production at the center. The political imagery of a center informed the urban visions pursued by socialist actors. By using Bucharest as a model, the government mobilized architects and archaeologists to create an urban landscape that was both socialist modern and specifically Romanian. Bucharest was not only envisioned as the socialist capital of the future but also as the historical center of the country. Within this vision, the Old Town represented the historical core of the city and, by extension, of the nation. By remaking the Old Court into a national historic site symbolizing Bucharest's *Romanian* past, the government also attempted to instill a sense of spatial and social order in the Old Town. As a pristine material representation of the nation, the Old Court was to replace people's perceptions of the Old Town as the city's commercial district—a site of an intense social, ethnic, and economic heterogeneity, whose unruliness socialist planners wanted to wipe out. In a similar manner in which the memory of a hero of the Haitian revolution was silenced by a palace that the Haitian king later built and gave it the same name (Trouillot 1995), the Romanian socialist government claimed its own national past in the form of the Old Court by silencing the politically inconvenient past of the Old Town, particularly its Jewish past.

This was not the only instance in which a socialist state aimed to erase the local Jewish past from the official historical narrative. Anthropologist Erica Lehrer's (2013) insightful ethnography of the rebirth of a Jewish heritage in post-socialist Poland reveals the diverging agendas that have informed the remaking of Krakow's historical Jewish district into a space of encounter, mutual discovery, and hopefully historical healing. However, while she points out the post-war efforts to expunge Jewish heritage, she does not examine in detail how the Polish socialist state actively intervened in or even coordinated such erasure. My analysis of the Romanianization of the Old Town, clearly supported by state authorities during the early 1970s, identifies some of the mechanisms of collective forgetting—and especially the role that particular urban visions and material forms played in the erasure of the Old Town's Jewish past under socialism.

The Old Town's multiple lives reveal the political employment of the concepts of "the center" and "the margin" in the process of state making under socialism and postsocialism. The transformation of some sites into heritage, accompanied by the denial of heritage quality to others, illustrated the spatialization of political power pursued by both socialist and postsocialist regimes. This book explores how centrality and marginality were spatially produced to sustain distinct political ideologies and accompanying property regimes, and how local actors adopted, adapted, or upended such neat spatial dichotomies.

Heritage: The Propriety of Property

In the 1990s and early 2000s, new calls for "heritage revival" in Romania signaled increasingly fierce struggles about how various groups wanted to remember their lives during the communist regime.[19] What was at stake in this debate was a critique of communism as a viable system of social and political organization. Some groups emphasized the social equality that stood at the core of the socialist ideology and argued that collective property was a prerequisite for the welfare state and a guarantee of social rights. Others opposed such views, proposing instead a radical decommunization, pointing out that democracy is not synonymous with an all-powerful state and that collective property never belonged to "the people," but only to those within the political system. It was the right to create their own heritage that ordinary citizens have tried to recapture from the state at the end of the communist regime. This book explores ethnographically the shift from (1) a centralized heritage regime, formed through the symbolic and economic monopoly of the state, to (2) a decentralized and multivocal model in which different groups claim the right to define their own heritage as a form of political autonomy—or even altogether reject heritage as an empty label.

As a linchpin among moral norms, historical narratives, social mores, and customary practices, heritage is a pivotal element of a property regime. Heritage produces and sustains a property regime through a circular model in which the ability to represent a marketable history reinforces the moral standing of a person or institution in a sociopolitical system. By claiming such moral standing while denying it to others, particular individuals or institutions could further accrue capital, prestige, and power. This book approaches heritage as the *propriety of property*—that is, a domain emerging at the intersection of moral codes, social expectations, and economic behavior that legitimize a property regime. It brings an anthropological perspective on property as relationships formed among people via things to bear on arguments that negotiations around heritage reveal who belongs and who is an outsider (Herzfeld 2009).

The relationship between property and persons has been a key focus of social theory. Marlyn Strathern (1988) coined the concept of the "dividual" to capture the profound interconnections between people and to challenge the idea of a defined, bounded self. Annette Weiner (1992) proposed the model of "keeping-while-giving" as a cultural practice of exchange that challenges liberal genealogies of ownership. Other anthropologists (e.g., Appadurai 1986; Brown 2004; Bryant 2014; Strathern 1999; Verdery and Humphrey 2004) have documented the complex creativity of the arrangements of rights and obligations that inform property regimes in various historical and sociopolitical contexts. These scholars have noted that a property regime presupposes a shared understanding of how individuals and groups are linked through things. Being an owner means an implicit social recognition; property signifies a social relation and not simply an act of ownership. As such, a property regime becomes a formative domain to define who belongs and who is excluded from a society. It identifies who knows and could tell about how someone came to own something and who does not possess such knowledge. And access to that knowledge often reinforces who is entitled to own, and thus be socially recognized as a person, and who is not.

Analysts have argued that heritage is not about the past but about the present—specifically, about the attempts of some groups to validate their sociopolitical claims not by appealing to a past but emphasizing their current cultural uniqueness. As anthropologist Michael Rowland (2004, 209) noted,

"Cultural property, defined as heritage, now plays a much larger role in defining the right to exist." Drawing on Verena Stolcke's (1995) observation that cultural difference has been increasingly coded in terms of uniqueness, rather than just idioms of race and ethnicity, Rowland has argued that this "right to exist asserts instead a claim to a unique identity supported and identified with an objectified notion of culture that may be gained or lost but not exchanged" (209). Thus, heritage becomes a framework for marginalized groups or individuals to appeal to the very logic of neoliberal capitalism—that of niche marketing, the uniqueness of products, and implicitly the unique new needs triggered by such products. However, this logic is turned on its head by those who are not yet fully visible on a global market of culture, so to speak. These groups emphasize their need to be recognized as irreplaceable, and appeal to affective tropes of loss and redemption, as Rowland put it, to transform heritage into an emotion, a sentiment—with an eye to gaining more visibility for their needs and hopefully more rights in the future.

But heritage cannot be invented overnight; notwithstanding its wider and wider diversity, not everything can become heritage (Berliner 2018).[20] Heritage has a particular conceptual stubbornness, which could be traced to how the term came into use.[21] Even though many people currently use both terms interchangeably, there used to be a clear distinction between *patrimony* and *heritage*, originating in the church's increasing authority in medieval Europe (David C. Harvey 2008, 22). Both terms emerged at around the same time (thirteenth and fourteenth centuries), but they designated two complementary entities.[22] *Patrimony* entailed anything derived from one's father (*pater*) or an endowment belonging by ancient right to a church. *Heritage* focused on the heir, who received what was being inherited or acquired from a predecessor— that is, from someone who was positioned in a kin relationship to the inheritor. In other words, while *patrimony* emphasized the origins, signaling an overly powerful father figure, *heritage* captured the importance of the destination, favoring a particular relationship with the heir as the recipient. By etymologically placing the agency on the relationship and not the source, *heritage* highlights the relationship between the present (and even the future) and the past and not just the past itself; it stresses the relevance of that interpretation of the past in the present and reveals its contemporary purposes. I will henceforth use *heritage* to signal that, like property, I approach it as a term and concept that emphasizes a relationship (between the heir and the father) rather than a point of origins (*pater*, father).

In medieval Europe, the Catholic church used a rhetoric of heritage to carve a clearer separation between the "private" domain of family and religious faith and the "public" domain of the rapidly expanding market, while it aimed to control both. Sociologist Max Weber ([1889] 2003) examined changes in property relations and inheritance practices in medieval southern Europe—exactly the context in which heritage emerged as a term to define the collective assets transmitted in the family from one generation to another. Even though he did not focus on the use and meaning of heritage, Weber's analysis allows us to understand how the term came to gain political resonance and become a potent instrument of social and economic differentiation. Focusing on family-based mercantile associations and craft-industry guilds, Weber noted that the associations relied on the formation of a common property fund and the element of "solidary liability," with all of the members being financially responsible for the others (172–75). Those strong bonds made them more trustworthy in the eyes of the creditors and led the associations to rapidly expand commercially. But these associations also challenged the economic monopoly and political power of the Catholic Church. That is, their increasing legal dexterity to span the divide between the private domain of the family and the commercial domain of the market went against the church's own agenda of keeping such dichotomies in place. As a rhetoric reinforcing particular practices and genealogies of ownership, "heritage" thus became an instrument for the church to capture and further reify a distinction between a closely guarded social domain of the family—including the religious congregation, allegedly characterized by a profound sense of belonging, mutual trust, and deep bonds—and an uncertain economic domain of the ever-expanding market, viewed as morally ambiguous. As an inheritance, heritage was not just simple wealth; it also signaled a socially acknowledged and thus morally dignifying relationship between a known ancestor and an heir.

This short inquiry into the origins of *heritage* shows that negotiations over heritage are not just over value and power. These negotiations are also informed by and often reinforce guiding narratives about moral behavior and social performance—especially when people themselves become commodified as heritage. In his superb analysis of the Pelourinho neighborhood of Salvador de Bahia, Brazil, John Collins (2015) has noted that the district's inclusion in the UNESCO World Heritage sites list prompted an implicit commodification of an idealized interracial history of Brazil. The impending gentrification has forced the residents of Pelourinho to seek to transform themselves—their knowledge, behavior, and social performance—into unique "cultural resources," which state officials can use as colorful proof of patrimony to bring in tourists. But the same residents also used their state-given role of embodying patrimony to criticize that very state through satire, mocking the documentary practices of state officials, and even stealing or forging archival documents to challenge the state's monopoly in deciding who can and who cannot be patrimony.

Unlike Pelourinho's residents, some of the state tenants who have lived in the semidecrepit houses in Bucharest's Old Town since the early 1990s want nothing to do with heritage. To them, it is as empty a word as the promises that they keep receiving from state officials—that their buildings, which are allegedly historic monuments, would eventually be repaired. They show no interest in an allegedly European past meant to be signaled by the new label of *historic center*. These tenants know that to have a heritage—to own social, economic, and symbolic capital—is a privilege that they would never attain. To them, heritage is the everyday labor they have put in defiantly making a home in a house that the state has abandoned, while fully knowing that the postcommunist state could care less about them and their history.

I would like to return here to Carmen, the young woman who has lived in Old Town all her life and whose critical comments opened this introduction. Born in the late 1980s and raised in a district that became rapidly impoverished after the mid-1970s, Carmen represented a history that the political elites of contemporary Romania wanted neither to acknowledge nor value in any way: the relatively recent past of the communist period. Still, like the other poor tenants in her run-down building in the Old Town, Carmen was someone still haunted by that past even though she was barely aware of it. It has haunted her economically and culturally because she was denied a place in a society and polity that has become increasingly individualistic and in which the gap between the middle class and the poor has rapidly widened within the last twenty years. The local authorities' strategic disregard of the dire situation of their state tenants, living in houses that could collapse at any minute, reveal a menacing state that has openly disparaged its social contract with the citizens—a state that, at the moment I am writing this in August 2018, proved that it could become even violent, using tear gas and water cannons to shut down massive but peaceful antigovernment protests.

Research Methods

As an inquiry into the politics of the past, this book's own trajectory echoes the convoluted dynamics of heritage making. Some things or experiences that appeared to me irrelevant at the moment of their occurrence came to take on new significance much later, when reexamined through a fresh analytic lens or filtered through other interposing explanations and events. In a sense, part of my insights into the politics of heritage in Romania comes from my own growing up there during the last decade of the communist regime. I still have vivid memories of the mandatory school trips to heritage sites across the country, including to the Old Court, sites meant to glorify the political leaders of the moment and those whom they deemed to be "politically proper" forebears. During the time I lived in Bucharest as a college student and an employee, between 1994 and 1999, I came to know the city in and out and to witness the rapid changes in its urban and social fabric. In addition to my personal experience and memories about Bucharest of the 1990s, I draw on interviews with architects, art historians, archaeologists, urban historians, historians, city officials, and state officials working especially in the field of historic monuments and historic preservation—a total of eighteen taped interviews in addition to more open, informal conversations. In many cases, I refrained from recording the interviews so that I would not make my interlocutors feel uncomfortable—especially in a context in which the people I talked to were not used to being recorded, and some even associated the word *interview* with far too inquisitive journalists or even to the former secret police. I took many notes during these conversations and added more details immediately after. Consequently, some quotations, noted in the book as "conversations," are approximate translations of what my interlocutors told me. I also consulted the collections of two of the most popular national dailies, *Adevărul* and *România Liberă* from 1990 to 2015, focusing especially on Bucharest and the Old Town. I also perused the online archive of *Revista 22* from 1990 to 1998 and 2000 to 2015. This is a political and cultural weekly that has gained a significant visibility and reputation in post-1990 Romania, functioning as a democratic forum for diverse voices and points of view.

Part of my fieldwork in Bucharest during 2007 and early 2008 included attending several workshops focused on heritage preservation in Bucharest, one organized at the French Institute (November 2007) and two held at the School of Architecture (May 2008). I attended several meetings of the Save Bucharest Association,[23] which began as a nucleus of civic-minded professionals concerned about the lack of public space, diminishing living standards, and lack of regulation of the city's urban planning. I also spent a lot of time walking in the Old Town, noting the emerging social and economic differences in the district, the contrasting aesthetics, the graffiti on walls, and overall the particular forms in which people used, inhabited, renovated, or radically altered the district's houses. I also paid attention to how people, Bucharest's residents, talked about the district. I struck up conversations with taxi drivers, people at the farmer's market, customers in newspaper kiosks, and sellers and shop owners, trying to gauge how they talked about the ongoing renovation projects happening then in the Old Town (2007–8). Would they choose to live there if they had the chance? What did they think about the gaps in the pavement, about the torn-up, narrow streets, waiting for months and even years for the new infrastructure to be installed? I noted the critical or laudatory qualities of their comments, observing how the changes were affecting people's daily interactions. I also took hundreds of photographs, which later helped me notice new details.

In addition to ethnographic fieldwork and interviews, the book is grounded in extensive archival research. To better understand the urban planning policies under socialism and the intersections between political decisions and aesthetic visions, I conducted research in the National Archives (Bucharest branch). To identify projects of historic preservation that had been launched in the Old Town, I worked in the archives of the National Institute for Historic Monuments, currently hosting the archival fund of the former Division of Historic Monuments, active under the socialist regime (1951–77). To learn more about the social composition and economic life of the Old Town throughout the nineteenth and twentieth centuries, I studied historical accounts of Bucharest, touristic guides, and travelogues published by foreigners visiting the city, as well as some of the business yellow pages of Bucharest during the interwar years (*Anuarul Socec*) and phone books. I found the phone books to be especially useful for me to reconstruct the ethnic composition of the businesses in the district. To identify the ethnic background of the individual business owners on Lipscani, the Old Town's main commercial street, I compared the names in all of the Bucharest phone books I was able to find (1938, 1947, 1954, 1958, 1965, 1970).[24] When perusing the phone books, I was aware of socioeconomic differences and implicit biases; I did not expect to find every resident mentioned in the phone book, given that having an individual phone line had been rather expensive during the interwar years and then became more difficult to obtain during the early socialist period (people needed to rely on specific "connections" to be able to have a phone line installed in their residences). However, when it came to identifying Jewish business owners, the phone books were an invaluable source, due to lack of other statistical data about the Old Town. To identify the names, I consulted a variety of sources, including an etymological dictionary of Jewish names, publications of the Jewish Romanian émigrés, and online discussion forums.

To learn more about how the local authorities viewed and talked about the Old Town after 1990, I relied on journalistic materials (e.g., interviews with the mayors and city councilors, investigations into real estate networks and their underground links to local officials, etc.). In addition, I consulted reports and plans published online, on the website of Bucharest's city hall (some reports that had been accessible during the late 2000s are no longer available online, but I have kept electronic copies). To learn about the legal status of particular buildings in the Old Town, I consulted the database on the website of the city hall, even though sometimes the online information did not match what I had learned from talking to the residents of the same buildings.

Although I conducted the bulk of my ethnographic research in 2007 and the first six months of 2008, I supplemented my fieldwork with shorter documentary trips to Romania in the summers of 2012, 2013, and 2015. In 2016, I interviewed a British architect about a project of urban renewal that a team of British and Romanian architects wanted to pursue in the Old Town. I also talked to a World Bank expert about his involvement with the redesign of Bucharest's transportation system. In May and early June 2016, I did another short round of fieldwork in the Old Town, talking to current and former residents. I had long conversations with three residents living in one semidecrepit building in the Old Town. In 2016, I also conducted a total of twelve interviews with professionals working in Bucharest, including architects, urban geographers, civic activists, investigative journalists, state officials such as the former minister of culture, and candidates in the local elections for Bucharest's city hall, as the local electoral campaign was in full swing during my time in Bucharest.

All these voices provided a rich array of perspectives on the Old Town's social meaning, economic value, and urban function, revealing its unique ability to function as a prism reflecting multiple negotiations and contradictory accounts, from people from abroad and the locals, from the powerful and the powerless. The diversity of these accounts challenges a unidirectional portrayal of the Old Town as either a site of urban decay or "Bucharest's cash cow," as one of my interlocutors put it. While conscious of various positions and motivations, I am less interested in gauging the accuracy of these accounts. Rather, I explore how many of these accounts employ the Old Town as a starting point from which they make a broader social critique, assume or deny responsibility, signal agency and defiance, identify unknown culprits and agendas, or, on the contrary, engage in various forms of erasures—of people, things, or value. I approach the post-1990 debates about the Old Town as a rich source to further illuminate new kinds of social dislocations produced by the incorporation of postsocialist Eastern Europe into global capitalism as well as to trace different groups' efforts to redefine meaningful community.

Organization of the Book

The book traces the multiple lives and political functions of one place, Bucharest's Old Town district, in the long arc from the beginning of communism to Romania's admission into the European Union. The chapters proceed chronologically, each focusing on a different political function that the Old Town fulfilled during distinct periods (the 1950s, 1960s, 1970s and 1980s, 1990s, 2000s, and 2010s).

Chapter 1 focuses on the plans to make Bucharest into a socialist capital during the 1950s and the political and professional debates surrounding these plans. Drawing on untapped archival sources, the chapter provides a historical context to better understand the 1950s (Stalinization and its aftermath) and the specific form that it took in Romania. The Communist Party aimed to solve the postwar housing crisis and launch a successful urbanization and industrialization with an eye to consolidating its power. At that time, politicians and architects viewed the Old Town as an urban eyesore, whose social and architectural heterogeneity challenged the architects' vision and plans to make Bucharest into a modern, aesthetically homogeneous and thoroughly functional city. But these negotiations about the city's form and function must be also understood as windows into larger conflicts among different factions within the Party leadership, as well as attempts of the Romanian communists to take a relative distance from the Soviets by relying less and less on their expertise. These negotiations reveal a fraught context in which the Romanian communists were also trying to figure out how to govern—how to strike the right balance between keeping a tight control on resources and decision making and relying on the experts' advice.

Chapter 2 begins with the moment when, in the midst of the socialist redesign of downtown Bucharest, the discovery of some medieval ruins brought the project to an almost complete halt. When the first archaeological digs opened in the city center in the early 1950s, their ultimate goal was to lay a clean slate for the transformation of Bucharest into a pinnacle of socialist modernity. The archaeologists' task was to "clean up" the area, ridding it of any remains of the past so that it could be closed down for good. But the discovery in 1953 of the ruins of the Old Court derailed the plans for remodeling this central area of the city. Accusing the architects of blatant disregard for national history, a group of archaeologists petitioned the state to remake the Old Court into a conservation site. After a long battle, the archaeologists received what they wanted: in 1972, a fully rebuilt Old Court officially became an open-air national museum. The tug-of-war between the architects and the archaeologists over the political and historical value of the site reveals a complex struggle for political and institutional visibility in the socialist system. Moreover, the resuscitation of the Old Court out of the rubble reveals how this fight made socialist leaders aware of how they could employ history as a political resource.

Chapter 3 addresses a particular attempt that emerged from the reconstruction of the Old Court. A group of architects sought to redecorate the buildings of the Old Town with elements deemed to represent "authentic Romanian architecture"—at the expense of the more eclectic style prevailing in the area. Drawing on archival sources that capture the debates around that controversial project, I suggest that the main goal of this undertaking was to offer a concentrated and politically purified historical narrative about the city, while also containing the old city to a clearly defined geographical nucleus in the midst of a modernizing capital. In the 1970s, the Old Town held out a tangible promise to state officials who hoped to reclaim history for themselves in the form of a "redecorated" historic center. But in the 1980s, the district was once again shunted to the margins as the regime took it upon itself to construct its own center—the Civic Center—as the spatial representation of a highly centralized system.

Chapter 4 focuses on the 1990s, the immediate years after the end of the communist regime, to inquire into the Old Town's marginality. I argue that this marginality was the result of a political strategy of affective devaluation. In the hands of the postcommunist elites, the Old Town's political function shifted to being an active border zone. Its marginality was deceptive; its real function was to divide time into clearly cut chunks separating the socialist past from the postsocialist present. The officials who came to power in Romania of the 1990s had been part of the former communist elites. They intentionally neglected the Old Town's run-down buildings and rejected any attempts at heritage revitalization because they aimed to use the district as a border. Districts such as the Old Town became spaces of abjection—spatial, tangible thresholds that enabled postsocialist politicians to deny their own communist past and to present themselves as newly reborn democratic politicians.

In the mid-2000s, under a new neoliberal government who sought to prove Romania's political potential to European Union officials, the district became once again a "center." The municipality launched the transformation of the Old Town into an urban brand, "a historic center" of a European capital. Chapter 5 examines how city officials employed the discourse of "Europeanization" not only to gain financial support from the European Union but also to launch an unprecedented control over city affairs. Europeanization became a justification for the local political elites to privatize public space, to redefine the relationship between the private and public domains, and to alter the criteria of political and social belonging: who deserved, and who did not, to be a citizen of Bucharest. The chapter also traces the long-term consequences of the broader privatization of the city into the early 2010s. It shows how city officials increasingly eschewed their own responsibility for the poor tenants and the state-owned dilapidated buildings in the Old Town. In fact, the local authorities used the ruined state of the buildings to create an aesthetics of contrasts meant to highlight the social polarization of the district and indirectly pressure the poor residents of the Old Town to move out from the city center.

In the conclusion, starting from these ethnographic observations, I develop a theory about the dual nature of socialist heritage. I argue that a postsocialist context still haunted by the ghosts of the communist order—the grandiose promises that the regime only partially honored and then only at huge human cost—offers a particularly rich angle from which to understand the nature of heritage as a double form of *marking*. As an illusionary search for essence, whether of an idealized past, a promising future, or an exemplary moral person, heritage reveals itself as a sign that can easily turn into a stain—a search for distinction, and a strategy of differentiation that contains at its core the potential for further isolation, marginalization, and exclusion.

Notes

1. Interview, May 18, 2017, Bucharest.

2. Lisa Breglia (2006, 14) has proposed an approach to heritage as practice, as opposed to one focused on heritage as artifact. Laurajane Smith (2006, 3) emphasized the processual and performative aspects of heritage, which entails a multilayered enterprise of "visiting, managing, interpretation or conservation . . . that embodies acts of remembrance and commemoration while negotiating and constructing a sense of place, belonging and understanding in the present."

3. Swenson (2013) points out that the production of heritage as an allegedly national project during the late nineteenth century emerged, in fact, through a transnational network of knowledge practices.

4. For the political role of materialities in the Soviet bloc, see, among others, Rubin (2012) for East Germany and Fehérváry (2013) for Hungary. For the production of socialist urban environments, see Lebow (2013) for Poland, Rubin (2016) for East Germany, Fehérváry (2013) for Hungary, and Maxim (2018) for Romania. For studies of architectural debates and urban visions underlying the building of socialism, see LeNormand (2014), Maxim (2018), and Zarecor (2011).

5. Two centuries later, at the height of the mid-nineteenth-century revolution that led to the formation of Romania as an independent state, the revolutionaries claimed Brâncoveanu as one of their forebears and a symbol of the fight for national autonomy. Then, in the 2000s, several centuries after his violent death, the Orthodox Church decreed the sanctification of Brâncoveanu and his sons as Christian martyrs, a move meant to make the church more visible as a political actor in contemporary Romania.

6. A description of the court is mentioned by Edward Chishull in his *Travels in Turkey and Back to England* (1747), quoted in Iorga (1939, 116).

7. The legend did not only circulate in historical accounts of the interwar period, such as Iorga (1939), but it also was revived during the communist regime. Eugen Barbu, a novelist and journalist who managed to gain the trust and support of the party leaders, published *Principele* (The prince) (1969), a novel inspired by the Phanariote period in which the leader of the beggars, Malamos, played a key role. A dark portrayal of foreign domination of the Romanian nation, the novel echoed and promoted the state-sponsored nationalism of the 1960s and 1970s, and consolidated Barbu's position as one of the "official" writers of the regime who benefited from serious favors and funds, including launching his own state-sponsored literary journal.

8. The name of the street, Lipscani, comes from Lipsca (Leipzig), where one of the most important fairs in late medieval Europe took place three times a year. Traders from

Wallachia and Moldovia went to the Lipsca fair for supplies twice a year. Their participation had become so significant by the mid-eighteenth century that when those traders seemed not to be able to travel due to the plague epidemics in the principalities, the fair organizers did not know whether they should still open the fair. See Ionescu-Gion (1899, 458) in Murgescu (1987, 139).

9. The novel's motto reproduces the comment made by Raymond Poincaré, a politician and future president of France, who said on his visit to Bucharest, "What do you expect? We are here at the gates of the Orient, where nothing is too severe" (Caragiale 2001, 53n1, translation from French).

10. Martha Bibescu, "Sugestiuni pentru înfrumusețarea orașului Bucharest," *Revista secolului 20* 385–87, nos. 4–6 (1997): 184. The original text was written in 1931.

11. When the town expanded, the fair moved from the initial location at the Sf. Gheorghe church, a site that currently is situated across Lipscani Street, down south, on the shore of Dâmbovița River. T. Evolceanu, "Concursul pentru sistematizarea Pieței Unirii din București," *Arhitectura RPR* 62, no. 1 (1960): 14.

12. Bibescu (1997, 183–84).

13. Bibescu (1997, 184).

14. More exactly, 6,173 out of a total of 20,176 businesses had Jewish owners, as noted by Rosen (1995, 93) citing *Aspecte ale economiei românești*, Consiliul Superior Economic, București, 1939, 207–8.

15. In 1937, the Bucharest phone book of that year recorded forty-six businesses (including banks) whose owners had Jewish names, twenty-one businesses owned by people with Romanian names, two shops owned by individuals with Hungarian names, one by someone with a Polish name, and one by someone with an Italian name. Obviously, I could not know whether some of the businessmen with non-Jewish names may also have identified themselves as Jewish. In addition, there were nine banks and forty-two businesses (mostly shops) whose names were neutral and thus did not offer any indication of the ethnicity of their owners (see "Abonații S.A.R de Telefoane, București și jud. Ilfov, August 1937"). In comparison, by 1947, there were fourteen businesses owned by people with Jewish names, twenty-three owned by individuals with Romanian names, and twenty-eight businesses with neutral names (including two banks) (see "Lista abonaților București, S.A.R de Telefoane, Iunie 1947").

16. In January 1941, the conflict between Antonescu and the Iron Guard escalated into a full-blown political crisis, when the legionnaires launched a rebellion and a gruesome pogrom against Bucharest's Jews, forcing Antonescu to enlist the army to crush the rebellion, ban the guard, and arrest thousands of its members. See Ancel (2005a, 363–400).

17. Among such economic policies, there were a series of labor laws that favored ethnic Romanian workers. See, for example, the 1930 Law for the Protection of Indigenous Work, the 1934 Law for the Employment of Romanian Personnel in Companies, the 1936 Law for the Professional Training and the Practice of Crafts, which offered significant advantages to the Romanians who opened up a business (lower taxes, etc.), and the 1939 Law of the Sunday Rest" (the last obviously targeting the Jewish employees and their Shabbat tradition of resting on Saturday, and not on Sunday).

18. By governmentality, Michel Foucault understood (1) "the ensemble formed by the institutions, procedures, analyses and reflections, the calculations and tactics" (Burchell, Gordon, and Miller 1991, 102) that produce power, and (2) "the development of whole complex of savoirs" (103). These are forms of knowledge via which power becomes practiced and

reproduced at a microscale, by the ways political subjects come to know what is right and what is wrong, what structures of feelings are politically "proper," and which are condemned.

19. For a larger discussion about history and memory in postcommunist Romania, see, among others, Kligman and Verdery (2011, 444–46) and Stan (2013).

20. David Berliner (2018) astutely notes the recent insistence on the "irreplaceability" of heritage and its role in triggering a connection via an empathy of loss.

21. As David C. Harvey (2008, 22) noted, heritage making, understood as an emphasis on one particular past to consolidate a social or political configuration in a given present, is far from being new. The appropriation and resignification of historical sites has been a practice since the ancient Romans had aimed to emulate the mythical figures and aesthetic forms of their former rivals, the Greeks.

22. For a comparative discussion of the institutionalization of *patrimoine* in eighteenth-century revolutionary France and of *heritage* via the private institution of the National Trust in eighteenth-century England, see Choay (2001). However, Choay does not explore the profound differences in the relationship between the state and church in the two settings: eighteenth-century England and France. The differences between the use of *heritage* and *patrimoine* pointed to distinct religious-political landscapes in which they emerged and were deployed and in shifting significations of sites linked to religious institutions. In comparison to the notion of *patrimoine* in France, where the historic sites simultaneously represented and constituted the state (as state possessions), the sites that ended up being treated as "heritage" in England continue to be separated from the state, being privately owned by the National Trust.

23. This association has since grown into a political party, the Save Romania Coalition.

24. The phone books are available via the digital collection of the Library of Congress.

1

TENSED URBAN VISIONS

Making Bucharest into a Socialist Capital

IN JUNE 1956, BUCHAREST'S CITY ARCHITECT, POMPILIU MACOVEI, found himself, once again, in front of the members of the government. He was summoned to the government's headquarters to inform the party leaders about the progress that he and his team had made on the planning of a socialist Bucharest. The Romanian communist regime viewed the transformation of Bucharest into a modern capital as the most tangible proof that the Party-state could and would keep its promises to deliver a better life and guarantee a brighter future. Since 1949, many architects had been working on Bucharest's master plan for urban development (henceforth, master plan), and their specific suggestions had already been discussed over and over again among the members of the government. However, all that talk led to nothing.

Five years after the work on the plan had started, the political leaders were still frustrated with the slow progress. Macovei tried to address their concerns by insisting on the pressing need for mass housing in a capital that was rapidly expanding, while noting the significant limitations of funds and, in particular, expertise. However, he could not prevent government officials' criticism. One of the ministers in the room, who was also an architect and the head of the State Committee for Architecture, complained about Macovei's presentation of the plan as being "too modest" and for failing to make Bucharest into "a future city that would be more optimistic, more luminous, as a communist capital should be."[1] At this point, Macovei lost his patience and retorted, "If we are too bold, we would break our neck!"[2]

This exchange captured the competing visions of state officials and of different architects commissioned to change Bucharest. A source of tension stemmed from the question of where they should start: to intervene first in the city center or to begin building new neighborhoods on the periphery. One of the major goals of the government was to find a rapid solution to the postwar housing crisis, because a successful industrialization was contingent on the government's ability to provide housing to workers. At the same time, the regime aimed high. They wanted to transform Bucharest into a radically new city, an "optimistic and luminous" capital, as the minister put it, standing for a new political ideology. In November 1952, Gheorghe Gheorghiu-Dej (Dej, henceforth), the party's first secretary and de facto leader of the country, presented Bucharest's transformation as a pursuit of national significance and a source of pride for every Romanian citizen: "Everyone in the country will find it a high honor . . . to visit the capital to see something different from the anarchy and disorder of the past, which we want to gradually eliminate within fifteen to twenty years."[3]

However, the architects had to acknowledge multiple limitations of labor, funds, and expertise. Such constraints created further problems. First, in a capital facing a massive population expansion, the lack of state housing forced many newcomers into the city to build their own homes in the form of rudimentary constructions often without access to water and electricity. These unauthorized houses defied the architects' attempts to bring order into the city via a centralized urban planning. Moreover, these constructions signaled the inability of the local authorities to gain and maintain control—not only over the urban development but also over the people's actions. The second problem was the narrow pool of expertise. The government simply could not find enough architects to work on Bucharest's master plan. The question was whether to continue to rely on expertise from abroad—that is, from the Soviets—or to seek alternatives within the country, such as the older professionals who had been marginalized due to their former political convictions. This was a particularly important dilemma in the conditions in which, after Stalin's death in 1953, the Dej-led government began seeking a relative autonomy from the Soviets. The debates around Bucharest's planning reveal the Romanian communist leadership's attempt to curtail the Soviets' control in a manner that did not appear to be overtly political.

And all these tensions derived from another: the infighting among different factions within the party leadership, which involved not only struggles for power but also different priorities and distinct visions about what a socialist society is and how it should be governed. After World War II, postwar Central and Eastern Europe became a laboratory for testing the possibilities and limitations of socialism as an alternative social and political order. All of the new regimes in the region mobilized architecture as a sign and tool of rapid modernization. Soon, architects gained significant political clout among the new structures of power as the experts who would literally "build socialism."[4] From the late 1940s to mid-1950s, the new regimes used the large-scale destruction caused by the war to justify rebuilding their urban landscapes according to the principles of socialist urban planning. Together or separately, architects from Czechoslovakia, Hungary, East Germany, and Romania traveled to Moscow to meet with and receive guidance from their Soviet colleagues.[5] These architects visited Soviet institutions of urban planning in order to see with their own eyes how they were organized and how they functioned, and then they reported back to their party leaders, bringing with them planning strategies to launch their own building projects at home.

Starting from the ongoing negotiations mentioned above, this chapter examines postwar urbanization in Bucharest as a process directly linked to state formation. It views state making as an attempt to extend control over and signal power via urban space, especially when a new political order was to be embodied by a new urbanity. This chapter argues that Bucharest's master plan for urban development served as an arena in which different political actors attempted to subtly assert their power through tense discussions about buildings, parks, streets, and squares. It follows the negotiations around Bucharest's master plan chronologically throughout the 1950s. It begins in 1949, when a team of architects began working on a plan for the capital that drew heavily on the 1935 plan for Moscow, and ends in 1959, when the authorities declared Bucharest's master plan completed.[6] I outline the main recommendations of the initial plan and follow them through their subsequent developments— exploring to what extent they were pursued and how the initial solutions were adapted (or abandoned) due to changes in the political context.

Before examining these debates, I offer a brief overview of the political and social changes occurring in Romania after the war. In contrast to other countries in the socialist bloc such as Czechoslovakia, the Romanian Communist Party had been nearly invisible as a political presence before and during the war. Once it came to power, it encountered a country deeply divided along class and ethnic lines. The party leaders had to work hard to gain people's trust. That became especially challenging when the new officials were trying to figure out how to govern—how to persuade institutions to work together in a centralized political system, how to envision and plan an entire economy, how to assess its future needs in detail, and especially how to reassure their citizens that they knew what they were doing, while they themselves were trying to find out.

A New Order: Romania's Sovietization

In November 1940, Romania entered World War II as an ally of Nazi Germany. However, Germany's economic exploitation of the country's resources and the staggering number of soldiers sent to fight for Germany on the Eastern Front deeply embittered the population. By 1943, emboldened by the defeat of Germany on the Eastern Front and the war's overall turn, the semilegal opposition sought to regain political power. The liberal and conservative historical parties responded to the call of the then illegal Communist Party to secretly form the National Democratic Bloc, whose aim was to annul Romania's military and economic commitment to Nazi Germany. This group of powerful politicians eventually persuaded the new king to oust Marshal Ion Antonescu and the country's pro-German government via a coup d'état in August 1944, and have Romania join the Allies.

Even though it changed sides in the eleventh hour, the country still had to pay a heavy price for its former alliance with Nazi Germany. In September 1944, Romania signed an armistice treaty whose terms were imposed by the Soviets. Although it recovered northern Transylvania, the armistice required Romania to comply with other harsh conditions, including ceding another part of its territory to the Soviet Union and paying $300 million in war reparations. The real cost of Romania's losses ultimately turned out to be much higher; it has been estimated at $2 billion.[7] In addition to economic losses, the war exacted a severe human toll: between 1941 and 1944, as many as 400,000 soldiers were killed or went missing, while on the home front 260,000 Romanian Jews and 25,000 Roma were deported to death camps.[8] Despite these losses, the armistice with the Allies seemed to have given Romanians a new sense of hope. The end of Antonescu's military dictatorship and the change of allegiance to the Allies initially triggered—despite the pain of war—a new wave of optimism among Romanians.

Derek Patmore, the same British journalist who had noted the colorful life of the Old Town when he had visited Bucharest for the first time in 1938, returned to Bucharest in late August 1944, shortly before the Soviet army entered the city. He wrote optimistically about a city that seemed to be coming back to life: "Already Bucharest's beginning to recover from violent events which liberated the country from German occupation. Bombed buildings are repaired and damaged shops and restaurants are opening again. . . . Bucharest, which, despite its Parisian elegance, has always been a mixture of east and west, has now become cosmopolitan again. Famous Athénée Palace hotel, which was shut when I arrived, has now reopened its doors, and its great bar [is the] meeting place for officers of many nations. Here one meets American [pilots], British RAF officers, members of the Allied Commission, Russian officers, and members of the Anglo-Saxon press."[9] In a city reeling from heavy bombing, Patmore found that the rich ate "plenty of caviar" in Bucharest's luxurious restaurants, while ordinary Romanians shared with him their elation about having the Transylvania region returned to Romania after the armistice. Patmore wrote of a country where people were "exulting over their newfound freedom," where new political groups were popping up like "mushrooms," where booksellers could not keep up with the demand for "English and Russian novels," and where theaters rehearsed a new repertoire of British and Russian plays to compensate for "four years of dreary German drama."[10] Drawing on his conversations with the political leaders of the National Peasants and Liberal parties, who returned to the limelight after Antonescu had banned them, Patmore noted that the new government was "bent on proving Romania's sincere friendship and intentions towards Russia."[11] In October 1944—the same month Churchill and Stalin drafted the now-notorious percentage agreement that brought Eastern Europe under the Soviet sphere of influence—Patmore ended one of his cables on a high note, one that captured a profound sentiment of relief and anticipation of the end of the war and the defeat of fascism: "Today Bucharest is proud to be liberated by the Red Army and as I walk through the streets I see the flags of Russia, Britain, and America in every shop window."[12]

The presence of Soviet troops was, in fact, the first sign that the sovietization of the country was already underway. Right around the time Patmore was cabling his articles, in October 1944, the Romanian and Soviet governments signed a memorandum that stipulated the number of Romanian forces that would join the Soviet army, as well as the units that would be demobilized or dissolved (Békés et al. 2015, 39). This accord violated the armistice agreement signed in September 1944, which had already reduced the number of Romanian troops necessary to maintain internal order and had replaced them with Soviet troops (39).

With direct support from the Soviets, the Romanian Communist Party exploited the tensions and frustrations ignited by the war and eventually maneuvered its way to fully control the government. This was quite an accomplishment for a party that had been banned during the interwar years, had rejected the post-1918 formation of Greater Romania, and had around one thousand members in 1944 (Tismăneanu 2003).[13] Once Romania switched sides and joined the Allies in 1944, however, the local Communist Party quickly intensified its political presence. First, it became part of the new government in the fall of 1944. Then, after several governments resigned in rapid succession between October 1944 and March 1945 in the face of street protests across the country, the king had to approve a coalition government strongly dominated by the communists, which included a communist prime minister.[14]

In March 1945, immediately after coming to power, the Communist-led government launched a land reform meant to redistribute property to poorer peasants, especially to those who had participated in the war (or whose families had).[15] Around six hundred thousand households received land, but they were not given property titles (Békés et al. 2015, 107). Gheorghe Gheorghiu-Dej admitted to Stalin that the delay in distributing titles was a political strategy for the upcoming elections, which were scheduled for November 1946: "We want to divide up property titles during the electoral campaign, as one of the ways in which to attract peasants" (107). He made this comment in Moscow, where the leaders of the Romanian Communist Party had traveled in April 1946 to meet with Stalin and receive his advice on how to win the elections. Stalin helped them prepare their political platform and suggested that they not mention more radical reforms, such as the nationalization of private property, in order not to "scare people" (109). He was also willing to support their campaign—more exactly, he agreed to give Dej $1 million dollars "to send out around 15,000 activists throughout the country for three months of propaganda work" (115).

The Communist Party formed a coalition with the Social Democrats and other parties on the left and won 84 percent of the vote in the November elections. This result led some foreign governments, including the US, to refuse to recognize the validity of the election and to accuse the new government of manipulating the results.[16] However, a confidential report prepared for the Communist Party estimated that the left-wing coalition still would have won around 45 percent of the votes in a fair election—not the majority of votes, as they had declared, but a significant number (Bottoni 2017, 41). This estimate indicates the depth of social and political divisions within a country torn apart not just by the war and the famine of 1945–46 but also by a radical social polarization between the rich and poor in postwar Romania, where 40 percent of the population was still illiterate (Békés et al. 2015, 109).

In July 1947, the leftist coalition government dissolved the previously dominant parties (the Liberals and the National Peasants Party). In November 1947, state officials pushed the Social Democrats to merge with the Communist Party and to form the Romanian Workers' Party. A month later, the communist government forced King Mihai to abdicate and declared Romania a popular republic. A wave of sweeping reforms followed suit. In February 1948, the government dissolved the parliament and replaced it with the Great National Assembly, the new legislative body of the state. New elections were organized at the end of March 1948. Following the elections, the Great National Assembly enacted the new constitution, which abolished private property and proclaimed the means of production as the property of the people.[17]

The nationalization of the industrial assets and of real estate occurred in 1948. The 1948 nationalization was one of the most significant means to form a material basis for the new state, in a process that started immediately after the war, before the communists officially came to power. As part of the postwar retribution, the post-1945 regime confiscated the assets (houses and land) of all of the ethnic Germans (though some of the houses were returned ten years later) (Tismăneanu et al. 2006, 543–46). However, the new state was not interested in making amends to the war victims either, especially to the Jews. Once the communists came to power, they forgot about their earlier promises to return Jewish property and defended the Romanians who had appropriated Jewish houses and business during the war (Ancel 2005, 246).[18] The collectivization of land was launched soon afterward in early 1949. All of the land that was not distributed during the agrarian reform in 1945 became state property. Although any attempt to resist was officially punished with three to fifteen years in prison and the confiscation of all of the individual's assets, the collectivization became a much more convoluted process, leading to widespread resistance and revealing a new state that was in fact weak (Kligman and Verdery 2011).[19]

At the same time, the new regime had ambitious plans to modernize society, launch a rapid industrialization, and provide housing to a growing urban population. The state's push for an accelerated industrialization, for which it needed a much larger labor force, along with the 1946 famine in the northern regions and the forced collectivization of agricultural land, prompted many peasants to leave their home villages for the cities. The nationalization of real estate offered a relative but temporary palliative to the postwar housing crisis, especially in the large cities. The state brought tenants to live with the house owners (Chelcea 2004) and redistributed some of the nationalized houses to institutions and individuals within the party apparatus. However, the growing number of migrants caused the postwar housing crisis to become only more acute.

During spring and summer 1944, Bucharest had undergone massive bombing, hit first by the Americans and then by the Germans (after Romania switched sides, joining the Allies in August 1944). The fabric of the city was torn apart. More than ten thousand buildings were fully or partially destroyed; 75,000 people lost their homes.[20] In addition, in the immediate years after the war, between 1948 and 1952, Bucharest's population grew from around 1,042,000 to more than 1,157,000.[21] In 1953 alone, 42,000 people arrived in the city, many of them trying to get away from the countryside and secure a job in industry.[22] Some of the newcomers tried to solve the housing problem on their own, despite the attempts of the local authorities to stop the unauthorized constructions. Approximately fifteen hundred small, one-story houses had been built under what state officials deemed "unhealthy conditions" throughout the city, and the trend continued.[23] People were desperate to have a roof over their heads, so they built such constructions in haste, many of them lacking basic utilities. At the same time, the state planners admitted that they could not keep up with this sudden population growth. Between 1948 and 1952, the local authorities built around fourteen hundred new apartments—in other words, the number of unauthorized constructions was higher than what the state could accomplish within the same time interval.[24]

In a 1952 meeting of the Council of Ministers (the government), Gheorghe Gheorghiu-Dej warned that it was "dangerous" for the state not to be able to provide housing to their workers.[25] At the same time, he declared that the government was not "indifferent about what we build, how we build, and who the builder [is]," alluding to the imperative to stop the unauthorized constructions that were proliferating all over Bucharest and to strictly follow a master plan.[26] State officials signaled their ambivalence, confusion, and especially frustration with how long it would take for these promises to become reality. The stenographic records of these meetings, alongside reports and earlier proposals prepared by architects, reveal a back-and-forth debate about what the central authorities wanted to make of Bucharest. What exactly was a socialist city? How did they want to achieve it? How many people would be allowed to live in the capital? Should the state authorities have exclusive rights over the building process, or should ordinary people also be allowed to build their own houses? How much of the existing urban fabric should, or could, be demolished? These questions led to incessant debates behind closed doors in government headquarters. Some officials had a few answers; others did not know much about urban planning but wanted to play the devil's advocate. But as they kept debating the fate of the city, they became increasingly aware that they had very few concrete solutions on how to tackle the project of building socialism. These meetings revealed a battle that was not always about urban planning alone but also about particular visions of what a communist state should be and how it should function.

The Soviet Blueprint

In June 1949, prompted by a phone call from Dej, Bucharest's city council (the equivalent of city hall in the communist administrative bureaucracy) commissioned a team of eleven architects to begin work on a socialist master plan for Bucharest, a pursuit ambitiously described as "an act of great importance for the current political moment."[27] The team prepared a draft of a plan for Bucharest that drew closely on Moscow's 1935 master plan.[28] The planners also sought Soviet advice at several stages in their work on Bucharest's plan. After their proposal was completed and reviewed by party leaders, the Romanian team intended to go to Moscow to discuss their work with Soviet specialists and modify the plan based on the latter's recommendations.[29] The Soviet team was then scheduled to visit the city to evaluate in situ the solutions proposed by the Romanian architects and to give their final approval.[30] According to the guidelines issued in 1951, it was the Soviets, not the Romanian leaders, who would have had the final say in the planning of Bucharest. However, this hierarchy of power, which in 1951 appeared obvious and incontestable, would change considerably by the end of the 1950s.

In the 1930s, Moscow's plan had emerged, in fact, as a compromise. As historian Karl Schlögel found in the text accompanying the master plan, the Soviet planners had emphasized the contrast between the past and the present, between "a true socialist city" and "the barbaric features of Russian capitalism," the latter reflected in "the narrow, crooked streets, the fragmentation of its districts by a plethora of streets and blind alleyways, the uneven development of the center and the periphery" (the 1935 Moscow master plan in Schlögel 2014, 37).[31] At the same time, the Soviets did not—could not—pursue a total erasure of this past, which would have entailed a demolition of kilometer after kilometer of streets and buildings in the city center. Instead, the planners proposed a middle way: "What matters in defining a plan for Moscow is to preserve the foundations of the city as it has developed historically, while . . . restructuring it by means of a thoroughgoing reform of its streets and squares" (38). Schlögel observed that the blueprint for a socialist Moscow included a number of major features: a cap on population (not to exceed five million); a relative straightening of the streets in the center, some of them widened, others newly built; "imposing new buildings" to be erected in the main intersections and squares, meant to "reconfigure the image of the city as a whole"; and ring roads that would go around the center and be connected radially via other roads to the outermost ring (38–39). These ring roads (in addition to the building of the metro) were designed to solve the traffic congestion.

Drawing closely on Moscow's plan, the Romanian architects came up with similar solutions.[32] They employed the same rhetoric about the contrast between the bourgeois past and the socialist present, about the capitalism that led to the uneven development of the city, marked by the radical contrast between a wealthy city center and the poor periphery. However, they were aware of their significant limitations of time and resources. The architects knew that they could not intervene much in Bucharest's center—especially not until they would have solved the housing crisis. Instead, they proposed some minimal interventions via a modernization of the main squares, and a system of thoroughfares that closely mirrored Moscow: three major traffic rings surrounding the city, connected by radial avenues that linked the city to the periphery.[33]

The political importance of Bucharest's master plan, and its further role in functioning as a template for the urban development of the other cities, was signaled by the government's decision to confer it a legal foundation. In November

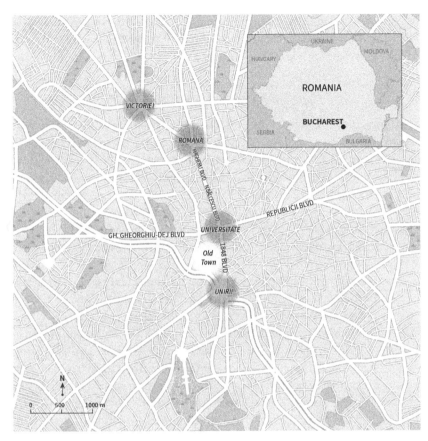

Map 1.1. The center of Bucharest around 1968. The four main intersections are marked by gray circles. Map by Daniella Collins, based on a map available at www.ideirubane.ro.

1952, the government issued a decree "on the construction and reconstruction of the cities and the organization of architectural activity."[34] The decree established a new institution, the State Committee for Architecture, set in charge of supervising the planning and building of all cities in socialist Romania. The committee functioned as a distinct ministry in the government, with its head holding the rank of a minister. In other words, the socialist transformation of Romania's cities had become such a vital project for the new government that it decided to create a separate ministry, rather than a subordinate department within the Ministry of Internal Affairs. The decree set out the main guidelines for Bucharest's development. It limited the perimeter of the city as well as its population (to a maximum of 1.7 million inhabitants) and laid out two long-term goals: (1) to smooth out the striking difference between the center and the periphery, and (2) to bring order into the city. However, the clear directives set out by the decree were further contested by different factions within the government as well as among architects.

A City as a System

In the government meetings about Bucharest's master plan, one of the words that constantly came up in the discussions to describe the current state of the city was *chaos*. The interwar elites had already pondered on Bucharest's chaotic development, debates that led to the formulation of a 1935 master plan. However, the 1952 decree deemed that earlier effort "a dead piece of work, with no technical and economic foundation."[35] By dismissing previous attempts to modernize the capital, the party appropriated the discourse of "order" and presented it as an intrinsic element of the socialist project. The interwar efforts were dismissed as useless, because the city allegedly "continued to develop anarchically and conform to the interests of the dominant class."[36] Ironically, some of the architects who had been involved in the design of the 1935 master plan later joined the team working on the socialist master plan.[37]

Even though the 1952 decree stressed the need for urban planning solutions that would highlight the contrast between the interwar and communist periods, it did not move beyond very general directives. In 1952, Macovei, as the new chief architect of Bucharest, was commissioned to develop Bucharest's master plan (drawing on the preliminary work done by the other teams between 1949 and 1952).[38] Macovei had already established himself as one of the most respected architects of the new regime. During his architectural studies in the 1930s, he had benefited from his apprenticeship under some of the best-known architects of the interwar years. He also became close to some of the members of the then-illegal Communist Party and financially supported the movement by contributing regularly to the "Red Help," a Soviet-sponsored organization that funded the activities of the underground communist parties.[39] On graduating from architecture school in 1939, despite his political allegiances, he had worked for the pro-fascist government, first in the Ministry of Internal Affairs and then in the Ministry of Propaganda, before spending more than two years, between 1941 and 1943, in Nazi Germany and fascist Italy as an attaché of the Romanian state.[40] He resumed his ties with the underground Communist Party on his return to Romania in 1943 but then fled Bucharest in spring 1944 to seek protection from the bombing. He reemerged only after Romania sided with the Allies in August 1944. Despite his radio silence during his two years abroad, when the party members did not know whether he was still loyal to their movement, he managed to quell their doubts and to persuade the Party of his loyalty. Disavowing his former career as a bureaucrat in the former pro-Nazi Romanian government, Macovei officially became a member of the Communist Party in 1945 and rapidly climbed the political ladder, joining the leadership of the Ministry of Constructions and then of the State Committee for Architecture. In 1952, he was appointed chief architect of Bucharest, a position that he held until 1958, when he began a new career as a diplomatic attaché, first in France, then in Italy.[41]

As Bucharest's chief architect, Macovei found himself in a prestigious but equally risky position. He and his team had to prepare a master plan that would decide how Bucharest would look and function for the next fifty years and beyond. Time was short; the pressure was high. In November 1953, two months after the team had started drafting the plan, Macovei was summoned to present the preliminary results to the Council of Ministers, led by Gheorghe Gheorghiu-Dej.[42] The discussions began at 9:00 a.m. and ended at 1:20 p.m. It was a long meeting but definitely not tedious; the stenographs of the discussions, totaling almost one hundred pages, capture an atmosphere of intense debate.[43] A close reading of these discussions shows that negotiations about urban space were negotiations over political power.

The meeting began with Macovei giving a lengthy presentation about the preliminary work he and his team had done on the master plan. He had to walk a fine line between displaying his own expertise and signaling his awareness of what everyone at the table took for granted: that in a centralized system, the political hierarchy mirrored the hierarchy of knowledge, meaning that the top state officials ultimately had the final word about everything. Macovei began by guardedly stating that he knew that the city's master plan was directly dependent on the future "socioeconomic profile of [the] city."[44] Yet there was no consensus, he cautioned, on what that profile should be: Was the capital to become an industrial hub or rather an administrative and residential area, with large industries moved elsewhere? And if it were to become an industrial center, what specific industries would be developed?

Without a clear idea about the future economic profile of the city, all that he presented, Macovei said, were merely "hypotheses."[45] Even though his team kept asking for more concrete information about the city's current economy, many of the ministers could not provide such data or offer predictions for the future. Macovei's team had requested data from forty-three central institutions; only seventeen had provided information.[46] The lack of coordination among these institutions led to a precarious situation: on one hand, the architects had to show rapid progress on the master plan; on the other hand, their plans would not amount to much if they did not address the city's economic and industrial needs. However, Macovei could not directly spell out this conundrum because the officials who represented some of these institutions were in the audience, and he likely did not want to risk his own position.

Instead, he quickly placed blame on previous city planners. He highlighted the contrast between the past and the present, describing a city that had developed as "a spider web of narrow and skewed streets," whose surface was mostly occupied by one-story houses, spread in disarray, which made Bucharest "look like an ordinary village, not the capital of the republic."[47] He noted the large discrepancy between the center of the city, with a density of 355 people per hectare, and the periphery, which had fewer than 10 people per hectare and lacked basic infrastructure (access to gas, sewage, and electricity).[48] Under these conditions, he suggested, Bucharest could barely aspire to be considered a modern capital.

The goal of the master plan was to create "a more cohesive city, a city that would work as a system,"[49] and with that goal in mind, he proposed several interventions. The first was the development of three major thoroughfares in the form of three concentric circles connected by several boulevards, an arrangement that would drastically improve traffic in and out of the city.[50] Buildings seven to eight stories tall would line the thoroughfares, followed by multiple five-to-six-story buildings on major streets opening from the thoroughfares, as well as lower buildings lining narrower streets.[51] Another intervention was to connect all of the green areas of the city to each other via new alleys. He also favored zoning—a strict separation between residential, commercial, and industrial areas—as a way to solve the allegedly chaotic current organization of city life.[52] Finally, he suggested placing a series of tall buildings in the main central squares that would alter the skyline of the city center.[53] All of these elements closely drew on Moscow's master plan. This obvious deference to the Soviets' urban vision should have made Macovei's proposal politically "safe," as he assumed that the Romanian leadership would approve a plan mirroring the Soviet blueprint.

The fierce debates that followed Macovei's presentation, however, revealed internal power struggles among the different factions in the party leadership. This infighting raises a further question: To what extent were the interventions into the urban fabric of Bucharest the product of carefully thought-out decisions, and how much were they influenced by chance, confusion, or political competition? To answer this question, I analyze the web of alliances and tensions among different political actors present at the November 1953 meeting, paying close attention not only to how these politicians commented on Macovei's proposal but also to how they supported, criticized, or ignored one another.

The discussions revolved around three points: the imperative to build quicker and to abandon unnecessary architectural embellishment, which was an indirect criticism of the socialist realist style promoted under Stalin and exported to all of the Soviet satellites in the early 1950s; the need to stop unauthorized constructions and to increase control by making local institutions more responsive to the government's requirements; and the lack of a qualified labor force and the need to search for an alternative to Soviet advice. In what follows, I focus on each of these points.

"The Plan Must Be the Dictator"

In the early 1950s, the architecture in the socialist bloc had to replicate socialist realism's monotonous monumentality. Famously epitomized by Moscow's "seven sisters"—the septet of nearly identical skyscrapers built under Stalin's personal supervision—socialist realism was the aesthetic byword for Stalinization. In architecture, it was represented by solutions that sought to be both modern and neoclassical, to include stylistic elements alluding to the past while subsuming that past under a monumental, triumphant socialist modernity (Zarecor 2011). Scholars have debated the extent to which socialist realism emerged as a critique of the architectural avant-garde of the 1920s, or if it was just a continuation of that radicalism. Addressing these questions, architectural historian Vladimir Paperny argued that the two periods should be viewed as a set of contrasts. He highlighted the stark differences between what he called Culture One, which expressed the "fluidity" of the Soviet avant-garde in the 1920s and a democratic horizontality in architectural vocabulary, and Culture Two, which represented the freezing absolutism of Stalin's epoch (Paperny 2002). However, art critic Boris Groys (2003) challenged Paperny's view by arguing that the tenets of the 1920s avant-gardes directly informed socialist realism. Groys noted that "the production of images in Socialist Realism served above all to depict the utopia of a happy future" in the form of "a new public with new eyes" (22–23) that the avant-garde artists always imaged as consumers of their art.

This utopia was soon to be exported abroad. According to Stalin's own tenet, any architectural project in the new satellites of the Soviet Union had to be "national in form and socialist in content." In 1950s Romania, the party leaders were careful to signal their political submission to Moscow by employing the same rhetoric and making sure they include it in official documents.[54] However, a year later, in the November 1953 meeting about Bucharest's master plan, Gheorghe Gheorghiu-Dej launched a new imperative. He requested an "industrialization of construction," calling for efficiency and an economical approach to building: "If we want the population to say, 'Yes, they are good managers [*gospodari buni*],' we should then do the things right. If we built a construction site, it needs to be well equipped, they need to know how much technology they need, what kind of architecture. As for the housing space, [we need to know] how much of it could be used, and how much for decoration, because there are some [architects] who assign 30 percent for usage, and 70 percent of the location is formed of dead angles. We need to abandon this approach."[55] Dej's demand for the industrialization of the building process and his criticism of "dead angles" signaled a pragmatic attitude, but it was also rather daring. Even though it was not an official call for change, it must be acknowledged like one for all practical purposes. By giving Macovei the green light to focus on function and not form, Dej indirectly asked the planners to abandon the prevalent architectural style of Stalinism and pursue a more functional architecture.

One of the first signals of political thaw was the distance that the new Soviet leadership took from the pursuit of socialist realism in architecture after Stalin's death. The style that had represented monumentality and political grandeur under Stalinism became associated with a waste of resources. In December 1954, at the All Union Conference of Builders and Architects, Nikita Khrushchev criticized the costly and gratuitous embellishment of socialist realism and called instead for the standardization of construction techniques and the building of "more economical and functional housing" (Senkevitch 1978, 592). That speech marked a new phase in the architectural practice of the Soviet bloc. It allowed—in fact, encouraged—the architects on the eastern side of the Iron Curtain to critically engage with the principles of postwar Western modernism (Popescu 2009, 109).

Placed in this broader context, Dej's open dismissal of dead angles in architecture was significant because it preceded Khrushchev's by more than a year—and it was made at a time when the directives from Moscow were not very clear, given the tense infighting for Stalin's succession. Dej's criticism of unnecessary "decoration" and his push for functional architecture and economical usage of resources signaled a deeper change in his political agenda. He began seeking relative autonomy from the USSR almost immediately after Stalin's death. His strategy becomes apparent if we pay attention to his behavior during the meeting about Bucharest's master plan. In that meeting, Dej did not make specific comments on Macovei's proposal to build in the periphery and postpone demolitions in the city center, which echoed the Soviet approach to planning. What preoccupied Dej most was the slow progress made in drafting the master plan and particularly the chronic housing shortage.

At the time of the 1953 meeting, Macovei estimated a deficit of forty thousand to fifty thousand apartments.[56] To meet the stringent housing needs, he proposed developing new neighborhoods mostly in larger areas on the periphery of the city, stressing that they could not afford to waste time and resources on demolitions in the city center.[57] However, the government still could not keep up with the increasing number of unauthorized constructions—which Macovei estimated to be around fifteen hundred in 1953.[58] In Macovei's view, the only solution to stop this phenomenon was for the state to allow the building of individual houses through a system of "cooperation." In his view, this system would have endowed ordinary citizens with a more active role in constructing their own homes while the local authorities still partially sponsored the construction and thus could control the final plans. Macovei argued that this policy would have stalled the spreading of one-story buildings, which at that moment made up 87 percent of the buildings in the city, and would have spurred, ideally, a shift to more modern houses with at least one extra story.[59] Although this solution seemed theoretically doable, no one else present at the meeting appeared to be persuaded by it.

The spread of unauthorized construction was visible proof that the new regime still could not make "order out of chaos," as they had promised. The housing crisis showed that what the authorities deemed to be the "chaotic development of Bucharest" was not necessarily a result of a "bourgeois" social order but rather was an immediate, improvised adjustment to the rapid social changes brought by the end of the war. These rudimentary, small houses also represented the agency of ordinary people and their determination to fight a state that did not trust its citizens to build their own homes, even though it was unable to provide housing for all of them.

The unauthorized houses revealed not only the limitations of a regime that promised a radically better society but also the laxed attitude of local bureaucrats who often ignored the illegal constructions. This story of local corruption and defiance ignited Dej's fury at the meeting. His anger was sparked not only by the disorganization and confusion around the master plan but also by his frustration with Bucharest's city council, whose bureaucrats could not control—or, worse, did not seem to care much about—the unplanned houses proliferating throughout the city. Stressing the need for a strict centralization of decision making, Dej launched into a lengthy tirade against all institutions that failed to obey the Party's orders:

> The master plan needs to be the dictator of construction in Bucharest. The city council has a large and kind heart, it is highly democratic, but such rotten bourgeois liberalism must cease now. No one can be allowed to squander state resources, to waste energy. . . . We need to train cadres—there are possibilities, and we should rely on the Soviet experience. In this regard, this is the only source that we can appeal to so we can receive help. . . . [We need] to stop haphazard work. There should be . . . an office that controls [all of the work entailed by the plan] that [everyone involved in the plan] obeys. If the city

council is not willing to fulfill that role, they should say so. Someone needs to monitor [the process]. We need to strengthen our control. We need to be extremely demanding with the architects and with everyone.[60]

His choice of words—saying that the master plan must be a "dictator," that the team must work as a "military unit"—revealed a leader highly preoccupied with retaining control. It also signaled that negotiations over urban space—who decided what to build and where, and to what extent people had a say in the location, size, and shape of their own homes—were implicitly negotiations of political power.

To regain control over the master plan and over Bucharest's urban space, Dej insisted on a stronger centralization. He asked that all the institutions responsible for the plan be subsumed under the State Committee for Planning led by Miron Constantinescu—and not under the State Committee for Architecture. Dej specifically asked Constantinescu to take over the project to "bring together some comrades with experience in this field to put together a plan that the Council of Ministers could approve."[61] In 1953, Miron Constantinescu was the head of the State Committee for Planning. A brilliant sociologist who had chosen to join the then illegal Communist Party in 1935, when he was nineteen years old, Constantinescu swiftly climbed the ranks, becoming part of the party leadership as early as October 1945. In 1949, he was appointed head of the State Committee for Planning, an institution with the rank of a ministry that was in charge of the organization and functioning of the planned economy.[62] This committee was probably the most important state institution after the Council of Ministers; Dej chose to supervise it himself during the first year, after which he passed his position to Constantinescu (Bosomitu 2015, 173). As one of the best-educated party members in a government formed mostly of former workers, Constantinescu was regarded with jealous admiration by some of his colleagues but succeeded in gaining Dej's support.

That Dej treated him as a loyal and bright ally becomes obvious from their interactions at the November 1953 meeting. At that meeting, in response to Dej's angered comments, Constantinescu defended Macovei by stressing the time constraints and the other tasks that some of the architects on the team had to attend to in parallel with working on the master plan.[63] Constantinescu then pointed out, "We have neither the specialists in construction, nor the technology and labor force . . . to be able to start constructing buildings of more than six or seven stories."[64] He brought up the example of Moscow, noting that the Soviets had not started with buildings of five to eight stories; their tall buildings were erected at a later stage, thirty years after the revolution. One solution, he said, was to intensify the training of specialists and speed up "the industrialization of the construction methods and materials." But he proposed another, more radical strategy, one that also packed a punch at the State Committee for Architecture.[65] Constantinescu advocated for more flexibility in the recruiting of architects:

> The team for the master plan must be strengthened. The team had to cope with a lack of specialists this year. . . . There are architects of great talent and experience who are still very little used. I think that the comrades in the Committee for Architecture must improve their methods of work and engaging [others].[66] There is a certain sectarianism here, which must end. We must engage highly experienced engineers and architects, but we must make them realign with the values of the supervision and line of the party and the government and discard their old beliefs.[67]

Although daring, Constantinescu's suggestion to reassign older architects to work on Bucharest's master plan was very practical. Even though few of these older architects had had any connection with the Communist Party before the war, they also possessed unique expertise based on decades of practice. It was not the first time that Constantinescu made such a suggestion. In November 1952, in another meeting of the Council of Ministers, which focused on discussing the 1952 decree and the future organization of the work on the master plan, Constantinescu remarked that "architects from the earlier generations" must be brought back. He used the example of an architect who had been a landowner and whose wealth had been confiscated by the state but whose professional value, he said, was dismissed.[68] However, at that meeting, another member of the government, Iosif Chișinevschi, replied, "We did not exclude him as an architect but as a landowner. We value him as an architect!"[69] Then Chișinevschi brought up a much larger problem: the lack of "qualified cadres."[70] He said, "We will be merciless when it comes to enemies, and we will punish any specialist who engages in actions against the party, sabotage, spying, or any diversion. But we should not destroy them just because they had been landowners. You cannot build only with people who are honest; they also need to be skilled. We should not let ourselves be influenced by some leftist elements . . . who love to attack, but when they are asked to work, they do nothing."[71]

Such remarks, made by a key member of the political establishment, signaled the government's increasing awareness that they had to rely on all of the expertise that they could find. This practical need, and not necessarily the Romanian communists' willingness to permit a relative relaxation following Stalin's death, might explain the new policies instituted in 1955, when the first wave of political prisoners had been released and brought back into the socialist labor force.[72] The party leaders worried, however, that this new group, and especially their "old beliefs," social background, education, and hidden expectations, could have potentially led to too much innovation, sparking a political reform that the party did all it could to prevent. The solution was then to tighten the government's control.

A Turn to National Stalinism

Dej's comments at the 1953 meeting made his penchant for increasing control crystal clear. He did not appear to be taken aback by Constantinescu's proposal to bring back old cadres. As he put it, "We need to search [for specialists] not only in Bucharest but also in other parts of the country. Bucharest is the heart of the country; there should be brought in workers, constructors, engineers, architects from other regions, and also employed older cadres."[73] However, he demanded total obedience from every employee at every institution.

By 1953, having already ousted some of his political rivals (i.e., the Pauker group, three prominent members of the Communist Party leadership [the Politburo] who had not shared Dej's political vision and had not shied away from saying so), Dej sought to gain full control over the Politburo and maintained that control by speaking with a forked tongue to the Soviets (Tismăneanu 1992; Bosomitu 2015, 213–44). His strategy was shown in the duplicitous way he reacted to the Soviet-endorsed de-Stalinization, launched by Khrushchev's 1956 speech acknowledging Stalin's crimes. That speech offered some hope to the satellites in the Soviet bloc that they could pursue their own path to socialism, less constrained by the Soviet model.

The most radical response to de-Stalinization was the 1956 revolt in Hungary, launched by reformers in the Hungarian Communist Party, a group led by Imre Nagy. Even though it began as an attempt to reform socialism, in the end the Hungarian elites wanted to cut all ties with Moscow and withdraw from the Soviet-controlled Warsaw Pact. The revolt was short lived: the revolutionaries were crushed by Soviet tanks, and Nagy and other government members were accused of treason. During the Hungarian revolt, Dej offered the Soviets full support, including military forces, and did everything Khrushchev asked, including allowing the Soviets to transport the Nagy group through Romania on their way to the Soviet Union, where they were tried and executed (Bottoni 2017, 94–95). Dej exploited the situation to gain Khrushchev's trust and persuade him to withdraw the Soviet military stationed on Romania's territory, which Khrushchev did in 1958 (103).

What was particularly significant about the November 1953 meeting around Bucharest's master plan was that the interactions at the table foreshadowed later political developments, such as Dej's pursuit of his own "national Stalinism," as Vladimir Tismăneanu (1992) called it. Dej's strategic distancing from Moscow and his assertion of a right to pursue a national path to communism was really a means to strengthen his domination at home and maintain an authoritarian hold on power that rejected any attempt at reform. The meeting also confirmed that Dej wanted to have the ultimate say in key decisions, and that those who had his ear used it to implement some small reforms, such as Constantinescu's proposal to hire older architects.

At the same time, the debates displayed the foibles of a centralized system. Theoretically, in the bureaucracy of the Party-state in which the government was subordinate to the party, party leaders made the decisions.[74] With Bucharest's master plan, however, party leaders could not offer much practical advice. No matter how much they tried, their comments revealed a shallow knowledge of basic principles of planning—and many of these comments contradicted one another, leading to even more confusing feedback. But the architects needed to signal that they understood the hierarchy, that the building plans had to be ultimately authorized by party leaders. Thus, discussions seemed to become more and more circular as both parties—the politicians and the architects—tried to avoid having the final say. The former did so because they did not have the necessary expertise but also did not want to admit their ignorance. The latter shied away because they did not want to be accused of disobedience (which would have quickly ended their careers). To get out of this circle, both turned to the third party: the Soviet experts.

The Soviets Come to Town

Dej's frustration with the relative lack of progress on the master plan—which he made no effort to hide in the November 1953 meeting—seemed to have catalyzed many into action. A few months later, the State Committee for Architecture reviewed the preliminary proposal produced by Macovei and his team. Based on those suggestions, in October 1954, the State Committee for Planning, led by Miron Constantinescu, submitted to the government and Bucharest's city council their report forecasting the city's socioeconomic development.[75]

Soon afterward, in January 1956, a team of seven Soviet specialists visited Bucharest. The engineers and architects working for the Soviet Committee of Urban Planning walked around the city and studied its topography. They also met with Macovei and his team as well as with specialists working on other urban projects (such as the city rail traffic and the reconstruction of Dâmbovița River, which crossed the southern part of the city).[76] They agreed with many of the proposals already outlined by Macovei in the 1953 meeting (the circular disposition of the major thoroughfares, which resembled Moscow's master plan; the focus on more peripheral area to build new residential assembles; and the use of the city's topography to develop a network of parks within the city).

The Soviet team, however, criticized other points. They found that the initial figure of 1.7 million for Bucharest's population ceiling—the maximum set by the 1952 decree—was too high and suggested reducing it to 1.5 million. They considered that the majority (75%) of the buildings could not be more than four stories high because Bucharest was located in a high-seismic area. The Soviet experts proposed the development of some "independent centers," farther from the city—basically, suburban residential areas—that would compensate for the limits set on the city's population. Other recommendations included keeping demolitions to 8 percent in the city center, rerouting and reorganizing the traffic, and expanding railway transportation.[77] The Soviets then returned to Moscow, probably assuming that their Romanian counterparts would follow their suggestions.

It turned out, however, that the Soviets' advice became yet another point of contention among the different parties. A few months after the Soviets' visit, in June 1956, Pompiliu Macovei was again summoned before the Council of Ministers to report on the revised version of the master plan.[78] There were clear tensions among the officials present at the meeting, which included the leaders of the State Committee for Architecture, Bucharest's mayor, and some of the architects on the master plan team. Macovei noted that he agreed with many of the Soviets' suggestions, especially the recommendation on setting the population cap lower and controlling who exactly would be allowed to live in the city. Ideally, Macovei said, the migrants should be mostly those who would join the "productive group," people who worked in the industrial sector, while the others be either pushed into production or forced out of the city. He echoed the Soviet model, noting that "people who were born in Moscow were then sent to live somewhere else."[79] But he said that the Soviets' solution—of establishing smaller towns outside the city area—was untenable for Bucharest. The bulk of Bucharest's industrial areas were still inside the city, which meant that workers must live within close proximity to their jobs.[80]

He admitted that such solutions would help solve the housing crisis: if the number of the city dwellers was going to rise to 1.5 million by 1970, they would need to build 118,000 apartments.[81] Three years had passed since the first master plan meeting, and the state was still grappling with the housing deficit. When Constantinescu confronted Macovei about it, asking him how many apartments had been built per year, Macovei answered one thousand. He compared Bucharest's situation to other capitals in the Soviet bloc (Warsaw, where twelve thousand apartments had been built per year, Sophia, with three thousand, and Prague and Budapest, with four thousand to six thousand).[82] Bucharest lagged far behind, and Macovei used this striking contrast to reject one of the main recommendations of the Soviets: to limit the city expansion.[83]

Macovei insisted that the city surface be extended, not constrained. The new residential zones thus could be primarily built on the city's periphery, which would entail minimum demolition.[84] He also complained that there were not enough factories producing construction materials.[85]

Figures, costs, functionality, economic needs—Macovei presented the master plan as an economic plan, exactly as Dej had requested three years earlier. But Dej was not present at this meeting, and Macovei came under criticism for lacking a coherent aesthetic vision. Chivu Stoica, the president of the Council of Ministers and the chair of the 1956 meeting, remarked that not much would change: "There will still be this mosaic of narrow and convoluted streets. Bucharest will not be a city with straight avenues and clearly aligned neighborhoods. The city will continue to appear as an unshapely mass."[86] Macovei replied that they had considered the aesthetics question and that the plan included a network of thoroughfares marked by major intersections. He said, however, that they could not straighten all of the streets into a modern grid because they still depended on the underground utilities infrastructure, paralleling the existing streets.

Nevertheless, more criticism followed. It became a larger debate between those who favored a master plan with a bold aesthetic vision and those who focused on functionality and on building as much as possible in the shortest time. The tension between aesthetics and function has been a major challenge in modern urban planning, but in the case of socialist Romania, it also spoke about distinct political agendas. Those who supported a realistic and economical plan, like Macovei and Dej, were mostly concerned with the housing crisis, which they anticipated could rapidly lead to a political crisis. The only solution they envisioned was to focus exclusively on building mass housing to satisfy the needs of a rapidly growing population. Those who highlighted the political significance of Bucharest's aesthetics did so by making comparisons to other capitals in the socialist bloc. They alluded to a subtler competition among the Soviet satellites, engaged in a peculiar race toward achieving a socialist modernization.[87]

One of the proponents of more radical interventions into the urban fabric was architect Nicolae Bădescu, the head of the State Committee for Architecture. He called the plan proposed by Macovei "modest" and argued for a bolder approach: "We need to approach the future more boldly. . . . If we keep going like this . . . in fifty, sixty years we will not have a capital that we could compare to Prague. It will be a functional city but not a beautiful, impressive city."[88] Criticizing the plan for lacking a vision of a "more optimistic, more luminous" city,[89] Bădescu alluded to a more latent conflict between the State Committee and Macovei's team: "We find that the version [of the current master plan] is not satisfactory. The version we pushed for was based on discussions with [specialists from] different sectors, but the planners rejected our proposal."[90] Macovei responded by noting, once again, that the current plan would not prevent a larger urban intervention in the future. But at that moment, he said, they just could not afford to be too bold. "The city is facing a housing crisis," he reminded the audience, "we cannot focus on the city's beautification right now."[91]

The 1956 meeting seemed to have sparked even more debates but led to no clear answers. In the absence of Dej, none of the members of the government dared to give clear directives—as if five years of discussions were not enough, and the politicians needed even more time for further debates.[92] Despite that ambiguity and the state authorities' unwillingness to come up with a final decision, June 1956 appears to be the last time the government discussed Bucharest's master plan. In the end, despite all of the debates, the planners stuck with their initial blueprint. The main guidelines of the plan remained what Macovei had initially presented in 1953: (1) the development of new residential districts in the periphery, (2) the redesign of the central squares with new tall buildings altering the cityscape, and (3) the opening of some new thoroughfares that connected the center to the new residential areas.

The June 1956 meeting was nonetheless politically important. At the time of the 1953 meeting, both the architects and the political establishment had to pay lip service to the Soviets and show that they were taking the latter's advice into account. But by 1956, they threw many of the Soviets' recommendations out the window, a choice signaling that the much-anticipated visit was just another formality to be checked off the list.[93] The appeal to Soviet expertise was not a professional imperative but a political one. For the architects who kept asking the government for a final decision and never received one, the Soviets' visit functioned like a backdoor strategy to receive the necessary validation so that they could pursue their own vision.

Between the time of the Soviets' visit in January 1956 and the time of the last government meeting about Bucharest's master plan in June 1956, things had changed. In February 1956, Khrushchev gave the famous speech condemning Stalin and his personality cult, launching de-Stalinization. Full obedience to Moscow was no longer necessary, and the architects' eventual rejection of the Soviets' recommendations reflected that shift. After the failed Hungarian revolt, the Soviet satellites learned that reform meant, however, only a relative autonomy and that the pursuit of their national interests could not radically diverge from Moscow's goals. In Romania, using the 1956 revolt as a justification for tightening political control, Dej launched a second wave of indigenous Stalinism disguised as a turn to nationalism (Petrescu 2009; Bottoni 2017, 102).

Even though he continued to court the Soviets, Dej declared in private discussions that "his party had matured and that relations between socialist countries should be governed by the principles of complete equality and national independence" (Tismăneanu 1992, 33). While he controlled the party with an iron fist, Dej also wanted to maintain the regime's legitimacy by honoring the social contract with its citizens. Mass housing and better living standards were among the key promises made by the Communist Party, and the state still needed to find a way to provide them.

Redesigning the City Center

In November 1958, at the party's third congress, Dej officially launched the call for speeding up the building process across the country. He asked all of the institutions in the field to do everything they could to "build as fast as they [could], as cheap as they [could], and as best they [could]," pushing for the industrialization of the construction process, praising the need for prefabricated materials, and so on.[94] It was an endorsement of what was already happening in the architectural field—and of what Dej himself had already requested in the 1953 meeting. This time, however, Dej's speech was an official signal of change, strategically echoing Khrushchev's 1954 call for a shift to functional architecture and efficient housing. All of the major cities in Romania pursued this building frenzy, but the phenomenon became especially obvious in Bucharest.

The same year (1958), Pompiliu Macovei moved on to a different position, and Horia Maicu became Bucharest's chief architect. Even though he had earned a reputation as a modernist architect in the interwar years, after the war Maicu became an ardent promoter of socialist realism and a high flier in the party system. He viewed Bucharest's master plan as a new opportunity for him to gain further visibility.[95] He became much more vocal about it—in contrast to Macovei, who had rarely, or if at all, spoken in public about the plan.[96] Responding to the political leadership's urge to build faster and better, Maicu claimed that he and his team of 350 specialists had come up with a new version of the master plan, one that reflected the new priorities outlined by Dej's speech.[97] In fact, he merely appropriated the work already done, because the blueprint that he presented to the Architects' Union in 1963 followed very closely the same tenets that the previous teams of architects had kept presenting over and over again to the government.[98] Granted, Maicu had a knack for knowing how to advance his career, as he had already amply demonstrated by swiftly adapting from modernism in the 1930s to socialist realism in the 1950s and then to a more functional architecture in the 1960s. However, he also directly benefited from an institutional change in the architectural field.

Starting in November 1959, a decree granted the chief architects of the cities, employed by local city councils, more leverage over central institutions of urban planning controlled by the State Committee for Architecture.[99] This meant that the specialists from the center no longer had the final say on large urban interventions; that power was transferred to local authorities (which until then had only executive, but not decisional, power in matters of planning). The decree also asserted that the local officials should no longer develop master plans for their cities, which would have entailed significant work and a long-term economic forecast. Instead, the building projects were to be pursued according to a short-term plan (*schiţa de sistematizare*), an outline of urban interventions for the following ten years, meant to address only the cities' most pressing economic and social needs. At the same time, the decree enforced stricter limits on city territory and specifically required the local authorities to forbid building projects outside that limit. This meant that the city officials had to turn their attention to more central areas.

In Bucharest, the authorities focused on the redesign of the main squares in the city, more specifically on University Square and Union Square. A competition for the redesign of University Square had already been launched in 1956, but those plans were eventually abandoned.[100] In contrast, the redesign of Union Square had a different story. It created a much more visible stir within and outside the architecture field, debates that eventually led to accusations thrown at the architects by other institutions with different stakes in the location. It was also one of the first competitions opened to all architects, and not just commissioned directly to Project Bucharest Institute, the institution in principle in charge of all the urban planning projects in the capital.

Bucharest's city council launched the public competition for Union Square on September 10, 1959, with the deadline set for November 10.[101] In architectural practice, a two-month deadline meant that the architects' teams had to work day and night if they wanted to cram all of the necessary thinking, consulting, and drafting, as well as complete the final design within such a tight time frame. Despite the short time line, however, the authorities received a record number of proposals—seventy-one, "the highest ever received in [an architectural] competition in our country."[102] Twenty days after the deadline, on November 30, 1959, the jury announced their final selection. The jury declared the winning proposal as a "clear and simple" solution that considered both the intense traffic in the square and the housing needs.[103] The winning team envisioned the square to be surrounded by tall apartment buildings, with three other apartment buildings placed in the center, and connected at the base by a large commercial space that would replace the immense market hall.

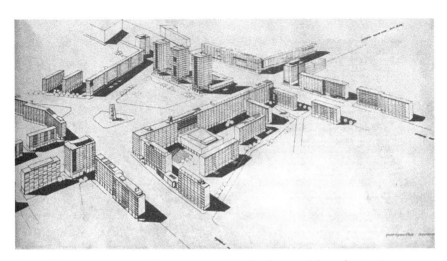

Fig. 1.1. The winning project of the 1959 competition for the remodeling of Union Square. *Arhitectura* 62, no. 1 (1960): 15. Photo by Sarah Andrews. Used by permission of *Arhitectura* journal.

The best proposals selected by the jury were then displayed in a public exhibit.[104] Architects as well as a larger audience could assess the projects and envision how Union Square would look in the near future. As it turned out, the unusual openness of the local authorities, who normally did not advertise the projects they had commissioned, proved to be their Achilles' heel. The jury's decision, and the competition itself, became highly contested. Immediately after the opening of the exhibit, in late December 1959, the Architects' Union organized a discussion about the finalists, attended by around two hundred architects, including some of the participants in the competition.[105] The latter complained that the competition guidelines had been confusing and that they received no clear answers when they had asked for further clarification. Some of the architects even questioned the jury's decision but were in turn criticized for acting as "prosecutors of the jury."[106] Others pointed out that the square could not be both an intense traffic node and a residential site, thus challenging the winning project. Amid all that talk, only one speaker observed that the competition did not take into account the historic monuments abutting Union Square, such as the Old Court and Manuk Inn. His remark, however, went unnoticed.[107]

The planned expansion of Union Square purportedly had a pragmatic purpose—that of improving the traffic in one of the most congested areas of the city. It also had a strategic one: to mark one of the key nodes in the city center. The expansion of Union Square, however, would have entailed the demolition of the southern part of the commercial district of the Old Town, including a historic inn and the site of the Old Court Palace, whose partial walls had just been discovered during the first excavations in the early 1950s. With one exception, all of the proposals selected by the jury aimed to actively erase the monuments from the city's geography. They envisioned replacing the seventeenth-century Manuk Inn abutting the square with longitudinal apartment buildings meant to hide the Old Town neighborhood and the Old Court Church.

Making a tabula rasa out of the Old Town neighborhood was the dream of many architects coming of age in the 1950s. The proposals for Union Square showed that the majority of architects considered the Old Town to be too old and cumbersome—that is, an obstacle in the modern development of the capital. But their dreams of demolition were not new either. As already discussed in the introduction, the elites of interwar Bucharest had already had a complicated relationship with the district, alternating between a fascination with and repugnance for the Old Town's colorful economic and ethnic mélange. The area remained one of the main commercial areas of the city but came to emblematize shoddy businesses and moral and urban disorder—an image that led Pompiliu Macovei to describe the area as a place filled with "money lenders."[108] During the interwar period, the Old Town kept its waxing and waning position on Bucharest's cultural map, with periodic attempts by city officials to redesign it or erase it altogether (Dobrescu 1934, 30–33, 51–52). Those attempts had been thwarted by political infighting and rapid succession of mayors with different urban visions. This time, in 1959, no obstacle seemed to be in the way; the architects proposed solutions, the authorities approved them, and the work on the square was set to begin.

But then an anonymous letter changed everything. This letter triggered a chain of questions, accusations, and self-justifications that eventually led not only to the indefinite postponement of the redesign of Union Square but to something the architects would never have imagined: the preservation and then reconstruction of the Old Court Palace, which would be resurrected out of almost nothing and transformed into a national historic site. The next chapter tells that story.

Conclusion

The transformation of Bucharest into a socialist capital was among the first large projects Romanian communists launched after coming to power. A combination of ambition and frustration underlay this enterprise. Their ambition was obvious: to transform a city that they viewed as the embodiment of chaos, poverty, and disorder into a modern socialist capital, and to prove that they were able to accomplish that. But they had a double frustration: with the present and also with the past.

What the state authorities found frustrating about the present was that unauthorized buildings continued to go up in the city despite their attempt to halt them. Urban planning in early socialist Romania became a political technology—a means to suppress an alleged disorder by closely monitoring urban space and by forbidding ordinary people to build their own houses. Instead, these people were asked to put their trust in a state that promised it would build for them—but could not deliver. In fact, as time passed and politicians and urban planners continued to negotiate the master plan, Bucharest's housing crisis only worsened. If in 1953, Macovei noted that there were around 1,500 unauthorized houses, between 1958 and 1971, their number rose to 11,500 (and the authorities estimated that the real number was actually double).[109] Bucharest's master plan thus functioned both as an end and a means. Yes, state leaders did want to transform the city into a modern socialist capital. However, they also used the discussions on how to pursue that project as a canvas against which they carried out their own internal power struggles.

During these prolonged discussions about the future form and function of socialist Bucharest, the Soviet influence gradually diminished, but both architects and politicians manipulated the Soviets' role for their own agendas. The former invoked the Soviets' advice to endorse their own ideas, while the latter used the Soviets as a cover up for what everyone already knew: that the party leadership had no knowledge about urban planning and that they eventually had to rely on the architects' expertise, while pretending that they had the final say.

However, what architects and politicians had in common, at least initially, was their frustration with the past as inscribed in Bucharest's space. Even though they quickly realized that they had to partially accept that past, because they had neither the techniques nor the resources to build skyscrapers overnight, they tried to minimize it. The competition for Union Square's modernization illustrates their intentions. However, by the time the authorities decided to redesign Union Square, the regime began to claim their right to carve out their own national path to communism. The *nation* as a category of belonging and as political rhetoric began to matter again. The urban past that the architects so despised suddenly turned into an invaluable resource for other professionals and, in the end, for the Romanian socialist state of the 1960s. The new nationalist turn opened the door to archaeologists to advance their own agendas.

Notes

1. ANIC, Fond Cabinetul Consiliului de Miniştri, Stenogramele şedintelor Prezidiului Consiliului de Miniştri, June 1956, file 6/1956, 139.
2. File 6/1956, 140.
3. ANIC, Fond Cabinetul Consiliului de Miniştri, Stenograma şedintei Consiliului de Miniştri, 13 noiembrie, 1952, file 11/1952, 21.
4. For Czechoslovakia, see Zarecor (2011); for Yugoslavia, see LeNormand (2014); for Romania, see Maxim (2018); for a comparative study of East Germany and Hungary, see Molnár (2013); for Albania, see Mëhilli (2017); for a comparative approach to modernism in the postwar Soviet bloc and beyond, see Kulic, Penick, and Parker (2014); for the Soviet Union, see DeHaan (2013).
5. See LeNormand (2014), Molnár (2013), Zarecor (2011). For Romania, see ANIC, Fond Cabinetul Consiliului de Miniştri, file 6/1952, 1–13. Architects Horia Maicu and Pompiliu Macovei led a Romanian delegation to Moscow, where they organized an exhibit of the architecture from Romanian People's Republic and received reviews from the Soviet architects. They also visited the Soviet Architecture Institute, and they learned more about the organization and functioning of the Soviet Architects' Union.
6. In 1959, Nicolae Bădescu, head of the State Committee for Architecture, declared the *sketch* of the master plan completed. That year, the government passed the 1678/1959 that officially promoted the sketch of urban development (*schiţa de sistematizare*) as the main instrument to be elaborated by planners and followed by the architects and builders. A fully detailed master plan for Bucharest was never accomplished. For Bădescu's declaration, see excerpts from ANIC, Fond CC al PCR, file 183/1959, 1–7, 11–12, in Stroe (2015, 174).
7. In addition to appropriating all German assets on Romania's territory and exploiting the population's resources to supply Soviet troops during their occupation of the country, the Soviets punitively inflated the level of reparations by using 1938 prices to calculate the value of goods to be transferred to the USSR, rather than their current value at the end of the war, which was much lower. See Bachmann (1989, § "World War II") accessed July 20, 2017, http://countrystudies.us/romania/22.htm.
8. Bachmann (1989, § "World War II")
9. ANIC, Fond 2904 Ministerul Propagandei Naţionale, file 1394/1944, 10–11.
10. File 1394/1944, 12.
11. File 1394/1944, 12.
12. File 1394/1944, 12–13.
13. Post-1918 Greater Romania was formed following the territorial accords at Versailles. A last-minute change of political tides during World War I, complemented by a shrewd diplomatic intervention during the Versailles Treaty, enabled Romania to gain the regions of Bukovina, Transylvania, and Bessarabia. This was a profound change from an ethnically compact state to a multiethnic polity, with a doubled territory in which the ethnically non-Romanian groups formed one-third of the country's population. For an analysis of the cultural politics of Romanization that the Bucharest authorities imposed especially on Transylvania's minorities, see Livezeanu (1995).
14. Petru Groza (1884–1958) was the leader of the left-wing party Ploughmen's Front, which he founded in 1933.
15. Law 187 of March 23, 1945, guaranteed "the expansion of the agrarian land of the households that owned less than 5 ha." See "Lege nr. 187 din 23 martie 1945 pentru înfăptuirea

reformei agrare," Camera Deputaţilor, accessed January 30, 2010, http://www.cdep.ro/pls /legis/legis_pck.htp_act_text?idt=1569. Originally published in *Monitorul Oficial*, no. 68, March 23, 1945.

16. "Acheson Declares Romanian Election Violated Pledge of Free and Unfettered Balloting," *Gazette* (Pennsylvania), November 27, 1946, 26, via Newspapers.com, accessed June 24, 2018, https://www.newspapers.com/newspage/65897935/.

17. ANIC, Fond 2904 Ministerul Propagandei Naţionale, file 1663/1948. Journalist Liviu Nasta to *New York Times*, August 13, 1948. Romanian journalist Liviu Nasta sent weekly reports to the *New York Times*, reporting on the social and political changes.

18. I thank Stefan C. Ionescu for providing me with a copy of this source.

19. ANIC, Fond 2904 Ministerul Propagandei Naţionale, file 1663/1948, 46. Nasta to *New York Times*, March 2, 1949. Nasta noted that during the 1945 reform, 1.1 million hectares had already been distributed to 860,000 peasants. The land that the state confiscated in 1949 amounted to a much smaller surface (15,750 hectares, or 0.5% of the total arable land of the country), previously owned by 14,120 people. This means that those peasants were well-to-do and able to make a profit out of their work and land, but they were definitely not very wealthy land owners.

20. APMB, Fond Direcţia Tehnică, dosar 10/1945, p. 2, in Olteanu (2014, 19).

21. Arhiva Ministerului Dezvoltării Regionale şi Administraţiei Publice, Fond Comitetul de Stat pentru Construcţii, Arhitectură şi Sistematizare, dosar 5/1958, f. 512, in Olteanu (2014, 19).

22. ANIC, Fond Cabinetul Consiliului de Miniştri, file 6/1956, Stenogramele şedintelor Prezidiului Consiliului de Miniştri, June 1956, 112.

23. ANIC, Fond Cabinetul Consiliului de Miniştri, file 6/1956, 193.

24. Direcţia Orăşenească de Statistică, *Anuarul statistic al oraşului Bucureşti*, Bucureşti (1959, 70), in Olteanu (2014, 20).

25. ANIC, Fond Cabinetul Consiliului de Ministri, Stenograma şedintei Consiliului de Miniştri, 13 noiembrie, 1952, file 11/1952, 16. According to the Constitution of the Romanian People's Republic of 1948, the Council of Ministers was the highest institution of the state administration, representing de jure the government. It included the president of the Council and several vice presidents and ministers. After 1967, the Council also included presidents of other central institutions. ANIC, "Prefaţă," Inventar Consiliul de Miniştri (1945–1955), no. 3135.

26. File 11/1952, 16.

27. ANIC, Fond: CC al PCR-Cancelarie, file 220/1949, 4. Dej called Bucharest's Provisional Committee on June 13, 1949, in Olteanu (2014, 14n43). For the purpose of simplicity, I will use *city council* to refer to the main administrative institution of Bucharest during the communist period, the official name of which was the Central People's Council of the Capital (Sfatul Popular Central al Capitalei, in Romanian). During the interwar period and until 1950, the city of Bucharest was divided in four sectors administered by four local city councils, which were subordinate to a central city council. After 1950, the main city council became the Central People's Council of the Capital, which administered eight local People's Councils. CIA, "Information Report: Municipal Organization of the City of Bucharest," August 27, 1952, https://www.cia.gov/library/readingroom/docs/CIA-RDP82-00457R013600180006-0.pdf.

28. ANIC, Fond Preşedintia Consiliului de Miniştri, file 5/1951, 100–105. Moscow's master plan was translated into Romanian and given to the Romanian team as a model to be followed.

29. File 5/1951, 99.
30. File 5/1951, 99.
31. File 5/1951.
32. Several teams subsequently worked on the master plan: one formed in 1949, another one in 1950, replaced by the one formed in 1952, led by Macovei. For information about the 1950 team, see Olteanu (2014).
33. ANIC, Fond Președinția Consiliului de Miniștri, file 5/1951, 30–31.
34. For the lengthy discussions on the decree and its earlier drafts, see ANIC, Fond: CC al PCR, file 5/1951, 1–100. The final version of the 1952 decree appears in ANIC, Fond: CC al PCR, file 103/1952, 13–32, as Resolution 2448/12 November 1952.
35. Horia Maicu, "Probleme de sistematizare a capitalei," *Arhitectura RPR* 90, no. 5 (1964): 9.
36. Maicu (1964, 9).
37. ANIC, Fond CC al PCR-Cancelarie, file 220/1949, 4. The Provisional Committee of Bucharest's city council commissioned the first team of architects, who began to work on Bucharest's master plan in 1949. The authorities condemned the 1935 master plan as having been a "failure," as was "any plan elaborated under the capitalist regime" (2–3). However, the same Provisional Committee was willing to include as part of the team two of the architects who had worked on the 1935 plan (architect Duiliu Marcu and urbanist Cincinat Sfinţescu). The team of planners was supervised by the "consultants," representing the political apparatus ranging from members of the Central Committee of the Communist Party, the State Commission for Planning, and the Romanian Academy, a team whose main role was to control and politically endorse the proposals outlined by the architects. The city council asked for help from other institutions that would offer resources as well as seek, acquire, and translate the Soviet technical documentation.
38. Pompiliu Macovei was appointed Bucharest's chief architect following a meeting of the Council of Ministers on November 18, 1952. Stenographs of the meetings of the Office of Culture of the Council of Ministers are cited in "Noiembrie 1952. Consiliul de Miniștri trasează planuri în construcții și urbanism," *Magazinul Istoric*, no. 2 (1998), http://www .itcnet.ro/history/archive/mi1998/current2/mi43.htm. The website (accessed April 20, 2008) is no longer available, but I kept an electronic copy. I tried to find the original file with the stenographs from these meetings, cited above, but the archivists at the National Archive told me it was not available (ANIC, Fond Consiliul de Miniștri, file 3039/1953).
39. ANIC, Comitetul Central al PCR, Secția Cancelarie, Fond 3293 "Dosare Anexe," file 72/1958, 4–5. This short characterization, named "Fișa de cadre," was an internal document about prominent party members and state officials, written by "informers," often collaborators of the secret police, representing a detailed profile of the activities, political links, kinship ties, and so forth, of each individual who was part of the party apparatus or even people of interest to the party. These files were updated periodically and included references and sometimes anonymous notes of criticism or even denunciations.
40. ANIC, Fond 3293, file 72/1958, 4.
41. During the 1960s and 1970s, Macovei kept a very high profile in the state apparatus, becoming the first president of the State Committee for Culture and Arts and, beginning in 1971, Romania's ambassador to UNESCO.
42. ANIC, Fond Consiliul de Miniștri, "Stenogramele ședințelor Prezidiului Consiliului de Miniștri și a Biroului Politic al Comitetului Central al PMR din luna noiembrie 1953," file 9/1953, 187, 190. Macovei noted that the team of twenty-five "technicians" (presumably engineers, planners, and architects) had started drafting the plan in September 1953 but that they had been collecting data for more than two years.

43. File 9/1953, 143–242.
44. File 9/1953, 191.
45. File 9/1953, 182.
46. File 9/1953, 190.
47. File 9/1953, 148, 152.
48. File 9/1953, 150, 156–57.
49. File 9/1953, 166.
50. File 9/1953, 164.
51. File 9/1953, 171.
52. File 9/1953, 165.
53. File 9/1953, 169.
54. See Miron Constantinescu's insistence that the language of the 1952 decree for the socialist building of Romania's cities include a clear reference to the tenets of socialist realism—that the architecture of the socialist epoch must employ "architectural elements national in form but with socialist content, based on the Soviet architecture." "Noiembrie 1952. Consiliul de Miniștri trasează planuri în construcții și urbanism."
55. File 9/1953, 238.
56. File 9/1953, 173.
57. File 9/1953, 174.
58. File 6/1956, 193.
59. File 9/1953, 192.
60. File 9/1953, 236–38.
61. File 9/1953, 238.
62. Established in July 1948 and closely mirroring the Soviet Gosplan, the State Committee for Planning oversaw all of the economic sectors, centralized data provided by the ministers, synthesized these data for the Council of Ministers to decide on the main objectives of the five-year plans, and translated these objectives into specific plans for each economic sector.
63. File 9/1953, 210.
64. File 9/1953, 212. The head of the State Committee, architect Nicolae Bădescu, had previously dismissed Macovei's proposal as rather provisionary and prepared in haste, even though he admitted that he had not had time to review it.
65. File 9/1953, 184.
66. In Romanian, "metode de muncă și atragere."
67. File 9/1953, 218–19.
68. The architect was Petre Antonescu. See "Noiembrie 1952. Consiliul de Miniștri trasează planuri în construcții și urbanism."
69. In 1952, Iosif Chișinevschi was one of the vice presidents of the Council of the Ministers. He also chaired the November 1952 meeting.
70. For a larger discussion of the communist "conversion" of some of the intellectuals and professionals who had been active during the interwar years, see Vasile et al. (2017).
71. "Noiembrie 1952. Consiliul de Miniștri trasează planuri în construcții și urbanism."
72. See the 1955 decree for pardoning the political prisoners who received prison sentences shorter than ten years for "war crimes and crimes against humanity." "Decret nr. 421 din 24 septembrie 1955 pentru grațierea unor pedepse și amnistierea unor infracțiuni," Marea Adunare Națională, Portal Legislativ, http://legislatie.just.ro/Public/DetaliiDocument/21461. Originally published in *Buletinul Oficial* 27, September 24, 1955.
73. ANIC, file 9/1953, 234–35.

74. The term of *Party-state* reflects the dual structure of power characteristic to communist societies, in which the communist party established the ideological agenda, controlled how state bureaucrats implemented that agenda, and surveilled state institutions from the central to the local level. The party bureaucracy closely mirrored the state bureaucracy, as in principle the two structures of power were linked by state bureaucrats who were also party officials. At the same time, there were tensions between the two sets of organizations, as they had distinct interests: the party bureaucracy focused on maintaining the ideological line, while the state bureaucracy tried to make that ideological vision work—which, more often than not, turned out to be a difficult task. For a more detailed description of the Party-state system and its particular dynamic in communist Romania, see Kligman and Verdery (2011, 58–61).

75. ANIC, Fond Cabinetul Consiliului de Miniştri, "Comunicaţie tehnică privind schiţa planului general de sistematizare a oraşului Bucureşti elaborate de specialiştii romîni," file 6/1956, 151.

76. "Comunicaţie tehnică," file 6/1956, 150–52.

77. "Comunicaţie tehnică," file 6/1956, 152, 154, 155, 161, 164.

78. ANIC, Fond Cabinetul Consiliului de Miniştri, "Stenograma şedinţei Consiliului de Miniştri, June 11, 1956," file 6/1956, 105–48.

79. "June 11, 1956," file 6/1956, 112.

80. "June 11, 1956," file 6/1956, 113, 119.

81. "June 11, 1956," file 6/1956, 115.

82. "June 11, 1956," file 6/1956, 116.

83. "June 11, 1956," file 6/1956, 108.

84. "June 11, 1956," file 6/1956, 108, 120.

85. "June 11, 1956," file 6/1956, 123.

86. "June 11, 1956," file 6/1956, 130.

87. This competition mirrored the broader Cold War competition between the two superpowers, the United States and the USSR, competition that was not fought just via the arms race but also through material culture, from modern houses to kitchens and television sets. For a global context of the famous "kitchen debate" between Khrushchev and Nixon in 1959, see Oldenziel and Zachmann (2009).

88. ANIC, "June 11, 1956," file 6/1956, 138.

89. "June 11, 1956," file 6/1956, 139.

90. "June 11, 1956," file 6/1956, 139. This is the episode mentioned at the beginning of the chapter.

91. "June 11, 1956," file 6/1956, 140.

92. There was also an elephant in the room, but one that had nothing to do with the master plan. The palpable tension between Miron Constantinescu and Chivu Stoica, two key members of the Council of Ministers, was very likely informed by a recent scandal within the party leadership. In a closed Politburo meeting held in early April 1956, Constantinescu launched an unprecedented attack against Dej, accusing him of corruption, incompetence, and a personality cult. The other members of the Politburo, however, formed a common front around Dej and, in turn, accused Constantinescu of treason. Secure in his position, Dej decided to show his magnanimity, declaring that Constantinescu had "lost his mind." Soon afterward, however, Dej retaliated. He did not physically eliminate Constantinescu, but he did end his political career. In 1957, Constantinescu found himself working as an obscure researcher in the Romanian Academy—a deep fall from his previous prestigious political ranks. Dej's death in 1965 and the coming to power of Nicolae Ceauşescu enabled

Constantinescu to gain a relative political rehabilitation until his own death in 1974. See Bosomitu (2015, 291–355).

93. For instance, the Soviet team strongly recommended that no new thoroughfares be built but that the existing streets would be repaired and widened. In the end, the Romanian planners dismissed this suggestion and pursued their initial idea. The first major thoroughfare built in the early 1960s was exactly the avenue that connected the center and the south. This project implied extensive demolitions in the center, but the local authorities nevertheless pursued it. The thoroughfare was called the North-South Avenue, currently Cantemir Avenue. See Panaitescu (2012, 123).

94. Gheorghe Gheorghiu-Dej, "Raport la cel de-al III-lea Congres al PMR," pp. 73–74, in G. Gusti, "Unele probleme privind reconstrucția de tip nou a orașelor noastre în etapa actuală," *Arhitectura RPR* 83, no. 4 (1963): 2.

95. Cătălin Gomboș, "De la Harry Goldstein la Horia Maicu: Arhitectul burghez care a stalinizat Bucureștiul," Artoteca.ro, accessed July 20, 2017, http://artoteca.ro/de-la -harry-goldstein-la-horia-maicu-arhitectul-burghez-care-a-stalinizat-bucurestiul-4260.

96. If he had had, it is very likely that *Arhitectura*, the main professional journal in the field, would have reported on that, but I found no such material.

97. Maicu cited in "Plenara Uniunii Arhitecților din R.P.R.," *Arhitectura RPR* 85, no. 6 (1963): 54.

98. Maicu (1963, 54).

99. This was decree 1678/1959. See "O importantă hotărîre privind activitatea de sistematizare a orașelor," and M. Locar, "Pentru dezvoltarea realismului socialist," *Arhitectura RPR* 65, no. 4 (1960): 6.

100. Augustin Ioan, "Concursuri de arhitectură în perioada comunistă," LiterNet.ro, March 10, 2006, https://atelier.liternet.ro/articol/3137/Augustin-Ioan/Concursuri-de-arhitectura-in -perioada-comunista.html.

101. T. Evolceanu, "Concursul pentru sistematizarea Pieței Unirii din București," *Arhitectura RPR* 62, no. 1 (1960): 14–16.

102. Evolceanu (1960, 16).

103. Evolceanu (1960, 17).

104. "Discuție de creație asupra proiectelor prezentate la concursul 'Sistematizarea Pieței Unirii București,'" *Arhitectura RPR* 57, no. 1 (1960): 20.

105. "Discuție," 20–23.

106. "Discuție," 21.

107. "Discuție," 22.

108. ANIC, "June 11, 1956," file 6/1956, 126.

109. Gheorghe Sămărsan, "Locuințele construite fără autorizație și sistematizarea Bucureștiului," *Arhitectura* 4, no. 143 (1973): 128–31.

2

MATTERS OF STATE

Archaeology, Materiality, and State Making

IN LATE DECEMBER 1962, AN ANONYMOUS LETTER LANDED on the desk of Nicolae Bădescu, the chairman of the State Committee for Architecture and, at that moment, one of the most powerful architects in the country. The letter was an anxious response to the impending redesign of Union Square, which presupposed the partial demolition of the adjacent Old Town district. Too scared to sign their names but also too outraged to remain quiet, the letter's writers appealed to the central authorities to correct what they saw as a blatant disregard for the history of the city. They asked for the plans for Union Square to be stopped and for the ruins of the Old Court to be transformed into an open-air museum.

The residence of the princes of Wallachia during the sixteenth and the early seventeenth centuries, the Old Court had been eventually abandoned and destroyed, and the land auctioned to merchants, who built their homes by using some of the original walls of the princely palace as part of the houses' foundations. "Caught" thus within the eighteenth-century buildings, which functioned both as shops and private residences, a part of the walls of the former palace was incidentally preserved. In the early 1950s, the ruins of the Old Court were still lying dormant in the foundations of the old houses. At that time, these walls carried no political significance. However, by the time the letter landed in Bădescu's hands in December 1962, some of the palace's walls had already been unearthed during several archaeological digs, making the Old Court a reality and feeding the archaeologists' dreams that a preservation and even a full reconstruction of the palace could be possible. A few years before, such dreams had seemed unattainable.

Before 1953, no archaeological digs had occurred in Bucharest's city center; the previous authorities never allowed them. When the socialist authorities requested that archaeologists conduct temporary excavations in the city center, the latter were elated. They described their research as the beginning of a "scientific study of the history of the capital, from the earliest times to the present" (Lăzărescu-Ionescu et al. 1954, 287). The city authorities, however, did not envision those digs to remain open for too long (Georgescu 1962, 7). As one of the reports pointed out, "one of the greatest difficulties that the research team had to face was the limited space that allowed for archeological research. . . . In most of the cases, we were forced to dig in the courtyards of the currently inhabited houses" (Lăzărescu-Ionescu et al. 1954, 464). Archaeologists' first priority was to search for possible historical traces that would help elucidate the city's origins. But their other, equally important, role was to "clear" the ground of potentially valuable artifacts. They had to prepare a historically clean surface onto which a modern city would be built.

The transformation of Bucharest into a socialist capital had been a key priority for the socialist government since its beginning. By comparison, archaeological research into the history of the city was on the periphery of the political agenda. However, the unexpected discovery of the Old Court offered archaeologists a unique chance to come to the forefront of political debates. They did so by appealing to the new nationalist card that the government started playing in the late 1950s in an attempt to strengthen their rule and gain relative autonomy from Moscow. From its appearance almost out of nothing to its transformation into a national historic site, the story of the Old Court bridges two distinct moments in Romania's communist history. It begins with the initial archaeological digs opened in Bucharest in 1953—the year of Stalin's death and the beginning of de-Stalinization. It spans the late 1950s, when the Romanian communist regime, led by Gheorghe Gheorghiu-Dej, launched a nationalist agenda that only intensified after 1965, under the leadership of Nicolae Ceaușescu. It ends in 1972, when Bucharest's city council finally decided to pay heed to the archaeologists' claims on the Old Court and to transform it into an open-air national museum.

This chapter begins with an analysis of the conflict between two professional groups. The first anonymous letter launched a lengthy and tense correspondence between architects, represented by the State Committee for Architecture, and archaeologists working in the Old Town, as mediated by a central institution: the Committee for Culture and Arts. This written exchange highlighted opposing goals: the architects wanted to build a new city, while the archaeologists wanted to keep the excavations open in order to produce a (new) history for Bucharest. The struggle over the meanings of the Old Court became more than just a bitter competition for resources in a centralized political system. It revealed a fierce struggle over the value of the "past," its specific shapes and chronologies, and the extent to which it could become a political resource in a socialist present.

In the second part of this chapter, I examine the arguments and material strategies archaeologists employed to create a privileged professional niche for themselves. They did so by emphasizing the alleged superiority of archaeological artifacts to prove "objective historical facts" over the documents of a presocialist ("bourgeois") historiography. I argue that by promoting the excavations as unique tools for the discovery of the past, archaeology as a method of scientific inquiry became implicitly a political strategy that directly helped the socialist state carve out a new historical map of the city. This map was perfectly laminated onto the teleological view of history advanced by the doctrine of dialectical materialism, which presented the communist regime as a pinnacle of progress. As such, the recodification of the past proposed by archaeology enabled this regime to retroactively carve its own history into the urban development of the city, a history perfectly fitting the state's ideological agenda.[1]

By promoting an imagery of history in the form of archaeological artifacts rather than written documents or even the nineteenth-century houses in the city center, archaeologists helped the state perform a multilayered operation. First, the new experts of the past enabled the party officials to exclusively highlight Bucharest's Romanian past and thus prove an ethnic continuity with the settlement and its earlier inhabitants. Second, the archaeologists provided material evidence for the early medieval development of the city, which theoretically laid the basis for the establishment of a socialist order, according to a Marxist teleological approach to history.

At first glance, the scales of the two projects—one pursued by architects, the other by archaeologists—could not be matched. While the remodeling of the city entailed massive deployment of resources, labor, and expertise, the archaeological digs in the city center were coordinated by a relatively small team of specialists. Symbolically, however, the two enterprises had similar revolutionary goals: whereas the architects aimed to give form to a world de novo, the archaeologists wanted to "unearth" a correspondingly pristine history, whose uncontested value appeared to be given by the very materiality of the artifacts in the ground. Both projects involved peculiarly similar dynamics: they were both concerned with different forms of "stretching," be that of the city's skyline or its own past. They both enabled the communist state leaders to present socialism as a sine qua non in the development of the nation.

Accusations

The letter that Nicolae Bădescu received in late December 1962 had originally been sent to the Central Committee for Culture, directly subordinated to the

Council of Ministers. In the archival file there was also a handwritten note attached to it, which read:

Comrade Bădescu,

We have received this from the Academy of RPR. I think that the staff of the Museum of Bucharest might have had a hand in drafting the document. What do you think?

Dinu V. December 24, 1962

Vasile Dinu (Dinu V.) was at that time one of the heads in the Department of Propaganda and Culture—the main institution that supervised the production of cultural knowledge and closely coordinated the work of the Committee for Culture and Arts.[2] That meant that someone at the Committee for Culture and Arts, where the letter had been sent, did not know how to handle the situation and forwarded it to the Department of Propaganda. Given the anonymity of the letter, we cannot assume that its writers were automatically associated with (or employed by) the Museum of History of the City of Bucharest (henceforth, the City Museum). But Dinu was an insider, someone who knew very well the intricate web of institutions and their internal hierarchies. At the moment of the letter's writing, all of the archaeological sites in Bucharest's territory were included in the jurisdiction of the City Museum. The museum had been established in December 1956, at the decision of Bucharest's city council. Simultaneously, the former Museum of Antiquities (the institution dealing up to that moment with the archaeological sites all across the country) had been renamed the Institute of Archaeology, being included in the Academy of the People's Republic (Panait 1962, 149). The City Museum belonged to the newly formed network of regional museums of history opened in the major cities. The communist state commissioned these museums to draft and display a local historical narrative that fit the new ideological requirements. They were also asked to administer the archaeological sites of local importance, while the Institute of Archaeology was entrusted with the sites deemed to hold "national significance." Given that the Old Court was one of the locations where the specialists from the Institute of Archaeology had not excavated, it would not have been too hard for someone who knew these hierarchies well to deduce that the letter's writers were the same archaeologists who knew the site because they had conducted research there—that is, the employees of the City Museum.

A map of the political and scholarly alliances and conflicts was being drawn in the background of the letter. One group of professionals, who claimed to be the only ones who cared about the city's past, portrayed themselves as an idiosyncratic David fighting a collective Goliath, who took the form of politically powerful but allegedly ignorant institutions and individuals charged with the urban redesign of the capital. The letter was just the beginning of a chain of back-and-forth accusations and justifications, which must be placed within the wider process of remaking disciplinary and professional boundaries in a centralized system of knowledge. In this network in which the resources distributed by the center became scantier, the various professional groups had to fight harder to assign stronger political significance to their specific research interests if they wanted to obtain further funding.

When the archivist brought two thick files to my desk, he admitted, a bit surprised, that their content represented a discovery for him as well, because he did not seem to remember having seen those files before.[3] According to him, those files had been somehow hidden during the reorganization of the archive, so it appeared that I was the first researcher to consult them. They included a large collection of correspondence between various political institutions on the subject of Bucharest's Old Court and proposals for the site's reconstruction, together with plans for the redesign of the Old Town district (plans that I analyze in the next chapter). The anonymous letter was the first document in the file, representing in fact its nucleus, as the subsequent pieces in the file emerged as different responses to it.

It was this letter that created the case of the Old Court and transformed it into a political issue. The debates that the site generated for almost a decade following the initial letter were visually captured by the different scripts on the cover. Very likely written at subsequent times, these scripts carried diverse descriptions of the file's content. They also signaled the changing political value of the Old Court, as it moved from being initially described as "the remains of the princely court," to being then marked as "the historic reservation," and later to being considered "the historic center of the Old Court." The scripts, with their different handwriting in distinct colors and inks, from a fountain pen, then a ballpoint, and finally a marker, visually captured an uncertainty about the "real" subject of the file: What was this site, what did it mean to different groups, and what should be done with it? The file's cover became thus a political palimpsest, with the documents therein appearing as not just evaluations of sites and buildings but also competing assessments of the political and heuristic value of the Old Court.

The anonymous letter opened with a statement:

    I. Some monuments of high importance for our country's history can be found in the immediate vicinity of Union Square. They are:
       1) the ruins of the Old Princely Court of Bucharest, and
       2) the Manuk Inn.
    1). The monuments had been identified and located during the archaeological digs carried out at this site by the Institute of

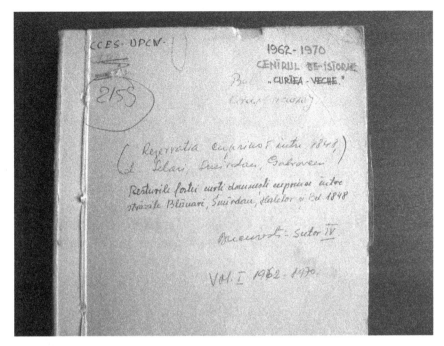

Fig. 2.1. The cover of the file "palimpsest." File 2159/1962–1970, the archives of Institutul Național al Patrimoniului, Bucharest. Photo by author. Used by permission of Institutul Național al Patrimoniului.

Archaeology of RPR Academy, in collaboration with the Museum of the City of Bucharest. The study had been carried out in order to meet the assignment given by the Party leadership to clarify Bucharest's historical development.[4]

By pointing out the Party's broader interest in bringing to light the "true" history of Bucharest and its origins, the writers tried to justify their decision to address the letter directly to the Council of Ministers (i.e., the government). They deplored the dire situation of the Old Court's ruins, in peril to be removed, noting that the site was "representative of the extremely beautiful Romanian architecture of the fifteenth to eighteenth centuries, being among the rarest artifacts of a princely court still existing in our country."[5]

The letter insisted on the historic significance of the Manuk Inn and the Old Court, accusing powerful individuals such as Bucharest's chief architect (Horia Maicu) and a minister (Nicolae Bădescu) of carelessness and even malevolence regarding the sites. The writers portrayed these highly placed officials as stubbornly pursuing their plans for the reconstruction of Union Square and not willing to find a compromise that would allow for the preservation of these sites. The document mentioned that the City Museum was one of the actors involved in the conflict, but it placed the blame squarely on the local authorities and especially on two institutions, both subordinates of the State Committee for Architecture, led by Bădescu. The first was Project Bucharest (Proiect Bucureşti), at that time a megainstitution that coordinated all of the major architectural projects in Bucharest.[6] The second was the Department of Historical Monuments (DHM), the central institution in charge of the preservation of historical sites and buildings across the country.

The letter's tone is highly unusual for a bureaucratic correspondence. It reads, in fact, more like a "classic" denunciation, a particular genre of political communication from a citizen to a higher authority regarding the wrongdoing of another citizen or lower-level institution. This was a practice that became widespread in Stalinist Russia and was later "exported" to the soviet satellites as a means of control, with the new regimes encouraging their citizens to act as the remote eyes of the state and report on (real or imagined) transgressions or abuse of power (Fitzpatrick 1996). Even though there were different kinds of denunciations, depending on who was writing them, to whom, and about whom, what they had in common was that they appealed to a higher instance to solve a conflict, and more often than not, their writers did not intend to have their identity known by those whom they accused of wrongdoing (Fitzpatrick 1996; Goldman 2011). The letter in question had both characteristics: it was anonymous, and it asked a central body (the government) to intercede for the archaeologists to solve their conflict with institutions more powerful than a museum. It accused these institutions and their leaders of negligence, corruption, carelessness, and even embezzlement of funds and of state property. To show how it stood as a denunciation, I quote extensively from the letter:

> The team of urban planners at "PROJECT BUCHAREST" had no knowledge about the existence of those monuments of high importance. . . . Following the interventions made by the team coordinating the archaeological digs in Bucharest . . . and the memos sent to the Party's Central Committee, the People's city council had been advised to pursue the preservation of those monuments. . . . A protocol [about this agreement] was signed three months ago between the museum and "PROJECT BUCHAREST." . . . However, up to this point, the [city council] has made no final decision regarding the conservation of the monuments . . . despite the imminent demolition works planned . . . for [the expansion of] Union Square. . . . On [the northern] wing there lies Manuk Inn, a monument of great importance for the country's history. . . . However, the architects of "PROJECT BUCHAREST" plan on replacing the inn with an apartment building. . . . They had not, however, inquired into the current state

of conservation of the initial architecture of the building, nor considered the possibility of preserving the inn and putting it to use. . . . The explanation for this situation is that:

1. All the problems related to this specific neighborhood and the existing monuments had been approached only through the interest of developing new buildings, with no serious, methodic concern to preserve the monuments, as it is done in other socialist countries.

2. The [DHM] does not properly care about the monuments of significance for the political and economic history of our fatherland, such sites being preserved only due to the intervention of museums or other institutions. . . . In contrast to other socialist countries, the department (despite its limited personnel) has not sought help from museums in the project of preservation of the historical monuments. . . . As for the Manuk Inn, they wanted to "restore" it under a totally new appearance in order to move their offices there (there is a project [on this reconstruction] already submitted to "PROJECT BUCHAREST"). The construction work was to be paid out of the fund reserved for monuments preservation. . . . Given that the demolition works, planned for the expansion of Union Square, are scheduled for the beginning of 1963, only now and not later could [these plans] be challenged and a decision on the conservation and restoration of this unique historical complex be taken. . . . It would have been commonsensical that such problems be solved by the local authorities of Bucharest. . . . Such a resolution is, however, not possible, because, on one hand, comrade H. M. [Horia Maicu], the chief architect of Bucharest had not carefully reviewed the projects designed by his subordinates. Therefore, even though he is aware of the situation of the archaeological monuments mentioned above, as well as the conservation state of the Manuk Inn, he would not change his opinion for obvious reasons. On the other hand, Comrade B. [Nicolae Bădescu], the president of the State Committee for Architecture, did not assume responsibility for the historical monuments. Every time he was informed of the critical state of those monuments, he did not appreciate their real importance and forwarded the memos to [other institutions].[7]

Obviously, the letter stirred up a hornet's nest within the State Committee for Architecture. A month after the first letter had reached this institution, the vice president of the committee drafted a response. The initial draft of this response had a defensive tone, accusing the initial document's writers of using "false information, insufficiently investigated data" in order to "discredit" the DHM.[8] In the archival file, this draft appears as heavily marked in red ink by a second reader (presumably, the chairman of the committee, Nicolae Bădescu), with comments asking that the response be "shorter, not polemical, [rather focused] on clearer proposals to solve the problems" (signaled by the initial letter).[9]

The response turned the accusations around by pointing out that the archaeological sites had never been entrusted to the DHM. Instead, the Institute of Archaeology and (in the case of the capital) the City Museum had been responsible for "archaeological monuments that emerged through excavations or are still buried in the ground."[10] In turn, the second letter accused those institutions—and especially the museum—of passivity, by suggesting that "the museum does not grasp the necessity of being actively involved and efficient in the scientific research underlying the work of restoration-conservation." Moreover, the letter stated that the State Committee for Architecture had already been aware of the "interesting artifacts preserved at the Old Court" and therefore had asked that architects working on Bucharest's master plan take it into account and planned for its preservation.[11]

However, the second letter still questioned the historical value of the walls unearthed at the site, asking for "further research that could ascertain the scientific and aesthetic value of those ruins and the extent to which this research must stop the imperatives of the area's redesign."[12] The State Committee for Architecture had already "recommended that work in the area of the Old Court be carried out gradually, under the supervision of specialists (archaeologists, art and architectural historians)."[13] While acknowledging the high value of the Manuk Inn as a historical building, the representatives of the committee pointed out that any attempts to preserve the inn must take into account the plans for Union Square. The response concluded that a proper preservation of the historical monuments within the city could not be pursued without the help and financial support of Bucharest's city council, help that had not been offered in the past. By emphasizing that the State Committee for Architecture knew what they were doing, that they were genuinely concerned about valuable historic monuments and that this concern informed their urban planning projects, the second letter sought to save the prestige of the committee and thus restore a hierarchy threatened by the first petition.

This written exchange must be understood through the institutional shifts that took place between the early 1950s and the early 1960s. The tug-of-war between the architects and the archaeologists over the political and historical value of the Old Court revealed, in part, a complex struggle for political and institutional visibility in the socialist system. Those competing agendas triggered frustrations among each group of stakeholders. The architects had to comply with the requirement that archaeological research be carried out before any further architectural intervention could be undertaken in the city center. The archaeologists, on the other hand, felt pressed to get their work done at an impossible pace—and sometimes, as the letter exchange suggests, they may have even been strategically "disinvited" from beginning an excavation.

A report on the archaeological digs conducted in the city center alluded to the power held by the architects and the managers of some construction sites in deciding whether to ask archaeologists to conduct preliminary research at their sites. Sometimes these managers chose to do so, but they equally could have "forgotten," as we can read between the lines of the following comment: "The activity of salvaging the relics of the past . . . appears as more necessary as a large part of Bucharest's surface undergoes ample changes. The large construction sites . . . often lead to the discovery of monuments of material culture. There have been numerous cases when the managers of the construction sites have contacted the Museum's specialists . . . to come to pursue archeological research on the large construction sites in the city" (Georgescu 1962, 7).

The architects working in the city, most of them trained in modernist principles, were mainly looking for an urban form that would satisfy a changing society of the present, while being very little or not all preoccupied with "the past." The past was not their business. The past was, however, the main business of the archaeologists who viewed the excavations in the city center as a once-in-a-lifetime opportunity. Suddenly, the district of the Old Town had to become extremely elastic so that it could accommodate the demands of the present (to be built) and of the past (to be preserved). To oppose the architects' plans to modernize Union Square, the archaeologists working at the Old Court made a bold proposal to state officials: if they were allowed to keep digging at the site, they would provide the new state with a politically proper past, a past that would add further legitimacy to the state in the making.

Starting from the tense correspondence revealing the broader conflict between the archaeologists and the architects, I examine the institutional and epistemic maneuvers through which a relatively marginal group managed to promote a site whose historic value was questionable—even among other archaeologists—and to transform it into tangible proof of the medieval history of the city. These maneuvers speak to the broader role that archaeology eventually came to play for the Romanian socialist state in consolidating a shift from (1) its political dependency on Moscow in the early 1950s to (2) an increasing cultural autonomy and the new rise of a nationalism with a socialist face during the 1960s and the early 1970s.

Archaeology as a Political Tool

In socialist Romania, archaeology became a political tool. During the sovietization of the early 1950s, archaeologists had tried hard to find traces of the Slavic culture in the artifacts they unearthed in an attempt to prove that the Soviet influence went way back into the past. However, once the political priorities changed and the regime openly embraced a nationalist agenda, archaeological artifacts had to become material proof of the nation's past. The shift in the official discourse made archaeologists switch their research interests—and publication topics—from attempts to discover the "Slavic connection" to searches for what they declared to be the "(proto) Romanian element."

From the end of the 1950s and the early 1960s, well-known archaeologists started publishing on the theme of "proto-Romanians" (Comşa 1959, 1968; Panait 1962). The term was used as early as 1958 (Nestor 1958) by one of the most powerful archaeologists of the time: Ion Nestor, the director of the Institute of Archaeology of the National Academy of Sciences (whose former right-wing sympathies during the interwar years were diplomatically forgotten under the communist regime).[14] This shift foreshadowed a broader "protochronist" treasure hunt that came to full bloom in the late 1970s and continued throughout the 1980s.[15] Launched by a group of scholars-turned-ideological entrepreneurs for the Party-state and heavily sponsored by the regime, this movement aimed to place the Romanian people at the core of the world's history by nonsensically arguing that "proto-Romanians" had exercised an ascendancy over all other peoples in ancient times (Verdery 1991, 167–214).[16]

The debates surrounding the Old Court show that the archaeological theory developed in the 1960s directly informed the protochronists' arguments emerging in the 1970s and 1980s. The materiality of the archaeological artifacts was employed to claim objectivity and thus grant the socialist historiography the status of "truth." By putting forward an interpretation of *historical materialism* that assumed that the material is the ultimate measure of truth, the things newly unearthed from the ground literally became the "scientific" basis on which entire disciplinary realms, such as literature and history, were being (re)built.

The first digs opened in the center of Bucharest in 1953 had explicitly followed the model of the excavations already pursued by Soviet archaeologists in medieval Russian towns. One of the first archaeological reports (Ionaşcu et al. 1954, 410) pointed out that their main goal was to reveal "the true multimillenarian history of the places we inhabit today," acknowledging that they drew on the Soviet precedent: "We will thus provide a just and objective report, similar to what the Soviet historians and archeologists have been doing for years via their ample archeological investigations in Moscow, Leningrad, Kiev, Novgorod, etc." (410).

Rewriting the history of "feudalism" on the basis of archaeological findings became an important pursuit all across the Soviet bloc in the 1950s. The Russian and then Soviet archaeologists had attempted to build the field of medieval (or feudal) archaeology in order to promote the highly disputed concept of pan-Slavism.[17] By adapting a pre-Soviet discourse on Slavic (linguistic and ethnic) brotherhood that legitimized the Russian foreign policy of expansion in Europe in the late nineteenth century, the Soviets sought to resuscitate the myth of Slavic kinship in order to substantiate a discourse of socialist transnationalism with the Soviet Union at its core.[18] They put a new twist on the "Slavic connection" by deeming it a crucial element for proving the ancient pervasiveness of Slavic culture across Central and Eastern Europe, a perspective that informed all of the archaeological work pursued in the Soviet bloc during the 1950s.[19]

In light of the prevailing Marxist historical paradigm, searching for feudalism and thoroughly documenting justified the existence and necessity of the communist regime. As historian Elizabeth Brown (1974, 1064–65) has pointed out, "by incorporating 'the feudal mode of production' into their design, [Marx and Engels] endowed it with seminal significance. Their followers came to view the feudal stage as a necessary prerequisite for the emergence of socialism, and socialist scholars and activists sought traces of it throughout the world." She points out that the problematic tendency of confining a variety of political and social forms of organization existing in a Europe of the Middle Ages under one conceptual umbrella of *feudalism* originated in the historical episteme of the eighteenth century. She writes, "The writers of the eighteenth century, like those of later times, assigned different meanings to the term féodalité, or, in English, 'feodality.' Some used it to designate a system of government, some to refer to conditions that developed as public power disappeared. By 1800 the construct had been launched and the expression 'feudal system' devised; by the mid-nineteenth century the word 'feudalism' was in use. . . . Since the middle of the nineteenth century the concepts of feudalism and the feudal system have dominated the study of the medieval past" (1064–65).

In other words, Marx's major concern with "the feudal mode of production" only reflected a more general interest in feudalism across the nineteenth-century historiography of medieval Europe. The concept became politically exploited later on by the Russian revolutionaries, especially Vladimir Lenin. He viewed czarist Russia as a feudal society in which the landlords still had significant power over the oppressed peasants, with an incipient form of capitalism emerging alongside feudal relations.[20] A socialist revolution, he asserted, did not need to wait for the capitalist phase to come into full bloom, but it came forth as a radical reaction to the feudal mode of production and its specific social stratification. In other words, socialism had to be built on the ruined foundations of feudalism—and a material proof of such foundations became a tangible guarantee that the socialist revolution had succeeded and that a communist future was in the making.

In the context of the Cold War competition, searching for feudalism became then a political task. Archaeology was called on to attest to the "superior development" of an early Slavic culture in comparison to those emerging in "the West." Proving the feudal origins of the major cities in the new Soviet satellites was a priority for the archaeologists working in the Eastern bloc. In Romania, Bucharest came to play that role. The first report (Lăzărescu-Ionescu et al. 1954) of the archaeological excavations conducted in the city in the early 1950s highlighted the strong Slavic influence on the local settlements discovered in those sites. It was the mandatory bow to Moscow and an impetus for other researchers to identify more connections to the Soviets, in the present and in the past. The reports also urged archaeologists to focus on the medieval period so they could have more information about the "feudal" times in the city territory: "Whereas [during the interwar times] there had been sporadic archaeological research, only within the domain of the primitive and slavery-based social orders, the popular democratic state gives special attention to archaeological research on the migratory period and the feudal order, as well as to the forging of a strong collective of specialists in feudal archaeology" (287). Archaeologists advertised their discipline as being uniquely equipped to confirm or deny the historical validity of textual sources and especially those that originated in the medieval and late medieval times.[21] These arguments remained in place after the government's turn to nationalism. This time, the medieval period—so-called early feudalism—was promoted as the time of the formation of the first Romanian states and symbolized the independence and the formation of the nation avant la lettre.[22] The search for medieval artifacts that would prove an earlier formation of the Romanian nation fit the new political priorities, and Bucharest played a pivotal role in the production of this narrative.

Even though the princely residence of the medieval principality of Wallachia had been the town of Târgoviște, and not Bucharest, that historical fact did not preclude the regime from promoting a narrative of the Romanian medieval past that centered on Bucharest. In 1959, the city authorities sponsored multiple events meant to emphasize and celebrate the city's quincentenary, given that the first reference to a "Bucharest fortress" appeared in a 1459 charter. In the same year, the Museum of Bucharest changed its official name to the History Museum of the City of Bucharest—the same museum whose specialists were believed to have sent the anonymous letter that opens this chapter. The widely circulating *Arhitectura* journal published a special issue commemorating the five-hundredth anniversary, with an assembly of photos and drawings meant to illustrate the historical origins of the city, as well as the contrasts between the capitalist past and the socialist present.[23]

This attempt to "stretch" the centrality of Bucharest back into the past, even to times when it was rather a politically peripheral location, was accompanied by scholarly efforts to confer legitimacy to this narrative. Starting in the early 1960s, the Romanian Academy, the country's highest forum of scholarly expertise, began publishing beautiful and expensive volumes about the history of Bucharest. One of these volumes (Elian 1965) focused on the analysis of a comprehensive collection of medieval inscriptions existing at that moment in the territory of the city of Bucharest (the book was published in 1965, but the project began in 1951). The analysis was accompanied by high-quality illustrations and some photographs of the inscriptions, including their transliteration from a Cyrillic script.

In their analysis of the medieval inscriptions, the researchers attempted to link distinct elements: materiality, feudalism, the Romanian nation, and the political focus on Bucharest. These themes became pivotal for historians and archaeologists in the early 1960s and onward. Once they constructed a narrative in which all these elements were made to appear as closely interconnected, scholars could begin the rewriting of history required by the communist state. The inscriptions were portrayed as unique sources of insight into the development of the Romanian nation since its origins. It was not the inscriptions themselves, in fact, but the procedure of identifying and selecting them that made the project uniquely suitable for political aims.[24]

The methodology of selection—of identifying "Romanian medieval inscriptions" and separating them from others of different provenance or usage—reflected a larger political agenda that sought to find evidence of Romanianness and to distinguish it from vestiges imputed to other ethnic groups.[25] The scholars involved in the project selected "representative" pieces according to their capacity to function as chronological devices, supposedly guaranteed by their materiality. Presented as an alternative means of unraveling "data of historical interest," the inscriptions underwent a careful curation meant to exclude those pieces that had no "historical value"—such as pieces inscribed only with the names of saints, without any other date, or those bearing the private names of "ordinary" people (in contrast to political figures). Also excluded were inscriptions on objects that "no matter their origins and historical importance, had not been produced in the territory of the Romanian [medieval] states [i.e., principalities] or had never circulated there in the past" (Elian 1965, 39)—meaning that they exerted no influence on the culture of the local population at that time.

A unique characteristic of the inscriptions that the medieval specialists presented as an additional proof of their accuracy was their "fixedness" (Elian 1965, 13), meaning that they were in fact very heavy stones and therefore much less portable. This characteristic made them less prone to be reinscribed with other data. This is how the researchers justified their approach: "The inscriptions make available data that are in general more certain than of other contemporary sources. . . . With a plain sequence of names and dates, the inscriptions are less *ad probantum* [less likely intended to prove something] than miscellaneous chronicles representing the interests of a group of boyars . . . doubtful stories or questionable arguments. . . . Within their strict and limited materiality . . . the veracity of the data they carry cannot be, in general, doubted" (15). In the eyes of these scholars, the inscriptions encapsulated the promise of rendering data "objective" via "their strict and limited materiality" (15). In a context in which writing (on paper) had become an increasingly dominant form of communication, it was the greater difficulty of generating information via alternative methods—that is, through techniques such as "carving, sewing, painting, and embroidering" (12–13)—that made specialists deem the inscriptions potentially more "accurate." Since they had to communicate the kernel of one event (e.g., by engraving one name and one date), these epigraphic forms were invested with the assumption that that kernel was "true" by default and therefore historically relevant.[26]

It is this focus on materiality as allegedly providing a guarantee of "historical truth" that enabled particular professional groups to enjoy a political limelight—and thus significant research funding. Archaeologists formed one of these groups, as shown by the ways they portrayed themselves as rescuers of Bucharest's past. This redemptive stance is reflected by the metaphors they used in their reports such as *salvage* and *discovery*. In one of these reports, on the first digs conducted in 1953 in Bucharest's city center, the archaeologists who took part in those excavations noted that "in addition to tracking down and salvaging some archaeological vestiges, the archaeological research carried out simultaneously with the construction work aimed to confirm the written sources [about the history of the city] on the basis of field research" (Panait 1962, 152).[27]

The first research reports published immediately after the 1953 digs had the role of popularizing the new knowledge-in-the-making. These reports aimed to "reflect the contribution of [the collective of the City Museum to] the great effort of the Romanian archaeologists to document, on the basis of dialectical materialism, the faraway past of our people" (Condurachi 1962, 4). Archaeology was called on to reject or verify "imagined legends" regarding the foundation of the city, such as the story that a shepherd, Bucur, was the founder of Bucharest (București meaning "Bucur's place" in Romanian).[28] According to the reports, the archaeological research carried out within the city should seek "information on historical periods for which data are still scarce," such as the fourteenth and fifteenth centuries for which little documentation existed—not to mention that archaeologists discredited even these limited sources as being "equivocal" (Georgescu 1962, 7). The report concluded that "knowledge on this subject should be acquired via archaeological research" (7). In other words, archaeological artifacts were to prove an unsweetened history of "what had happened," as Michel Trouillot (1995, 113) put it, and not just of "what is said to have happened"—that is, an interpretation of history presented by written documents that were purportedly corrupted by the previous political regimes.

These scholars in socialist Romania were not the first to become drawn to a "cult of the artifact"—that is, archaeology's extolling objects over texts as the ultimate source of historical truth. As art historian Tony Bennett (1995, 147) remarked, such a sacralization of the artifact led to the birth of the nineteenth-century modern museum, which functioned as "repositories of the *already known*." The museums, Bennett argued, promoted the belief that the artifacts' materiality guaranteed a more pristine and thus more veridical rendition of history, while they were in fact the very means through which a thing becomes "a rhetorical object, . . . as thickly lacquered with layers of interpretation as any book or film" (146).

The case of the Old Court, and the controversies that it later triggered among other archaeologists, illustrate the perils underlying such a cult of the artifact. The debates surrounding the Old Court, its heuristic validity and historical importance, were ultimately debates about the ability of artifacts to deliver and guarantee the "historical truth" and the extent to which some professionals could intervene and "adjust" that truth to fit a convenient narrative of the present. More importantly, these debates emerged not only at the crossroad between distinct professional gazes and agendas, such as urban planning and archaeology, but also through some tense collisions among archaeologists themselves. If initially, the archaeological digs at the Old Court, conducted in early 1950s, brought new evidence about the early Slavic presence on this territory, by the late 1950s and early 1960s, the same research—and sometimes even the same artifacts—provided incontestable proof of a national independence allegedly achieved as early as the sixteenth century. The existence of the princely palace that purportedly symbolized an independent polity of the medieval ("feudal") period became a sign of the nation before that nation even existed.

Fluid Chronologies

The shift in the political value of the Old Court must be set against a tense background formed of a mix of ideological changes, controversial methodologies, an intense struggle for funding, and particular conflicts of interests among archaeologists. Archaeologist Florin Curta did not participate directly in the excavations at the Old Court, but he had direct access to what he called "the gossip within the archaeologists' guild." Here is how he described what he viewed as "the total chaos of 'the Old Court episode'":

> It became an ugly story. They had to prove that the artifacts were from the time of Vlad the Impaler [the first prince who built the palace in the fifteenth century]. During the excavations, they found the vaults, which used to be the top of the palace's rooms. But after the court was abandoned, the ground became elevated over time, and the vaults became lower chambers, which functioned as a waste landfill for the [rapidly developing] commercial district established around the court. The archaeologists who found the pottery next to the vaults dated them to the time of the building of the palace [the fifteenth century]. But those artifacts were actually from the eighteenth century, having being thrown there as garbage. . . . These findings were not accompanied by any documentation, despite this being right at the time when they did the most extensive excavations [he referred to the research conducted between 1967 and 1971]. The digs were done with no stratigraphic analysis and no profile. After that, the [medieval] archaeologists working in Bucharest [those affiliated with the City Museum] could no longer be taken seriously—everyone laughed about their digs.[29]

These comments reveal that the Old Court became a hot terrain for different groups of archaeologists to exert or challenge claims to expertise, professional visibility, and access to resources. With an eye to receiving more research funding, the archaeologists digging at the Old Court had to prove its importance for the early medieval history of the city. Consequently, they strove to find as much evidence as they could—even to the point of stretching the dating of some of the artifacts a few centuries back to make them consistently "match" the official narrative of the city's medieval origins. Such was the case of the pottery found in the ground covering the walls of the court (the vaults), which archaeologists claimed to be contemporary with the walls, but which in fact originated in a later period, after the Old Court had been abandoned and made into a landfill for the eighteenth-century merchants living in the area.[30] Stretching time— that is, dating artifacts to match the political priorities of the moment—seemed to have been a strategic choice made by some of the archaeologists working at the site. If we compare the two reports of the two sets of excavations (in 1953 and 1958–59), we find significant discrepancies between them, as each made distinct arguments based on different chronologies.

The excavations at the Old Court began in 1953 under the coordination of archaeologist Dinu V. Rosetti. He had gained significant experience during the 1930s, when he conducted numerous excavations in Bucharest's periphery

‹ *Curtea Veche* » — *Macheta ruinelor degajate în 1967 — 1968*

Fig. 2.2. Model of the ruins of the Princely Palace. 1967–68. *Arhitectura* 113, no. 4 (1968): 27. Photo by Răzvan Voinea. Used by permission of *Arhitectura* journal.

(at that time, no archaeological excavations were allowed in the city center) (Rosetti 1932). He had also played a key role in the establishment of a municipal museum in Bucharest in 1929, which eventually became the City Museum in 1956 (Rosetti 1971). Under Rosetti's lead, the first excavations at the Old Court led to the unearthing of a part of the initial foundation of the Old Court Palace (more precisely, the western corner of the palace, shown in fig. 2.2).

This foundation—of which only the western corner of the wall was preserved, being enclosed within a house built later on the premises—turned out to be part of a large (thirty-two-meter-long) vaulted hall (Lăzărescu-Ionescu et al. 1954, 483). The construction method and material used for this wall led the specialists to date it to the middle or even early sixteenth century. Invoking the "beauty of the construction and its vaults, and the fact that it is the sole construction left from the old buildings of the princely court," the team proposed that this room be classified as a "historical monument" and be "transformed into a lapidarium" (487).

The first research report on the excavations at the Old Court appeared in 1954 as part of a larger study (Lăzărescu-Ionescu et al. 1954) of all the excavations opened in the center of the city—with Rosetti authoring the section on the Old Court (461–538). The report presented the Old Court site as the kernel of a continuous social life, extending all the way back to the Neolithic era. In contrast to other sites dating to the fourth and fifth centuries that had been discovered at the periphery of Bucharest, the archaeologists argued that "at the Old Court, one found much larger and intensively inhabited settlements," where "a

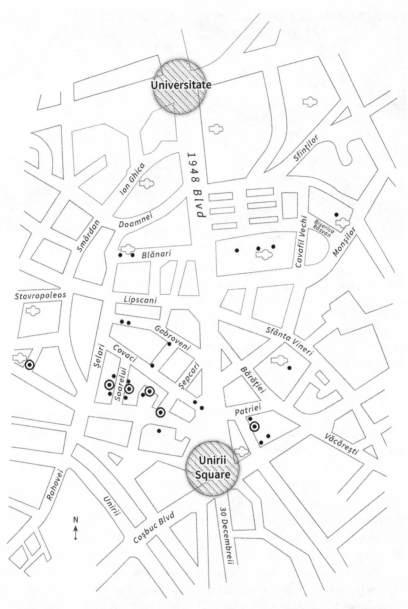

Map 2.1. The plan of the excavations conducted in the Old Town between 1953 and 1959. The black dots mark the locations of all digs; the white circles note the locations dated in the fourth century. Map by Daniella Collins based on Rosetti (1959, 148). Used by permission of Muzeul Municipiului București.

vital life had pulsated" (473). The urgency of proving the continuous habitation of this site comes forth in comments such as, "the settlement at the Old Court presents therefore the characteristics of a settlement where an indigenous local culture had been developed. As the locals had quasi-permanently been engaged in defense fights, the inventory of the material culture is quite poor" (473). That is, instead of raising the hypothesis of a more dynamic habitation of the area, comprising more diverse population movements, the argument remains stuck within the continuity paradigm of the culture-historical model.

This report also dated some of the pottery to the sixth century and identified it as "Slavic," arguing that the local population adopted "the Slavs' way of living" (Lăzărescu-Ionescu et al. 1954, 537). This analysis came under harsh scrutiny in 1958, when another archaeologist claimed that what the first team, led by Dinu Rosetti, had described as pottery of the sixth century had a much later origin, belonging to the twelfth or thirteenth century (Diaconu 1958). Then, more than a decade later, a third archaeologist added another twist to the debate. While he challenged the second periodization, bringing back the pottery to the time framework already established by Rosetti (the one between the fifth and seventh centuries), he claimed that this pottery belonged to an autochthonous Romanic culture, preceding and therefore not proving an alleged contact with the Slavs (Teodorescu 1964, 1971).[31]

When he explained to me the controversy around the earlier excavations at the Old Court and of the dating of the artifacts collected from that research, archaeologist Florin Curta suggested that Rosetti had dated the pottery found during the 1953 excavations by relying on his own earlier research at other sites around Bucharest. In the 1930s, he had found similar pottery and Byzantine coins from the Justinian dynasty (sixth century) in Bucharest's periphery. In 1953, however, he chose to view the same coins as signs of the Slavic presence. As Curta put it, "In the 1930s, no one would have attributed those artifacts to the Slavs, but things changed after the war. Archaeologists from the Soviet Union as well as from other European countries began viewing the sixth century as the moment of the large battles between the Roman Empire and the liberating Slavs—[a way of] extending the Cold War conflict into the past."[32]

Despite its ideological biases, however—such as the attempt to work within the framework of a continuous habitation of the site, as well as to prove the presence of "Slavic culture" in the area—the report on the 1953 digs offers detailed explanations of the methodology employed. It includes details on the dating of the artifacts via comparison with similar material found at other sites, stratigraphic drawings, pictures and drawings of pottery and coins, photographs of the stages of excavations. In contrast, the (much shorter) report on the second stage of research in the area, conducted in 1958–59, neither gives as many details nor presents a stratigraphic analysis (Rosetti 1959). The 1958–59 Old Court excavations were also smaller in scope than the 1953 digs. They were intended only to precede the building of some new apartment buildings on the southeast corner of the Old Town district and, more importantly, were meant to be the final excavations in the area.

Once on the job, however, the archaeologists tried to exploit the new nationalist turn of the political establishment and to persuade the authorities of the importance of the site for national history. The research report on the second excavations reflects their strategy. Pottery that Rosetti had first identified as "Slavic pottery" produced in the sixth century, for example, was reanalyzed by Rosetti (1959, 153) and now placed in the ninth to eleventh centuries—that is, the beginning of the Middle Ages. In the report, the sixth century is no longer linked to the "Slavic culture" but rather used as a material proof of "early feudalism." Thus, the pottery was presented as tangible evidence of the first "feudal" states that had been formed in the territory of contemporary Romania. This reference is crucial, as it points out not only the political turn away from the "Slavic connection" but also the rising importance of the early Middle Ages for the new theory of history advanced by the socialist state, which aimed to establish the continuous presence of a Romanian nation from feudalism to socialism.

The pottery was thus used to "prove" that the settlement was a central one for the early feudal history of the city, and that the sixteenth-century princely court came later to be established "directly" on the site of this earlier settlement. The report contended that "starting in the first half of the fifteenth century, there [was] more frequent habitation on the site that would likely host the walls of the Princely Court at the end of that century" (this places the princely palace in the fifteenth century, not the sixteenth, as the earlier report had found). Having established this key moment in the history of Bucharest—the early medieval period of the ninth to eleventh centuries—the report then stated that "the centuries to follow [covering the period between the twelfth and fourteenth centuries] are still very poorly documented" (Panait 1962, 143).

In sum, the archaeologists picked and chose evidence as they saw fit. No matter that they found no evidence of habitation during the period in between (just a few centuries!), the archaeologists dismissed the lack of evidence as a consequence of a more recent period, the "bourgeois" interwar years, when the urban interventions, they said, destroyed those strata of material culture. They "squeezed" their artifacts into historical time slots that were deemed representative of the nation, stitched together a chronology out of disparate evidence, and made it appear to look like a historical continuum. This is exactly what they needed in order to claim that the Old Court had been continuously inhabited from early medieval times to the present: a proof of a chronologically flawless past for a perfect socialist present.

The distinct chronologies of the two reports reflect the political priorities of distinct political moments in the communist period: while the first report identifies the beginning of the site's habitation in the fourth to sixth centuries, in order to claim the Slavic connection, the second document amends this conclusion by setting the key moment four centuries down the road, somewhere between the ninth and the eleventh centuries. Yet the two reports share a key argument: both assume and seek to prove a theory of historical continuity. Although both reports acknowledge the lack of archaeological data covering important stretches of time (the period between the fifth to the fourteenth century is absent in the first report; in the second, the lacuna runs from the ninth to eleventh centuries to the fifteenth century), both also start from the premise that the site had nevertheless been continuously inhabited. While both analyses provided no evidence for their theory of continuous habitation, they claimed that such evidence would be provided by *future* excavations, thus subtly asking for more funding.

The fluid chronologies of the artifacts collected from the Old Court site under two excavations occurring at distinct political moments tell a rich story about how the socialist state sought to create its own heritage through archaeological evidence and less so through written documents. Recently unearthed and thus untainted by any "bourgeois" interpretation of history, as textual sources allegedly were, the archaeological artifacts met several criteria crucial for the socialist regime. Their "newness" befitted a new state. This same newness likewise made questions of ownership moot: the artifacts belonged to the state, as state property. They were also mobile, which meant that they could be brought into museums as signs of the ancient past of the socialist present. Such artifacts represented crucial ideological props for the state, prompting a renewed interested of the communist government in archaeology. Starting with late 1950s, the government began to fund extensive archaeological campaigns, encompassing vast and long-term excavations across the country that led to an impressive collection of materials.[33]

Again, it was not only the artifacts per se that mattered but rather the project of amassing and ordering them within a comprehensive (and centralized) assembly meant to construct a persuasive historical narrative. Commenting on the political implications of archaeology in the Balkans, Timothy Kaiser (1995, 108) noted that

> another consequence of the nationalist-inspired historical revival in the Balkans has been the adoption of essentially historical methods in archaeology. Chief among these methods is the use of artifact typology as a

means of chronology-building and of delimiting cultural boundaries. With their typologies and analyses of artifact style, archaeologists have sought to construct a history of the Balkan past in the absence of written records. While a preoccupation with artifact typology is hardly unique to southeast Europe, it does seem that the enterprise is widely regarded as the most serious and important aspect of archaeology. Careers and reputations stand or fall on questions of chronology and typology.

Archaeologists in the Soviet bloc worked with a culture-historical model that favored "long-term historical continuity" over other possible interpretations of the data because they were mostly interested in proving the existence of distinct groups that continuously inhabited a territory—that is, document-ing the existence of the nation much earlier than it existed as a concept and a polity (Anghelinu 2007, 6). It was a direct application of the precepts of the Soviet archaeologists. The Soviets had drawn on the cultural-historical para-digm launched by nineteenth-century German archaeologist Gustaf Kossina to promote the myth of a superior German culture, but the Soviets turned this theory on its head to advance their own myth of pan-Slavism, arguing that Slavic groups had had a unique culture and therefore represented a particular "nation" (Klejn 2012, 27, 112).

Under the Soviet influence during the 1950s, archaeologists in socialist Romania tended to favor an empiricist agenda, which they continued during the political turn to nationalism from the 1960s onward (Dragoman and Oanță-Marghitu 2006). As archaeologist Mircea Anghelinu (2007, 6) has noted, many Romanian archaeologists working at that time found the cultural-historical paradigm more politically palatable and tended to shy away from adopting a dialectical approach, one that would start from an analysis of archaeological findings to derive a theory about change and internal developments. Instead, they approached dialectical materialism as a simplified and more rigid version of Marxism (11), one that almost erased the dialectical and focused exclusively on the material. In other words, the more one dug out of the ground, the better a researcher she or he proved to be. This meant an increasing number of new sites being opened, which led to a larger and larger archaeological collection that would then be displayed in key locations for political propaganda, such as the regional museums of history. In addition to the major operations of national-ization and collectivization, this process of agglomerating artifacts functioned as another form of channeling resources to the center (Verdery 1996)—the key strategy by which the communist state aimed to consolidate its power.

In fact, large quantities of artifacts hoarded in museums did not necessar-ily mean more value, even though their presence was meant to prove the con-trary. Some archaeologists chose to hide the most valuable artifacts they found, sometimes even in their own houses, bringing instead to museums pieces of secondary value and relying on the ignorance of their political supervisors to get away with it.[34] But the sheer quantity meant more than quality. It had a clear political purpose. The archaeologists were barely keeping up with the rhythm of the excavations, receiving generous funds from the government for more and more digs, even though they had little time left for the analysis and publication of their findings.[35] But this was precisely what the state needed—an accumulation of things and not necessarily of value. In fact, such dual process of digging immense quantities of artifacts, only to hide away the most valuable ones, reflected the workings of the broader system in which a centralized economy enabled an expanding illicit, secondary market operating in its shadow.

Writing about the role of archaeology in Israel, anthropologist Nadia El Abu-Haj (2001) has underscored how archaeological research in British-occupied Palestine promoted an imaginary of a state before the Israeli state actually existed. She notes an obsession with collecting "sometimes seemingly inchoate data" (78), decoding that very act of amassing evidence as a political project, the creation of heterogeneous evidence of Jewish presence. El Abu-Haj pointedly notes that

> the labor of fact collecting helped to assemble [a view] of the (present) land by way of the dots that mark locales of ancient Jewish presence. This work of fact collecting needs to be understood as part of a wider cartographic project, one that was not limited to map making, but was very much about "world-making" (Haraway, 1997:132). . . . Relics were fetishized as unmediated empirical evidence, . . . [presented as] facts of ancient Jewish history through the perspective of which the land was fashioned as an old-new Jewish national home. This material-symbolic (re)inscription of the land connected the dots not only in space but also through time. (79)

While El Abu-Haj emphasizes the pursuit of place making (the "cartographic project") that informed such searches for a material proof of Jewish origins, I would argue that the heterogeneity of those collections was equally important as its geographical locations. It was this heterogeneity, in the form of an overwhelming quantity of things that defied easy classification, that added political heft to those earlier projects—that is, before a more systematic attempt was made to identify more significant archaeological material and disentangle it from that mass of objects. That large collection of relics, whether or not it was considered archaeological proper, created a rich material foundation for the imaginary of a new state before that state (post-1948 Israel) even appeared on the map. The more things, the richer the imagination, and thus the stronger and more "real" that state would appear in the minds of those longing to bring it into being.

If we try to apply this interpretation to the case of socialist Romania, we can see why the act of collecting was just as, if not more, important than the correct identification of chronology and typology, as Kaiser argued. In the early years of the socialist regime, at least, the archaeological artifacts unearthed in an intensive campaign of excavations throughout the country added a much-needed gravity—and gravitas—to a revolutionary political project. Heaps after heaps of objects of the past, ordered and collected in the new museums of history that appeared in every city in the country, supplied the new state with a new history. The overwhelming quantity of these objects enhanced their political value, making them more visible and thus more compelling as a form of historical evidence. That archaeology became a pivotal propaganda tool of the communist regime is also illustrated by the state-sponsored promotion of Romania's archaeological sites via international expositions—such as the one organized by the Romanian Commission for UNESCO in mid 1960s.[36]

Moreover, by taking Marx's materialist conception of history ad literam, archaeologists promoted their findings and their discipline as the most ideologically appropriate source of knowledge production. Objects, including archaeological artifacts, never have a straightforward meaning, but their meaning comes from the particular political and cultural context of their use. However, instead of approaching the archaeological material as a "text" in which they could discern systems of thought, meaning, and social action (Moreland 2001; Patrik 1985), archaeologists in post-1945 Romania chose to regard the archaeological record as raw matter, free of any political meaning, and thus as carrier of an objective historical truth. The new archaeological collections had a multilayered function: they materially magnified the state and they extended that perception of the state into a manicured past that fit the ideological priorities of the present.

Of course, this argument could be extended to many other sites opened in Bucharest and elsewhere. But how did the archaeologists working at the Old Court manage to persuade the authorities to keep the site open and eventually make it into an open-air museum, while other sites nearby were closed down? The artifacts were the first step for the archaeologists to win the battle over the Old Court site. Despite their fluid chronology, these coins and fragments of pottery functioned as a proof and a promise that a larger part of the Old Court walls would come to the surface if only the archaeologists were allowed to dig further. The chronologically malleable artifacts and the immovable walls complemented one another, mutually enhancing one another's political value and promoting the Old Court as being the most important historic site in the city.

Competing Regimes of Value

At the Old Court, the archaeologists used the discoveries during the 1953 and 1958–59 campaigns to pressure the state authorities to keep the site open. The anonymous letter of denunciation that accused Nicolae Bădescu and other architects of crass disregard of Bucharest's history played an important part in that plan. The stir that it had caused allowed the archaeologists to buy more time and, more importantly, to gain the authorities' support to open other research sites in the Old Town. The subsequent excavations, the broadest and longest-lasting (1967–71) led to "the discovery of riverine stone walls" (Panait 1980, 9) that specialists identified as having been part of the first palace that the Wallachian prince Vlad the Impaler had built it in the fifteenth century. This long-awaited "discovery" had, in fact, been what the archaeologists had hoped they would find right from the beginning, since their earlier digs in the early 1950s. They had known about this palace, mentioned for the first time in a 1459 charter as "the fortress of Bucharest" (8). This palace was the material proof of a medieval Bucharest, a tangible evidence that accompanied and solidified the charter as a valid historical document and justified the archaeologists' request for the reconstruction of the Old Court and its transformation into a national open-air museum.

The story of the Old Court illustrates a case of spatialization of political power that competed with the regime's pursuit of power through the redesign of urban space, which I discussed in the previous chapter. Nicos Poulantzas (1980, 114) has argued that the modern states have relied on a particular revaluation of the relationship between space and time, as state making entailed both a historicization of a territory and a territorialization of history. I have already showed how the archaeologists won their fight with the architects by assigning historicity to a territory—in this case, by presenting the Old Town as a mere background for the vestiges of the Old Court. This pursuit was, however, not enough; other archaeologists could step in and bring proof of medieval artifacts collected from other sites.

To secure their position, the archaeologists working at the Old Court had to make their project resonate more deeply with the political imaginary of the present. To territorialize history, in socialist Romania, and in the socialist bloc in general, meant to implicitly pursue a spatial centralization, one that mirrored and extended the project of creating a heavily centralized political and economic system. The walls of the fifteenth-century fortress allowed the archaeologists to claim that the Old Court was the historic nucleus of the city: its place of origins, its axis mundi. Winning this argument was particularly important for the teams working at the Old Court because they knew that other groups could easily dispute it by claiming that other sites were equally, if not more, historically significant because Bucharest never had one center to begin with. In our conversation, Florin Curta stressed this point:

> What made the archaeologists declare the Old Court the most important historical site in Bucharest? Bucharest is a polyfocal city; it does not have a real center, because it emerged as a conglomeration of settlements. The fifteenth-century vaults [found at the Old Court site] did not mean much. Other sites such as the second palace from Mihai Vodă were equally important.[37] The main question is how the political leaders became persuaded to fund the research [and then open the site as an open-air museum]. There was a lot of maneuvering to receive the OK from the Party. It was not [the state authorities] that dictated the archaeologists [what to do]. It was the specialists who fed the political discourse.[38]

In the end, the archaeologists of the City Museum promoted the Old Court as the city's place of origins and persuaded the political establishment to acknowledge that position. In 1969, the Council of Ministers passed a decree that officially declared the Old Court "a historical site of national importance" (*rezervație istorică*), the only one of its kind in Bucharest.[39] The museum of the Old Court was officially opened in 1972 and set under the supervision of the City Museum (Panait and Ştefănescu 1973, 5). On its opening, the City Museum began to publish touristic guides and albums, advertising the Old Court as "the heart of the city" (Almaş and Panait 1974). Even though Bucharest had never had a clearly delimited center, the archaeologists used the Old Court to create a historic nucleus of the city, offering the socialist state a tangible representation of the political center of the past, conferring historical continuity and thus legitimacy to the socialist system.

To understand why this pursuit was so important, we must go back to the initial exchange of letters, which captured the unequal relationship between the architects and the archaeologists. The writers of the initial letter did not dare to directly confront the architects, because they were aware that the ruined walls of the Old Court held very little value in comparison to the modern buildings planned to be developed in Union Square. Initially, the Old Court and the new Union Square were part of two competing "regimes of value" in which two competing political agendas informed how things circulated, were exchanged, and captured or lost value. However, the archaeologists eventually managed to merge these regimes of value by making the Old Court appear as important, if not more, as a modernized Union Square. In this process, they gained unexpected political capital.

A persuasive theory about the emergence of a regime of values has been proposed by anthropologist Arjun Appadurai (1986). He urged scholars to consider "the social life of things," the ways in which they capture or lose value in motion, at different moments of exchange and (re)valuation. He thus launched a new direction in the anthropological study of materiality, in which he tried to go beyond Marx-influenced arguments about fetishization in which things would be seen as totally flexible recipients of meaning. Appadurai sought to recuperate some agency of things by arguing that the trajectories of things did not simply reproduce a dynamic web of social and political relations but that they contributed actively to further shaping such relations. However, he did not inquire into the temporalities of value making and unmaking. For instance, under what circumstances does the value of a thing in the present become dependent on another thing from the future?

The case of the Old Court illustrates how time itself becomes as important a variable as exchange in constituting value. However, in this case, time is not the temporal duration that informs the social life of only one thing, moving through various phases of its existence. Time is the very glue that binds together two distinct things (or sets of things), with one gaining value only from the promised existence of the other in the proximal future. The first walls that archaeologists discovered at the Old Court in 1953 had a questionable value, heavily contested by architects as well as other archaeologists. However, the ruined walls gained further meaning when archaeologists advertised these artifacts as anticipating more significant discoveries in the future—that of the entire foundation of the Old Court (which indeed the archaeologists unearthed in later excavations, but which in 1953 they were not sure they would find). The first walls captured value in the present because they functioned as signs of value in the future. By creating a connection between the first set of walls and the entire foundation of the court that would appear through more excavations, the archaeologists challenged the architects' monopoly on "the future." An Old Court that could be fully brought to surface and ideally reconstructed would be as valuable as a modernized Union Square, which so many architects wanted to redesign and make into an epitome of a socialist urbanity. The archaeologists gained political capital from these symbolic transactions because they successfully merged two distinct regimes of value into one.

In their analysis of the materialities of colonialism, more precisely of the Europeans' attempt to replace a form of currency (cattle and beads) with coinage in early nineteenth-century South Africa, anthropologists Jean and John Comaroff (2006) showed that distinct regimes of value could coexist and be negotiated in a social space, especially a social space characterized by intensive encounters such as the one between the colonizers and the colonized. They noticed a paradox: that for a regime of value to be effective and valid—that is, to survive drastic political and cultural change while undergoing transformation but not erasure—it needs to rely on persuasive techniques of commensuration via which distinct media become interchangeable.

In short, a regime of value is powerful enough not when it endorses but rather when it negates difference (Comaroff and Comaroff 2006, 109). Commensurability—the ability to persuade others that cattle, coins, and beads are interchangeable, that they have the same value in making (or breaking) social relations, and consolidating or challenging mores, morality, and prestige—is sine qua non for creating new zones of contact, for enabling cultural and economic translatability, and for endorsing new clusters of political and economic power. Only when formerly "incompatible" things appear as commensurable could they engender "new lines of distinction, new languages of value, new forms of inequity" (109). By becoming more semiotically supple, these things seem to radiate an agency that makes those who suddenly accept their commensurability believe that such things gain "magical properties" and could "make history of their own accord" (109). But what appears as these things' magical qualities that enable social change are, in fact, an effect of some groups' ability to persuade others to "see" how these once incommensurable things could now be exchanged—how cows could become coins, and then contracts, and then capital.

These semiotically supple things could be cattle transformed into coins and contracts in nineteenth-century South Africa. They could also be old walls unearthed from the ground that initially few wanted to have anything to do with but that eventually would be elevated to the status of Bucharest's most valuable historic site—the historical core of the city. Initially, the tensions and mutual accusations between the architects and the archaeologists regarding the Old Court resembled the early colonial situation described by the Comaroffs in which cattle and coins were incommensurable, being part of distinct regimes of value grounded in distinct moralities, political hierarchies, and expectations of social relations. Initially, at that particular political moment, the plans for a new city center, with large squares, spacious boulevards, and modern, functional buildings were part of a regime of value that had no place for some ruined walls of a long-ago-forgotten palace. In short, history was incommensurable with modernity.

However, the archaeologists found a way to bring history into the political discourse, but they did so through the back door. First, the archaeologists needed to make that history palatable to the new leaders. And they did so by appealing to a teleological interpretation of history that fit the ideological priorities of the epoch. By simplifying Marx's interpretation of history as a product of the means and relations of productions, the archaeologists employed a theory of history that became increasingly popular at that time—that is, an overly deterministic view of history as one that evolved in specific stages, from slavery to serfdom in the Middle Ages, to capitalism, to socialism, and finally communism. The Old Court represented a material proof of the medieval past of the city that further guaranteed a socialist present and a communist future.

Second, the archaeologists digging at the Old Court added a historical dimension to the concept of "the center," thus challenging the architects' monopoly on the city center. The idea of "the center" was pivotal within a socialist system, designating both a planned economy and a political process which decision making was, at least in theory, concentrated in the hands of a few. The architects initially believed that they held undisputed control over a spatial dimension of this center. The record number of proposals that the city council received regarding the planned redesigned of Union Square revealed the high stakes of this particular location. The winning team would have had a strong say in transforming Bucharest into a functional modern city with a clearly defined city center, marked by Union Square. However, instead of allowing the architects to capitalize on a future city center, which existed at that time only in the planners' sketches, the archaeologists offered the regime a center that had already been there: the Old Court.

Suddenly, the ruined walls of the Old Court appeared as commensurable with the planned walls of the new, modern buildings—and soon they became even more valuable than the latter. In the end, the new city center that would be represented by a modernized Union Square did not materialize. Instead, the archaeologists managed to assign the Old Court's walls a new political relevance. They did so by merging two distinct regimes of value, characterized by distinct temporalities, into a smooth and continuous narrative of the nation's origins, one in which the walls came to represent a medieval past that was suddenly "glued" to the socialist present. The promotion of the Old Court as the political center of the past reinforced the power of the "center" in the present and thus played a key role in the process of state making in 1960s Romania.

The production of the Old Court as a socialist heritage site must be placed in the broader context of the production (or erasure) of value under socialism. I suggest that the socialist state created its own regime of value not only by hoarding goods and means of production at the center, as Katherine Verdery (1996) persuasively argued, but also by altering the relationships among distinct things, the ways in which they were linked one to another (or disconnected one from another). In 1950s Romania, specific forms of materiality (such as artifacts uncovered in archaeological excavations) became more relevant than others (such as nineteenth-century buildings) as potential carriers of historical "truth." These artifacts gained more value than old buildings because

Fig. 2.3. The partially reconstructed walls of the Old Court. The marks on the wall are traces from the eighteenth-century houses erected on the site and demolished in the 1960s. Photo by author, May 2016.

they could be moved into new collections and be reordered so it would fit a new historical narrative. Thus, the formation of a new regime of value under socialism involved a paradoxical process of freezing mobile things into collections—whether for display in museums as "the people's property" or even "borrowed" indefinitely by party apparatchiks for their official villas.[40] Mobile things, such as paintings, art objects, and archaeological artifacts, gained value only when they became centralized in new museum collections. By contrast, fixed material forms, such as old mansions, castles, and places of worship that had already gained historical value during previous political times, would be turned into alienable things. The value that they had acquired before 1945 became the very source of loss of value under socialism. Their former significance evoked worlds that contradicted those promoted by the new state. Therefore, the communist authorities sought to divest such buildings of their histories by making them into ordinary hospitals, hospices, or boarding schools and sometimes by abandoning them altogether.[41] These processes of reordering things to enhance or erase their value were part and parcel of the making of the socialist state.

Fig. 2.4. The Old Court Museum in 2016. Note the highly heterogeneous collection of artifacts. Photo by author, May 2016.

What was particular about the Old Court was its newness—the fact that it literally emerged out of the ground right after the new regime came to power. It was pristine from a political point of view, not tainted with any other political connotations that other old buildings had inevitably acquired. It was not just that the archaeological artifacts collected from the site could be politically "tamed" by being dated and then redated according to different agendas. The walls themselves could be claimed by the regime as its own history, a material proof of the history of nation, vestiges that had the unique quality of being both old and new and thus much more politically malleable.

Conclusion

Throughout the socialist period, the state invested massive resources and energy in the rapid transformation of Bucharest into a model socialist city. But the archaeologists working at the Old Court managed to persuade the political establishment that they needed a past to ground the promised socialist future. By calling on Marx's theory that a feudal order is a prerequisite for socialism, the archaeologists sought to promote the Old Court as uncontestable proof of the city's medieval origins. They offered the state an extraordinary opportunity to expand itself, not only in space through city planning but also in time by presenting the communist period as a corollary of the medieval ("feudal") past.

Archaeology helped the Romanian socialist state consolidate its legitimacy. Archaeological methods and artifacts were favored over historical documents as more pristine sources with which to write a new past on which to build a socialist future. But the supposed objectivity of archaeological data—their very materiality—provided a convenient facade for the archaeologists digging at the Old Court to hide their manipulation of the chronology in the service of ideology. Moreover, it invited others to follow suit. These individuals were not just the literati, historians, art historians, and literary critics who wrote book after book of purportedly scientific studies that extolled the uniqueness of the Romanian nation. They were also architects who sought to bring more national authenticity into the city by starting nowhere else but in the Old Town district—the same place that their own colleagues had wanted to demolish in the 1960s but that by the early 1970s was officially acknowledged and advertised as the historic center of Bucharest. As it turned out, archaeological artifacts were not the only ones that could become chronologically fluid. Some architects wanted to transfer that fluidity onto the Old Town's houses, making them into time-traveling vehicles of nationalism.

Notes

1. I owe this point to Oana Mateescu.

2. Vasile Dinu was also professor at the University of Bucharest and the chair of the Department of Scientific Socialism. See Vasile and Tismăneanu (2013).

3. I would like to thank Iuliu Şerban, archivist of the National Institute for Historic Monuments, for helping me identify these sources. The archive of this institution (referenced henceforth as AINMI, Arhiva Institutului Naţional al Monumentelor Istorice) has a dramatic story, having been on the verge of being destroyed twice in the last fifty years. The archives of the former Commission of Historical Monuments, active during the interwar period but abolished in 1947, had been rescued at the last moment in 1947 by historian Oliver Velescu. He preserved them until the Department of Historical Monuments (DHM) was established in 1953, as part of the State Commission for Architecture and Construction. The archive of the interwar commission was then divided in two: the majority of the files had been sent to the archives of Bucharest's city council, while a smaller part remained in the archive of DHM. Then, after the second dismantling of DHM in 1977, the archive was temporarily placed in a basement, but then a shelf of files fell on the door and blocked access to the archive. This accident was a blessing in disguise, because the archive was thus kept intact until 1990, when it was returned to the recently reestablished Commission for Historical Monuments. Between 1990 and 1993, a team of archivists, including Iuliu Şerban, read and classified the entire collection.

4. AINMI, "Notă privind situația monumentelor," file 2159/1962–1970, 2.

5. "Notă," file 2159/1962–1970, 2.

6. When the new communist government launched the project of a socialist master plan for Bucharest in 1949, the Institute for Urban Design and Constructions was established as the main office entrusted with the development of the plan and subordinated to the Ministry of Constructions. Project Bucharest became the more powerful version of the initial institute, emerging as a by-product of the government's 1952 decision to grant more power and autonomy to the architectural field.

7. Excerpts, "Notă privind situația monumentelor," file 2159/1962–1970, 2–9.

8. "Notă . . . (urmare notei Academiei R.P.R.)," file 2159/1962–1970, 10–15. This passage was deleted with a red pen by the second reader on page 10.

9. File 2159/1962–1970, 10. Those comments were addressed to "Comrade [Vasile] Bumbăcea," apparently the one who produced the first draft of the letter responding to the accusations of the first memorandum. At that time (January 1963), Bumbăcea was vice chairman of the State Committee for Architecture. See *Arhitectura RPR* 62, no. 1 (1963): 60.

10. File 2159/1962–1970, 11.

11. File 2159/1962–1970, 14.

12. File 2159/1962–1970, 10.

13. AINMI, file 2159/1962–1970, 16.

14. During the interwar years, Ion Nestor made his political views clear in a manifesto that he and two friends published in a literary magazine that, starting in late 1920s, openly supported antisemitic and fascist writings. In the manifesto, they praised "the historical continuity," noting that "the shying away from breaking from the cultural traditions represents our autochthonism, is what brings us life, and connects us to . . . a millenary past." Sorin Pavel, Ion Nestor, Petre Marcu-Balș, "Manifestul Crinului Alb," *Gândirea* 8, nos. 8–9 (1928): 317.

15. One of the most famous protochronists, art historian Răzvan Theodorescu (1974), enjoyed a thriving professional career under the socialist regime as well as afterward. He argued that "the first superior forms of medieval political, religious, and artistic life" had emerged "only and only" within the territory between "the two extremities of the Romanian Danube" (9). To support his argument (17, 32, 35, 43), he cited at length archaeological research, such as Comșa (1959, 1968) and Nestor (1958, 1964).

16. For an analysis of the scholarly employment of the idea of historical continuity in postcommunist Romania, see Niculescu (2004–5).

17. After 1945, when Eastern Europe was recognized as a Soviet sphere of influence, the International Congress of Slavic Archaeology was founded to encourage closer relations among Slavic nations. See Trigger (1990, 210). For arguments that the Slavic ethnicity as a homogeneous group was itself a construction of Byzantine authors, see Curta (2001a).

18. As Russian archaeologist Pavel Dolukhanov (1993, 150) noted, "From the very beginning archaeology in the USSR was largely viewed as a device for official communist indoctrination. The study of material remains . . . was regarded as an instrument for promoting Marxist dogmas in relation to the socioeconomic development of preclass and early-class societies."

19. For a review of the institutional support of a "Slavic archaeology"—that is, an archaeology focused on the Slavic ethnogenesis—in the post-1945 Soviet bloc, see Curta (2001b, 2005). For a discussion on the development of archaeology in socialist Bulgaria and Romania, see Bailey (1998) and Stamati (2015, 2016), respectively. For a survey of different

approaches taken by Romanian historians and archaeologists with regard to the "Slavic influence" over the genesis of the population living in the territory of current Romania, see Curta (1994).

20. Vladimir Ilich Lenin, "The Development of Capitalism in Russia," in *Collected Works*, 1896–1899, via Marxists.org, accessed June 30, 2018, https://www.marxists.org/archive/lenin /works/1899/dcr8ii/index.htm.

21. This argument is obviously not new. It has stood at the core of much larger debates on the relationship between archaeology and history. For a succinct and original discussion of this topic, see Moreland (2001).

22. I thank one of the anonymous readers for their observation that Romanian historians in the 1960s sought proof of "Romanian" continuity starting with Dacian times and described Burebista, the "king" of the Dacians (ca. 82–44 BCE), as the first leader of the "Romanian state," when Dacia was just a colony of the Roman Empire. However, the linchpin between the socialist present and the allegedly Dacian past was the early medieval period— or early feudalism, as the archaeologists in Romania called it. In order to prove the continuity theory, the archaeologists needed to assert that the Dacians were the forbearers of the people living in Bucharest's territory during the medieval period.

23. Horia Maicu, "500 de ani de existență documentară a orașului București," *Arhitectura RPR* 5, no. 60 (1959): 3–16.

24. See Foucault's argument (1970) that the modern episteme—the mode of knowledge prevalent in modernity—stopped relying on resemblance but focuses instead on identity and difference. In this case, chronology becomes more important, hence the political importance of history as a discipline.

25. Timothy Kaiser (1995, 103) points out that the Romanian archaeologists have focused very much on the products of the current ethnic majority.

26. I thank Britt Halvorson for pointing out to me that the very assumption that inscriptions would communicate "facts" is a specifically historical one, built on a particular understanding promulgated through print capitalism.

27. The archaeological digs in the country began in 1949, but the first excavation in the city of Bucharest began only in 1953. See Lăzărescu-Ionescu et al. (1954, 285–87).

28. For instance, as a result of one of the first digs opened in the city center (in the Radu Vodă Church area), the researchers dismissed some of the first (mid-nineteenth century) attempts to popularize historical accounts of Bucharest's origins as "fantasies." Those accounts include Gr. Musceleanu, *Calendarul antic pe 1875* (București), and Al. Pelimon, *Bukur, Istoria fondării Bucurescilor* (1858). Both documents mentioned a church that had been initially built of wood by Bucur himself, which then was rebuilt in stone by one of the Romanian princes, Mircea the Old. The researchers argued that an archaeological study of the site "definitively clarified the origins of the church, [which] had been built in the eighteenth century and it is not in any case linked to the city's origins nor with its founder." See Ionașcu et al. (1954, 458–59).

29. Phone interview, March 8, 2009, followed by an email correspondence, April 10, 2009.

30. Florin Curta, email communication, April 10, 2008.

31. I thank Florin Curta for pointing out these references to me.

32. Email communication, April 10, 2009.

33. Historian Cristian Vasile noted that extensive funds had been channeled into archaeological research during the 1950s and 1960s. Email communication, December 2, 2016. Florin Curta confirmed this information, email communication, September 11, 2018.

34. Florin Curta, email communication, September 11, 2018.

35. Florin Curta, email communication, September 11, 2018.

36. "Participation de la Roumanie a la mise en oeuvre de programme de l'UNESCO," UNESCO archives, File X07.2I (498) A 562, Romania—Briefing for DG, 15.

37. Mihai Vodă was a church on a hill near the Dâmbovița River in Bucharest's city center. Another team conducted archaeological research on the site in 1959 and again during 1960 and 1961. The research led to the discovery of two palaces, one of which was dated to the late seventeenth century and deemed to be the largest feudal building discovered until then in Bucharest's underground (Cantacuzino 1965). During the building of the Civic Center in the 1980s, the church was initially scheduled to be demolished, together with other constructions on the hill. At the insistence of specialists, the church was slid (on rails) 300 m down the hill from its initial location.

38. Phone interview, March 8, 2009.

39. AINIM, file 2159/1962–1970, 123–26. The decree authorized city council to restore and preserve the area of the Old Court. Approved by president of the State Committee for Architecture, Nicolae Bădescu, August 29, 1969.

40. Archaeologist Eugenia Zaharia wrote about the uncertain period 1948–51, when many art collections and museums had been dismantled and some important objects were "lost" without trace. She also talked about the reorganization of the Royal Palace into the Art Museum, when many objects were "given away" at the request of the new authorities. Eugenia Zaharia, "Colecții și muzee distruse" [Destroyed collections and museums], *Ziarul Financiar (Ziarul de duminică)*, January 16, 2006, http://www.zf.ro/ziarul-de-duminica/colectii-si -muzee-distruse-3015923/. See also Grama (2019).

41. Many incidents of destruction and looting in the immediate years after the war were signaled to the central authorities in Bucharest, but the authorities did very little to prevent this devaluation. In 1948, the president of the Hungarian People's Union of Romania wrote to the state secretary of nationalities about the dire situation of many mansions and castles in Transylvania: "In most places, the peasant victors did not only occupy the estate and the park, but they also destroyed the castle, using its material to build houses or other sites." However, nothing came out of this petition. AINMI, file 3842/1947–1948, 7.

3

TIME-TRAVELING HOUSES AND
HISTORIES MADE INVISIBLE

IN 1967, ARCHITECT CONSTANTIN JOJA MADE AN UNEXPECTED proposal to Bucharest's city officials: to make the Old Town's houses travel back in time. Specifically, he wanted to redesign their facades in a style that allegedly represented the architecture of the eighteenth century, a time that Joja associated with the beginning of the Romanian nation. This proposal came in the context of local authorities' decision to designate the Old Town as Bucharest's historic district and their commissioning a team of specialists to make it happen. Most of the Old Town's urban fabric had been built during the nineteenth and early twentieth century, forming a heteroclite assembly of architectural styles in which the straight lines of modernist buildings of the 1920s and 1930s alternated with sinuous decorations of the art nouveau facades of the early twentieth century and cast iron balconies with intricate patterns embellishing the nineteenth-century houses. This amalgam of styles may have been visually appealing to some, but not to Joja.

Joja declared, "Since we want the Romanian architecture to be displayed in its full value in the area [of the Old Court], the renovation project will center on the adoption of the urban civil constructions of the eighteenth century," which in his view represented "the most authentic [architectural style] of the epoch."[1] What he regarded as a genuinely Romanian architectural style took the form of two-story houses, with their balconies enclosed by a series of small windows to add additional insulation in hot summers and freezing winters. He wanted to draw on this style to redecorate the facades of "ninety-two currently degraded houses" in the Old Town as well as those of other, newer buildings.[2] He also recommended that architects survey other districts planned for demolition, identify "older" buildings that presumably displayed a "Romanian specificity," and save them from destruction by "transplanting" them to the Old Town. In his view, such a collection of houses, no matter how anachronistic, would have transformed the district into the historic center of a modern city. It was a strategy similar to one already employed by archaeologists to transform the Old Court into a historical site of national value. Like some of the chronologically fluid artifacts at the Old Court, these time-traveling houses were to become, in Joja's hands, equally fluid. Together, houses, artifacts, and the rebuilt palace of the Old Court would have constituted a perfectly coherent assemble, fitting the state's ideological needs—a proof of the site's historical continuity, from early medieval times through the eighteenth century (allegedly the beginning of the modern Romanian nation) until the socialist present.

Even though Joja's vision to make the Old Town into an architectural pastiche never moved beyond the proposal stage, it accomplished something else: it made the Old Town—and not just the Old Court—much more visible for both architects and politicians. The historical development of the Old Town over the course of the twentieth century is shot through with ambivalence, as different political elites at distinct moments swung back and forth between viewing the site as valuable or worthless. When one party wanted to abandon or raze the district, other actors found ways to upend those plans. These oscillations became even more visible under a centralized system that monitored and streamlined debates. The constant struggle over the meanings of the Old Town reveals how various actors manipulated the city's past in order to gain control over the city's future.

While the previous chapter focused on the political "resurrection" of the Old Court and its transformation into a heritage site for the socialist state, this chapter explores the state's ambivalence about the political value of historic buildings at two moments of the socialist regime: (1) the relative political and cultural openness of the mid-1960s and early 1970s, and (2) the authoritarian context of the mid- and late 1980s. It does so through an analysis of the particular material forms, urban aesthetics, and temporal frameworks that various professionals called on to create a palatable historical narrative for the state officials. I analyze two episodes in particular: (1) the 1970 attempt to transform the Old Town into a historic district purportedly displaying a Romanian style, and (2) the liminal situation of the district during the mid- and late 1980s, when its demolition appeared imminent in light of the construction of a new Civic Center. I examine the different lives of the Old Town as a window into the relationship between place and politics. I analyze how buildings and people became signs of political order or disorder; how debates about what constitutes "proper" historic preservation signaled other choices, such as political dissent or obedience; and how, no matter how much the regime wanted to stifle lives and ways of being that it deemed "improper," the Old Town's inhabitants found ways to undermine the system as they kept breathing life into the place and making it a home.

The Emergence of National Communism

From the time of the discovery of the Old Court's ruined walls in 1953 to the time it was rebuilt as an open-air museum in 1972, socialist Romania underwent many other changes. By the early 1960s, the political tides had shifted. De-Stalinization was in full swing. The socialist satellite states sought various paths to reform, and national interests took precedent over those of the Soviets. Gheorghe Gheorghiu-Dej, the party general secretary and the state president, died in 1965, and Nicolae Ceauşescu became the new leader, intensifying and expanding the nationalism that Dej had launched in his last years of presidency. At the beginning of his regime, Ceauşescu appeared to be interested in economic and cultural exchanges with Western countries. He managed to gain a reputation for open-mindedness when he was the only Eastern European communist statesman to publicly oppose the USSR's invasion of Czechoslovakia in 1968. It soon turned out, however, that Ceauşescu's main interest lay in setting up an increasingly nationalist agenda with an eye to building his own minuscule empire.

The early 1970s marked a turning point in the cultural politics of Romanian socialism. In a 1971 speech that came to be known as the "July theses," Ceauşescu requested that all cultural production focus on matters of national interest and that any Western influence be dramatically curtailed. His speech triggered a nationalist campaign that culminated in the mid-1970s with the so-called protochronist rhetoric promoted by intellectuals who sought to advance their careers by singing hymns to the regime (see the previous chapter). The nationalist rhetoric was in full bloom, bolstered by the protochronists' claims that the forebears of the Romanian people (the proto-Romanians) had been at the center of world history. Some archaeologists joined this chorus by "discovering" alleged evidence of the earliest *Homo sapiens* in Europe near Ceauşescu's home village, Scorniceşti (Rady 1995 in Light and Dumbrăveanu-Andone 1997, 33), and thus "proving" a historical continuity between the first linguistically articulated leaders and Ceauşescu himself.

By trying to manicure the past, streamlining complex histories of centuries-long multiethnic cohabitation into a narrative that favored exclusively Romanians and effectively deleted the heritage of the ethnic Hungarians, Germans, Jews, Roma, Italians, Russians, and Armenians who lived for generations on the territory of modern Romania, the communist regime tried to make itself more palatable to the ethnic majority and force the minorities to forgo their ethnic traditions. As Katherine Verdery (1991) has argued, the state-promoted national ideology was meant to compensate for the regime's increasing authoritarianism, while maintaining a relative consent from its people. But in the process, the meaning and the constituency of the people had changed. Non-Romanians' reaction to the state's nationalist policies was to flee or to distance themselves from their ethnic origins (as fight was no longer an option). In 1948, the population consisted of approximately 85% ethnic Romanians, followed by approximately 10% Hungarians, 2.2% Germans, 1% Jews, and a much lower percentage of Roma and other ethnic groups.[3] By 1977, these numbers changed to 88% Romanians, 8% Hungarians, 1.6% Germans, 1% Roma, and 0.1% Jews.[4] In 1960, Romania officially allowed Romanian Jews to emigrate to Israel, and they did so en masse (Rotman 2004, 89–104). The mass emigration of ethnic Germans and Jews reached its peak in the 1970s. In 1977, after decades of negotiation, West Germany persuaded the Romanian state to sign the agreement for the families' reunification, which triggered the mass emigration of ethnic Germans (with Germany paying thousands of dollars per immigrant in exchange of exit visas) (Dobre et al. 2011).

The state-sponsored pursuit of ethnic homogenization (Romanianization) through culture and education was accompanied by other authoritarian policies. The strategy of modernization through space had been part of the regime's ideology right from the beginning, but the late 1960s marked an important shift in the state's politics of urban planning. With the reorganization of Romania's territorial units in 1968, the state launched a grandiose project of urban planning known as *sistematizare*. This is how anthropologist Steven Sampson (1984, 75) described this policy: "In the Romanian context, *sistematizare* is more than just a method for the physical transformation of villages and towns. It is, firstly, an *ideal* of how spatial planning should be integrated with economic planning (*planificare*) and socialist development. Second, systematization is a *program* for developing (or in some cases phasing out) each settlement in the country, from hamlet to metropolis. Third, systematization involves an *organizational structure* in which national objectives, regional imbalances and local potentialities are to be harmonized into a centrally administered State policy, codified by law." *Sistematizare* was thus a project of spatial intervention through aesthetic and geographical homogenization. As Romanian specialists admitted to the UNESCO delegation who visited the country in April 1989, "the central purpose of the rural systematization program was to speed up the country's modernization."[5] The policy allegedly targeted a rapid modernization through the standardization of urban planning and through a forced urbanization of Romania's villages.[6] The Romanian authorities claimed that this policy of extreme urbanization was meant to improve the living conditions in the countryside. In fact, it was merely a new bureaucratic label but with significant social effects. By elevating the villages to the status of urban settlements, at least on paper, state officials made it more difficult for villagers to leave their places of origins and move to cities—in the conditions in which the urban area were already overpopulated, and state authorities continued to struggle with the housing crisis.

At the same time, *sistematizare* was also an ideological technology: by rearranging how cities and villages were linked one to another and making them further dependent on a center (the central government in Bucharest), a key goal was to produce a mental shift in the ways people from different regions thought of themselves in relation to this center. Supplementing nationalist policies, this shift targeted especially the multiethnic region of Transylvania, which the regime wanted to closely control. The political establishment aimed to intervene in a long-term symbolic competition, one that began right after Transylvania's inclusion in Greater Romania in 1918. The two sites, Bucharest and Transylvania, symbolized different historical times in the political trajectory of the Romanian modern state. Bucharest, the capital of Romania since the unification of the two principalities, Moldavia and Wallachia, in 1859, represented the center par excellence of a modern, politically independent Romania. However, Transylvania continued to be looked on as the "cultural heritage of Romania" (Pop and Porumb, 2004)—the region at the heart of Romania's political identity, for which tens of thousands of soldiers fought in World War I and II, and which, throughout the twentieth century, Bucharest's politicians never ceased to view as a hotbed of ethnic tensions and political dissent that needed constant policing (Bottoni 2018; Livezeanu 1995).

We could understand the political significance of the transformation of the Old Town into Bucharest's historic district only if we placed the project within the broader context of *sistematizare*: the regime's attempt at remaking a Bucharest-centered national imaginary through a shift of perception. It was not just an attempt to change people's sense of belonging to a particular symbolic geography. It also aimed to alter people's perception of the past through space. Given that the Old Town had been for centuries a home not just for Romanian but also Jewish, Armenian, Italian, German, Hungarian, Turkish, and Greek traders, craftsmen, bankers, lawyers, and physicians (Iorga 1939), the alteration of the Old Town's historical narrative was particularly important in light of the nationalist rhetoric. But the nationalization of the district's history also reflected a local ethnic homogenization that began in the early 1960s.

After the nationalization of 1948, most of the small businesses in the district closed down, their shops folded into the socialist economy, while their private residences usually located on the second floor of the buildings became state property. The modern apartment buildings that appeared in the 1920s and the 1930s in between nineteenth-century houses were nationalized (Chelcea 2004), no matter the ethnicity of their owners.[7] Those whose residential space was smaller were able to keep their apartments, or had to accommodate new tenants in their homes. The mass emigration of the Old Town's Jewish residents in the early 1960s (Waldman and Ciuciu 2011), alongside many other Romanian Jews, seemed to offer a temporary solution. In exchange for passports, state authorities forced them to sign over their houses to the state without compensation (Rotman 2004).

As the former owners departed, their houses and stores became redistributed in the centralized economy. Some were rented to the Artists' Union to function as workshops for painters and sculptors and as art galleries in which the union could sell their work. Other spaces became offices of various central institutions or warehouses. The shops, restaurants, and hotels alongside the main streets of the district kept being open, only now serving the state economy.[8] The better apartments in the modern buildings were retained for people within the system, those who had enough political clout to receive a central apartment from the state authorities for the minimum rent. The private residences in nineteenth-century buildings became part of the state housing fund and were rented to poorer people who were willing to pay the price of living in the city center: put up with less-than-perfect conditions such as lack of central heating, one bathroom at the end of the hallway shared by several households, and so forth. Slowly, the multiethnic makeup of the place began to change, but its social heterogeneity endured. If before the war, the district's residents made up a mix of middle-class entrepreneurs, low-class shopkeepers, and workers and servants who had migrated from the country side (Patmore 1939, 27–28), by 1960s the Old Town became a place where bohemian artists lived and worked next to state tenants who wanted to live in the center and tailors and furriers who kept a small business in their own living room.[9]

Even though the Old Town had been a combination of commercial and residential space for more than two centuries, its impending transformation into Bucharest's historic district was implicitly an economic enterprise, meant to bring tourists and shoppers in, but gradually expel its residents. In 1967, approximately 4,800 people were estimated to be living in the area.[10] By 1970, according to a survey, around 2,900 people lived in the district, distributed in 1,300 households.[11] Even though the commercialization of the area was a declared goal, no one among the state authorities or the specialists involved in the project openly admitted that they wanted to get rid of the residents or at least make them as invisible as possible. But this was likely one of the goals of Joja's proposal: the radically redesigned facades of the district's old houses, whose balconies would become closed verandas, would not just become architectural vehicles of nationalism but also strategic cover-ups to conceal their poor tenants.

The Revival of Interwar Nationalism

Freud (2003, 124) described the uncanny, or the "unhomely" (*das Unheimlich*) as a derivative of the "homely," something that is known, familiar, and thus reassuring—but that suddenly goes awry. Its danger resides precisely in the qualities of proximity, comfort, and trust that a thing, place, or person used to radiate. Socialism's "uncanny" became the nineteenth and early twentieth centuries, which were officially portrayed as an era of rampant capitalism leading to dire poverty and of a dominant class concerned only with its own interests. The nineteenth century was problematic for the socialist regime because of what it represented: a new Romanian state, formed as a parliamentary monarchy officially recognized by the Western powers in 1877. Independence brought a significant economic advantage to Romania and spurred rapid economic development in the late nineteenth and early twentieth centuries, especially in Bucharest (Hitchins 1994). While that period was indeed characterized by many of those traits—political nepotism, overt antisemitism, radical social polarization, with an impoverished, illiterate peasantry disconnected from an urban middle class—it was also a time of an intense artistic and social experimentation. During late 19th century and throughout the interwar times, Bucharest became a hotbed of cultural wars between modernists and traditionalists, between liberals and conservatives, a modern Babylon and a place of contrasts that kept attracting diverse crowds, cultural canons, and capital. After 1947, the communist regime declared all that social, aesthetic, and political diversity to be "anarchy" and "disorder" and sought to purge it from the official historical narrative and from tangible representations of that past, such as historic buildings.

It was the social and aesthetic heterogeneity of the Old Town that challenged the state's priorities of social and urban order. The only solution was to redesign the facades of the Old Town's nineteenth-century houses in a manner that would belie their time of origin, making them look more "national" than they indeed were. The stylization evocative of the eighteenth century that Joja wanted to imprint the old houses was a pretense for most of them, given that most of the district had been destroyed by fire in 1847 and had to be rebuilt according to the architectural fashions of the late nineteenth century (Mucenic 1997, 36). Historical accuracy, however, did not seem to pose a problem to Joja.

When he tried to persuade the communist politicians to make the Old Town into a historic district with an eighteenth-century flavor, Joja emphasized that style as being "authentically Romanian." However, the style that developed at the end of the eighteenth century, which Joja deemed to represent "Romanian civil architecture," was in fact a product of a period (the Phanariot era)

Propunere de reconstrucție a unei clădiri de pe str. Lipscani

Fig. 3.1. Proposal for the remodeling of a house in the Old Town. Drawing by Constantin Joja in *Arhitectura* 113, no. 4 (1968): 18. Photo by Răzvan Voinea. Used by permission of *Arhitectura* journal.

that nationalist historians were not willing to include in the official history of the nation. In the eighteenth and early nineteenth century, the Ottoman Empire attempted to strengthen its control over its Romanian principalities by anointing foreigners (wealthy Greeks from the Phanar district of Istanbul, in particular) as temporary princes. Even though the Phanariots were highly educated promoters of the Enlightenment and launched important cultural reforms in the principalities, interwar and then socialist historiography chose to portray the Phanariot period as a time of economic and cultural decline with a strong Ottoman influence and a period of crisis for the Romanians fighting for their national identity.[12]

However, Joja's proposal to bring back the Old Town's houses to the architectural style of the eighteenth century seemed to ignore such critical views of the Phanariote period. Its main focus lay somewhere else; the redesign of the houses' facades was an attempt to remove the "uncanny"—in the form of now rejected styles, people, and visions of history—from the urban landscape. It aimed to transform the Old Town from an unruly site, a meeting place of various styles and ways of living, into an orderly, aesthetically homogeneous "historic district." Purified of the "foreign elements of nineteenth-century French influence" and redecorated according to what Joja deemed to be an authentic

"Romanian architectural style," the Old Town's architecture would travel back in time, similar to some of the artifacts that archaeologists found next to the walls of the Old Court.[13] Those time-traveling houses would join the artifacts in fitting the ideological needs of the present: the reconstructed Old Court meant to stand as a tangible sign of the medieval past would be surrounded by houses representing the beginning of the modern Romanian nation.

Joja's proposal, then, must be approached as a double intervention in perception: in the ways visitors and tourists viewed the district and in the relationship between the place and its residents. He viewed it as an opportunity to invent a "new" past. Joja appealed to a set of strategies that aimed to alter the relationship between the district, its houses, its residents, and its visitors. First, he proposed that the district be made a pedestrian-only area, an intervention that would have brought about a new rhythm of interacting with and perceiving the place (Merleau-Ponty 2012). It was thus a shift of focus, from the residents to the visitors. It was the visitors who were invited to linger, to become pedestrians, to enjoy the place and see it with new eyes. Second, Joja wanted to put the district's residents literally out of the picture. Closing down the open balconies was a social intervention as well. The closed verandas would have covered the colorful signs of the poor living in the shabbier buildings, from the laundry hanging up to dry, to their own faces and bodies leaning on the balconies, smoking and people-watching. It was these lower-class people that Joja and the city authorities sought to render invisible. Not knowing what to do with them, in the conditions in which the housing crisis remained a problem throughout the 1970s, state authorities found more than appealing a plan of aesthetic redecoration that also whitewashed the district's increasing social polarization. Joja's proposal was thus more than an attempt at beautifying history via an architectural redesign. It also represented a practical strategy to literally screen off the unwanted elements of the nation.

We could better understand Joja's vision if we placed it within his particular political and professional trajectory. The irony was that the national past that Joja praised was an invented past—very much like the search for the architectural expression of a "national style" during the interwar period (Popescu 2004a, 2004b). It was in the interwar years that the search for both a "National Style" (Popescu 2004b), an architectural movement that focused on a selective inclusion of vernacular style into modern architecture, and a more daring modernism (Machedon and Scoffham 1999) had emerged as opposite answers to autochthonous calls for modernization. Both aesthetic visions continued to inform socialist architecture, especially during the 1960s, even though the architects officially denied such influences (Ioan 2002; Popescu 2004a). In fact, the architectural debates about the aesthetics of the city, far from being products of a new ideology, mirrored and continued the debates of the interwar period (Maxim 2018).

Joja's case illustrates the cultural ties between the interwar nationalism and its cultural brokers during communism, ties that both the authorities and architects tried to deny. His penchant for identifying and promoting a "Romanian style" had been a constant of his career. When he began to work as an architect in the 1930s, his professional agenda was heavily informed by his far-right political allegiances. He joined the ultranationalist and antisemitic Iron Guard. By 1940, he was one of the official architects of the guard, as the head of the planning committee of the Legionnaire Movement.[14]

Joja's interest in the Old Town also had its own history, dating back to his professional beginnings.[15] In 1935, a writer made some rather scornful remarks about the cultural festival that took place in the center of Bucharest every spring. He wrote, "The month of Bucharest was born mainly out of the need for the sensational. . . . It is an invitation to jamboree. . . . The city officials ask us to celebrate this [new] capital of 1935—their work of art. To enhance our wonder and admiration, they reconstituted a part of the past of this city under the form of dioramas representing major monuments, street corners and scenes of the past, and they lay them in front of our eyes side by side: old and present images of Bucharest."[16] In 1935, the "old" Bucharest was represented by some of the nineteenth-century sites that used to be located within the perimeter of the Old Town and that despite their demolition continued to be part of the local urban imaginary.[17] To celebrate Bucharest's past, a group of young architects built temporary replicas of these sites, which made the Old Town appear as an eerie combination of old and new. One of the authors of this project was "young architect Constantin Jojea"—the same Joja who more than thirty years later would attempt, once again, to make the Old Town as Romanian as possible.[18]

In 1948, Joja was thrown in prison for his former political affiliations.[19] On his release in 1952, he resumed his practice. When Bucharest's city council commissioned him to lead the team that would redesign the Old Town in 1970, he viewed the project as a once-in-a-lifetime opportunity. The authorities took him at his word: that the style he proposed was indeed "Romanian" and consequently that the restoration of the Old Town would produce a more nationally authentic urban environment.

While it won over the state officials, Joja's proposal raised eyebrows among some architects and caused consternation among others.[20] A long correspondence ensued between the Department of Historical Monuments, whose specialists opposed Joja's plans, and the officials who wanted to get the project started.[21] In April 1968, these diverging views reached a much larger audience when a public debate on the reconstruction of the "old historic center of the capital" was

Fig. 3.2. Proposal for the remodeling of an interior courtyard. Drawing by Constantin Joja in *Arhitectura* 125, no. 4 (1970): 40. Photo by author. Used by permission of *Arhitectura* journal.

organized at the Architects' House in Bucharest. Invited to present his project, Joja emphasized his innovative perspective on the area's restoration.[22] However, other architects reacted strongly to Joja's views. Some of them rejected such radical interventions in the architectural style of the district; others found that the closed verandas that Joja deemed "authentically Romanian" were overly "pretentious";[23] and others described such verandas as "a decadent derivation" of the originally open porches (*pridvor*).[24] Instead of a "renovation based on imagination," Joja's opponents suggested that the Old Town's houses be preserved with "the forms and motives that they had initially displayed, as much as they are still present: modest but original."[25] His critics argued that "an abuse of [redecorated] facades ...would falsify the true character of the district's [mixed] architecture."[26]

Still, Joja found some supporters among architects well placed in the political system. One of them shifted the weight of the debate from the redesign the Old Town to the historic importance of the Old Court. As Joja's proponent curtly put it, "Some specialists understand 'restoration' by rejecting any clearance of the vestiges of the parasitic constructions. [This translates] in our case [as] the refusal to accept the demolition of the nineteenth- and twentieth-century buildings, which mutilated the palace and which throughout all this time have masked valuable evidence/traces. .... How could we seriously support the viewpoint that the walls of those taverns, whose construction meant the mutilation of an ancient monument, be displayed together with vestiges of tremendous historical value?"[27] In other words, Joja's proponent criticized other architects for their insistence on keeping the original architecture of the nineteenth-century houses, accusing them in turn that they wanted to preserve buildings that "mutilated" the Old Court as a national historic site (even though the houses targeted to be redecorated were located somewhere else in the district).

Such arguments allow us to understand why the redesign of the Old Town appeared so palatable to state officials. Joja planned to make the Old Town into an extension of the Old Court, two sites "performing" different parts of the Romanian past. The Old Town would be turned into a pastiche of the eighteenth century, meant to represent the national essence in a particular aesthetic form. Moreover, by isolating an architectural element—the closed verandas— and promoting it as the quintessence of Romanian vernacular architecture, Joja wanted to create a narrative that linked the village to the city in a political fantasy of national homogeneity.

The Political Need for a Historic Center

The harsh criticism that other architects expressed about Joja's plans reflected a broader opinion shared by many architects at that time that "'the old area' of Bucharest was an irremediably condemned area, meant to be replaced by new buildings and built assemblies."[28] One of best-known architects of post-1989 Bucharest, Alexandru Beldiman, was a student in the mid- and late 1960s. This is how he commented on the Old Town and Joja's renovation plans:

> I look back at my evolution as an architect and I cannot identify a moment when I had any interest in this chapter [the Old Town], until much later, in the 1990s, and that was under a specific circumstance. Probably if you asked my own professors, none of them cared about the Old Town either [*nimeni nu dădea doi bani pe Lipscani*]. They were modernist architects. And modernist architecture started from the principle of doing tabula rasa [with the past] and reconstructing from zero. . . . One of the architects who is currently [late 2000s] a strong proponent of historic rehabilitation was a student in the early 1960s. His graduation project proposed the erasure of the entire Old Town and its modernist reconstruction. . . . This was the spirit of the epoch![29]

Beldiman's comments convey the aesthetic vision shared by a large part of the Romanian architects in the 1960s. To the new generation of architects smitten with modernism, the Old Town represented nothing more than a bunch of old houses that occupied highly valuable space in the city center. Many of these architects saw the solution for the Old Town not as renovation but demolition. In 1973, *Arhitectura* journal, the main professional publication in the field, conducted a survey among 130 architects about how they envisioned the actual center of the city and what exactly was the city perimeter within which that center should be located. Many of the respondents thought that Bucharest should develop as a polycentric metropolis in which a smaller civic center would complement the larger central area in the middle of the city. More importantly, when queried whether there should be interventions in the city center (the area defined by the first major traffic ring), more than 80 percent said yes.[30] They differed in terms of where the new buildings should be placed and how much of the existing urban fabric should be demolished, but the majority was clearly in favor of modernizing the city center. Some architects commented on the intensity of social interaction favored by the Old Town's particular topography in which the sinuous commercial streets were linked one to another by narrow shortcuts and pedestrian-only passages, creating a tight and vibrant social space.[31] However, it was the particular pattern of the Old Town's streets, and not the houses per se, that these architects valued.

For the architects seeking modern solutions, Joja's plans appeared idiosyncratic to say the least. However, as a person "who believed very strongly in his ideas," as architect Beldiman described him, Joja knew how to gain the city officials' attention by seizing the new ideological priorities of the regime, such as the turn to a nationalist rhetoric. To what extent did Joja's plans succeed? Between 1967 and 1971, the renovation project continued to be debated

Fig. 3.3. Manuk Inn in 2016. Photo by author.

alongside the negotiations around the archaeological excavations at the Old Court site. Eventually the eighteenth-century buildings on Soarelui Street that cut through the Old Court site were removed. The ground level on the site was lowered in order to leave room for the newly unearthed walls of the princely palace, which was fully reconstructed and opened to the public as the Old Court Museum in April 1972. Under Joja's guidance, the restoration of the adjacent Manuk Inn began in 1969; it was later reopened as a hotel and restaurant. However, Joja's dream of remodeling some of the Old Town's houses never materialized.

I could find no documents that would explain why the authorities of the city council did not pursue Joja's plans despite their initial support. I presume that in addition to the strong opposition voiced by many architects, including the specialists in historic preservation from the Department of Historic Monuments, the financial aspect also played a key role. After all, decorating so many houses with closed verandas would have absorbed valuable funds at a time when the main goal of the local authorities was to build more housing. What matters, though, is how close Joja came to turning the Old Town into his own architectural fantasy.

Theorist Svetlana Boym (2007) has argued that in addition to plans that came into fruition, we could decipher political visions from projects that never materialized. She urged us to explore nostalgias "for the unrealized dreams of the past and visions of the future that have become obsolete" (10). She wrote, "A history of nostalgia might allow us to look back at modern history not solely searching for newness and technological progress but for unrealized possibilities, unpredictable turns and crossroads" (10). Joja's plan to redecorate the houses of the Old Town represented such a project. The renovation of the district envisioned as a journey back in time to an idealized eighteenth century failed to materialize, but Joja paradoxically managed to perform another type of time traveling: once seen as "too old" and therefore worthless, the Old Town became simply "old," with city authorities willing to see it as a place of potential value, even though the exact source of that value was uncertain. Joja's vision, though never completed, was important because it revealed the state's pursuit of an aesthetically and narratively coherent national history.

Some saw Joja's project as an aberration, but others praised it. These contestations brought visibility to a place and a time that other professionals and politicians were initially inclined to reject. Architect Nicolae Lascu, who began his practice in the early 1970s, told me that the very concept of historic district was relatively a new approach to understanding Bucharest's particular urbanity: "It is not clear to me when and how the idea of a historic center appeared [in the professional discussions of Bucharest's architects]. It was a concept that emerged bit by bit. Very few architects showed an appreciation of this type of urban fabric, which was drastically different from Transylvania's historic [fortified] cities. In Bucharest, the discovery of the historic court [the Old Court] very likely played a role [in associating the historic center of the city to the Old Town]."[32] If the historic district did not exist yet as a concept, Joja's plans and the debates that they triggered helped the Old Town transform from a nonplace (Auge 1995) that most of the architects chose to ignore into a site with a powerful identity. By incessantly talking about the unique value of the "historic district," Joja promoted a new symbolic geography of Bucharest with the Old Town at its core. This new imagery of the city dismissed the particular configuration of historic Bucharest as a multifocal urban space, promoting instead a vision of the capital that matched the unifocal model of the (Western) medieval town, developed around a single historic kernel. Even though Joja's plans remained unrealized "futures that have become obsolete," as Boym put it, they still produced "unpredictable turns," more specifically, a shift of perception. This shift had long-term consequences.

First, the making of the Old Town into the city's historic district enticed specialists and larger audiences to begin envisioning an old Bucharest

Fig. 3.4. Image of eighteenth-century Bucharest, woodcut, Leipzig, 1717. Public domain.

reminiscent of popular images of (Western) medieval towns. Such images had become all the more ubiquitous in architectural journals since the mid-1960s. They echoed the 1964 Venice charter, a movement launched by European architects that sparked wider interest in the preservation of historical cities in Western Europe in the face of modernist urban planning. Among other measures, the Venice charter advocated the rehabilitation of the "historical districts" of Western European cities.

In the context of mid-1960s Romania, this new insistence on historic preservation must also be put in the context of the government's attempt to keep Moscow at arm's length while focusing on its national affairs and seeking a relative economic rapprochement with Western countries.[33] This strategy was accompanied by a cautious political opening toward Western Europe, as well as an endorsement of cultural arguments that emphasized Romania's historic links to European culture and history.[34] The attempt to promote the Old Town as the historic district of a European city, with the Old Court as its historic nucleus, must be understood as part of a broader agenda to demonstrate the Europeanness of Bucharest—an agenda with its own complex history but one that at that specific political moment was openly welcomed by the state authorities.

However, by promoting the view that Bucharest had only one historic center and consequently having the historic district solely circumscribed to the limited perimeter of the Old Town, Joja and his supporters indirectly enabled the symbolic erasure and the eventual demolition of all of the other historic areas that were not part of the district—even though they all had been part of eighteenth-century Bucharest. The Old Town became the geographically condensed representation of the city's history, thus allowing the authorities to proceed with the modernization of the city center while deterring any criticism that the regime was not concerned about Bucharest's past. In the end, the Old Town functioned as a token that the regime used to create a thoroughly new center by demolishing a large part of old Bucharest.

The New Civic Center and Its Impact on the Old Town

In March 1977, an earthquake struck Romania, hitting Bucharest the hardest. The loss of human lives and material resources was significant, but the government sought to capitalize on this event by exaggerating the trauma so as to garner more support from abroad. Ceaușescu's government also viewed the earthquake as an opportunity to drastically alter the city's urban fabric by building a new center, the Civic Center (Light and Young 2015). The construction of this center was Ceaușescu's attempt to further consolidate his authoritarian position and project an image of a strong and independent leadership (O'Neill 2009). His plans also resonated with the disregard for old Bucharest shared by many architects of the postwar generations and echoed earlier attempts of urban elites to bring order into the city (Popa 2004). After the end of the communist regime, well-known architects who had participated in the planning of the Civic Center refused to assume responsibility for this urban concept, portraying it solely as a product of Ceaușescu's megalomaniac vision. At the time, however, many of those professionals had viewed this plan as the final chance to modernize the capital after many thwarted attempts (Popa 2007).

The building of the new Civic Center was Ceaușescu's paradoxical response to a challenge of his own creation. Faced with a debt crisis in 1979, Ceaușescu decided that "debt-financed development and policy independence were incompatible" (Ban 2012, 743) and chose instead to pursue Bucharest's modernization by relying exclusively on the country's internal resources. The government's focus on fully paying off Romania's external debt and achieving economic autonomy precipitated a rapid decline in the living standards. However, the political establishment completely disregarded the dire situation of ordinary Romanians. While people were spending hours in lines to buy bread, oil, and potatoes and were sleeping in tents installed in their own bedrooms so that they could survive the cold winters in their unheated apartments (Anghelescu et al. 2003, 118), Ceaușescu spent immense resources on rebuilding the city according to his megalomaniac dreams.

Despite attempts made by a few Romanians living abroad to draw the attention of international organizations such as UNESCO to what they portrayed as a "cultural genocide" of the history of the city, immense constructions sites opened in the city center.[35] No international actors could or would have wanted

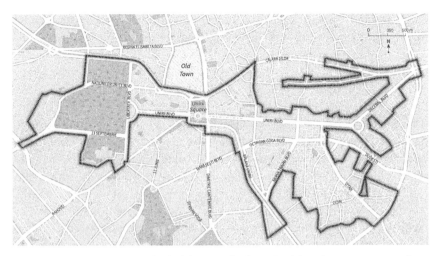

Map 3.1. The perimeter within the dark lines marks the scale of the urban interventions that the socialist government launched in the early 1980s for the construction of the Civic Center and the People's Palace. Map by Daniella Collins.

to intervene in a project viewed as a matter of a state's internal affairs.[36] With the exception of the small residential clusters left behind, the bulldozers erased a large part of historic Bucharest. Plans for the new Civic Center began to be outlined in 1977, but the project was launched in 1984, with the demolition of the majority of the eighteenth and nineteenth-century buildings and churches in a central zone of about five hundred square kilometers, more than the surface area of Venice (Light and Young 2015). On the construction site, twenty thousand poorly paid workers labored nonstop in three shifts (O'Neill 2009, 96), while other forty thousand people had their homes demolished in front of their eyes and had to move out to other areas of the city (O'Neill, 104). In place of the razed neighborhoods, a gigantic building appeared: the House of the People (Casa Poporului), intended to amass all state institutions in a single edifice— the most tangible representation of a heavily centralized authoritarian state.

The House of the People introduced a new axis in the city's geography: a large ceremonial avenue framed by equally imposing apartment buildings meant to host the Party elite. Behind those new constructions, clusters of residential areas were left, for the time being, intact—a state of limbo that eventually saved them when the regime collapsed. Some of the churches were literally moved out of the way, being kept but hidden behind the buildings lining the broad boulevard. The construction was still going on in December 1989, when people across the country took over the streets and launched the revolution that brought down the communist regime. The Civic Center was never finished.

Large avenues leading nowhere and steel skeletons of never-finished build-ings remained in the urban landscape for decades—dystopian remnants of the unfulfilled promises of a regime that had promised radical equity and a bright future for all.

If we open a map of the Civic Center, we see that it borders the Old Town district. In fact, the remodeling of Union Square, which had provoked so much debate in the late 1950s and early 1960s (see chap. 1), before being postponed for decades, was eventually completed as part and parcel of the Civic Center proj-ect. Why did the planners stop at Union Square? Why did they not demolish the Old Town? Throughout the 1970s, the regime found the Old Town politi-cally useful. Even though Joja's proposal for the redesign of the houses' facades was never pursued, the city officials sponsored other restoration works on some buildings on major commercial venues (Lipscani and Blănari Streets), in paral-lel with the reconstruction of the Old Court Palace.[37] The architects who coor-dinated later restoration works had been part of the initial team led by Joja, but they tried to be more conservative in their approach and restore, rather than redesign, the historic houses. The second stage of the renovations began in 1975 and focused on the renovation of a glassmakers' workshop (the Glass-makers Courtyard), located behind the Old Court.[38] Other renovation works were planned for some of the historic inns, which were to be turned into period restaurants.[39] However, many of these blueprints had never been pursued. One reason was that the city council dissolved its historic preservation office in 1977 and afterward commissioned various builders to focus on different projects. These teams had no training in historic preservation, and consequently they chose more economical reconstructions that did not include painstaking resto-rations of the historic architecture.[40] Another reason was the 1977 earthquake, which damaged many other buildings in the district that had to be demolished. The empty spaces that the new demolitions left in the street fronts only height-ened the air of neglect exuded by the other semidecrepit buildings.[41]

After 1977, no other restoration work was carried out in the Old Town, even though plans kept being drafted and architects kept pleading for the value of the district. In 1981, Ceaușescu approved a new plan for the renovation of the district, but when he visited the site again in 1983, he asked for those plans to be revised and for new constructions to be built on the empty lots left by the build-ings demolished after the earthquake.[42] This was a sign that by the mid-1980s, the government ceased to view the Old Town as a valuable historic site that needed to be preserved as such. In the eyes of the government, the area was becoming, once again, "too old," but the regime was undecided about what to do with it.

In summer 1987, the central officials asked Bucharest's city council to launch "a competition for proposals for the restoration of the Old Town and the reconstruction of the Lipscani commercial area."[43] Some of the architects who had previously worked in the area in the early 1970s proposed the renovation of the facades on the main commercial street, Lipscani. They insisted on the restoration of existing buildings, and they suggested that the new constructions to be built on the empty lots mirror the historic style of the district. They even brought back the proposal initially made by Joja that "some buildings or parts of historic buildings could be brought in from some other [neighborhoods] undergoing demolition."[44] Most importantly, they tried to persuade the government that the district be preserved as an architectural reserve, because only under this form could it function as a point of contrast with the new city: "It is the architectural assemblage, and not the individual buildings, that will be set in contrast with the rest of the new city."[45] The very existence of the historic district, they argued, would attest to "the grand leap forward made by the city in the socialist era."[46]

The architects' response must be read against the background of that political moment. Their mobilization around the Old Town signaled that they had more information about the real plans of the government and that they viewed the proposal launched by the city council as a pretext to begin demolitions in the district. The architects were aware that their pleas for the Old Town's preservation might fall on deaf ears. This is why they emphasized the commercial value of the district. They tried to win the central officials over with arguments about economic efficiency, stressing the surprisingly high revenues that the small shops on the Old Town's narrow streets brought to the state budget—30 percent more than what the larger, modern shops located on the central boulevards generated.[47] They argued that the preservation of the district as "an open-air museum of feudal Bucharest" would entice foreign tourists to visit and thus become a stable source of hard currency for the state budget.[48] However, the architects' proposal seems to have led nowhere, because a year later, in May 1988, the Architects' Union called for a larger meeting of its members to find ways to forestall the demolition plans. They hoped that the public meeting would bring more visibility to the uncertain fate of the Old Town. Those attending the meeting prepared a written response, in which they insisted, once again, that a careful restoration of the district's buildings would transform it into a thriving commercial and touristic quarter that would no longer need state funds; on the contrary, it would become a self-sustained economic enterprise that would bring more profit to the state.[49]

Despite all these plans and negotiations, no funds came into the district. But neither did the bulldozers. It is also very likely that the central officials did not want to bring the bulldozers into the Old Town (yet) because they did not want to fully disclose that the state-promoted concern about the national history was just a facade. In the end, the previous efforts of state officials and archaeologists in the 1960s and 1970s to portray the Old Town as the historic core of Bucharest had not been in vain. By the 1980s, not only archaeologists but also architects regarded the Old Town as the city's historic district, a unique representation of national history. Even if they wanted to eventually demolish it, state officials had to at least pretend that they had tried to salvage the district in order to prevent the tensions with the concerned architects from escalating even further.

Indirectly, then, the Old Town functioned as a deal maker between the state and some professional groups in the massive project of demolition and rebuilding of downtown Bucharest; by delaying the Old Town's demolition, while signaling uncertainty about the district's value, the regime made architects and other professionals focus solely on this site and seek ways to protect it, while forcing them to accept the demolition of other historical parts of the city. This does not mean that state officials did not try to find alternative ways to alter the urban and social fabric of the Old Town. Only that in comparison to other areas that had been demolished almost overnight to make room for the new Civic Center, in the Old Town the state's intervention took the form of a more subtle degradation.

The Dark 1980s: Decay and Defiance

When I asked her to tell me about what happened with the Old Town in the 1980s, Mariana Celac had a lot to say. A well-known architect who had worked in Bucharest for decades and knew the city inside and out, she had been one of the few intellectuals who openly asserted their political dissidence in the 1980s, defying the professional and social marginalization that derived from their courageous stand. She pointed out that the officials' neglect of the Old Town was a form of passive aggressiveness that was part and parcel of the active plans for urban modernization. This is what she told me:

> Between the abandoned restoration plan in the early 1970s and the beginning of the Potemkin village [this is how she called the new Civic Center], nothing much happened. I believe—though I have no written proof—that this passivity relied on the premise that those [old buildings] should be left to die their own death. Even this was not an official plan; it was a dream, a vision that led to specific decisions. Such as the official decision to stop any investments in the restoration of old buildings. It relied on the vision of extending the Civic Center to the entire territory of Bucharest, of replacing all the old things with an image of an *ex novo* capital. Nothing would be restored. Everything would be allowed to decay as the socialist city advanced. The decision of no longer investing funds in restoring old buildings began in the early 1970s, but the earthquake gave these plans a serious push forward, which was only amplified

by the full mobilization of all resources for the new center [the Civic Center built in mid- to late 1980s].[50]

Housing officials in Bucharest's city council cared little about the conservation of historic buildings, but they tried to use them strategically. The buildings came in very handy as temporary housing for the poorer population. As shown in chapter 1, ever since the end of the war, one of the main concerns of the central authorities has been Bucharest's limited housing reserve, especially in the conditions in which the city's population grew constantly (between 1966 and 1972, it grew from approximately 1,367,000 to 1,510,000).[51] Despite the state's recognition that they still have not solved the housing crisis, and the 1973 new law allowing the construction of individual housing, Bucharest's city council was extremely reluctant to give construction authorizations. To justify their decision, the local authorities invoked the strict plans of urban development (the master plan) and the requirements that any new construction in Bucharest must be at least four-stories high. Moreover, the same authorities did not allow the house owners to demolish their old, low-comfort houses and use that land to build new and more comfortable individual homes, even though almost 30 percent of the city's population lived in such improper conditions.[52] According to city officials, these people were to wait until their neighborhoods were demolished as part of the master plan, and only then did they have the right to petition the state for a new apartment.[53] The authorities' stubbornness did not leave people with many choices. Some decided to build without a construction authorization, and the number of Bucharest's illegal constructions continued to grow in the 1970s.[54] Others, especially those who had no means to build on their own, were more willing to accept housing repartitions in very old buildings in districts that were planned to be demolished soon. They hoped that once the demolitions started, they would have a higher chance to be moved into new apartment buildings.

The second group was the main target of what Mariana Celac called temporary repartitions. She viewed such temporary repartitions as subversive strategies employed by the authorities to accelerate the decay of the older buildings. They moved in people who did not want to live there in the first place, and were not interested in repairing these buildings or improving their living conditions—thereby rendering their demolition more acceptable. She described this strategy as a "planned urban decay," adding a sarcastic twist to a term (*planning*) that was the official cliché of the time, a direct reference to the centralized system and the planned economy. She said,

What happened in the Old Town also took place in other historic districts, though they were less important to the urban fabric. All such places were subject to planned urban decay. This strategy even had a name: it was called second- or thirdhand repartition. The district's traditional residents left for the new apartments in other areas, because all of the maintenance work and building improvement ceased in the district [planned for demolition]. A proletarian population came to live in those [semiabandoned] houses, a marginal world, people with large families, who could live with no amenities, with just an outhouse and water from the pump. . . . This policy exposed such semiabandoned enclaves to an urban degradation that [planners and state officials would then exploit] to justify an exhaustive cleansing [of the area] and [its] replacement with new buildings.[55]

In describing this population shift as a strategy of "planned urban decay," her choice of the term was only partially sarcastic. In fact, such an operation accompanied earlier interventions in the city's urban fabric, begun in the early 1970s as part of a major plan for expanding the thoroughfare network in the city. Celac explained,

A screen of new buildings was erected alongside those thoroughfares, with no conceptualization of the relationship between the street front and what lay behind [those tall buildings]. If you go in the back of those apartment buildings, you see streets that end right there [disconnected from the boulevards]. . . .

The front yard and the backyard, as I called them, the difference between the facade and hinterland remained a fatal inconsistency of a modernization project that was theoretically meant for all the people, and especially for the wretched of the earth. A project that degenerated into this arrangement: the front yard and the backyard. The backyard for the masses, the front yard and the champagne for the chosen few![56]

When I noted the immense social and economic discrepancy between the residents of the upscale apartment buildings lining the boulevards (especially at the Civic Center) and the "crowd" brought in to occupy the empty houses in the "backyard" enclaves, architect Celac used my comment to further her argument. Employing the striking image of a uniform and lengthy rug unrolled across the surface of the city, she argued that the presence of these people was intrinsic to the plans for a future demolition of the entire urban fabric of Bucharest: "This is precisely why I believe that this was the first stage in a broader plan; a vision that such an urban development would eventually be [brought into those enclaves, as well]. [The state] used [those people] just so to justify the rug-like operation (*operația de tip covor*) that would come next."[57]

The old houses in the Old Town represented such an enclave, one of the "backyards" with less-than-proper living standards where the city council sent the poor and relatively poor tenants. Ovidiu, a social geographer who has studied the housing situation in socialist Bucharest, confirmed Celac's analysis

Fig. 3.5. Mailboxes for different families sharing the same house in the Old Town. Photo by Alexandru Stoinescu, 2001.

of "planned urban decay," except that he emphasized the planning dimension less, putting more stress on the complex social and political changes occurring a few decades earlier. In our conversation, he pointed out that after many of the former Jewish homeowners had left the Old Town, a poorer population took their place. As Ovidiu put it, "They lived with their luggage by the door, ready to catch the first chance to move somewhere else [that was better]. They put themselves on the [housing] list at their factory, paid bribe after bribe to ICRAL [the state housing office] until they could finally receive a better place. They would leave, and some other tenants would take their place. But during this time, no one bothered to paint the walls, to take care of the building. Every occupancy cycle would further degrade the [already decrepit] houses."[58] By the mid-1980s, according to Ovidiu, "Everyone knew that the area was doomed to be demolished in short order, so the only ones willing to live there were marginal people who had no alternative, including many Roma. Then the revolution happened, and they were left in place. They have been living there for twenty-six years."[59]

During our separate conversations about the Old Town, both architect Celac and Ovidiu portrayed the residents of the Old Town as indirectly or even directly participating in the degradation and destruction of the place—their passivity about the degradation of the historic buildings, combined with their extreme lack of resources, made them appear as the human counterpart of the nonhuman destroyer: time. My interlocutors described the Old Town as a socially liminal space, with a social structure always in flux and an occupancy cycle that became shorter and shorter.

However, the marginal people who ended up in the district by the 1980s, when it was planned to be demolished, ironically turned into its protectors. They did this in a way that went against the mores and atmosphere produced by an increasingly intrusive police state. They were the ones who kept the district pulsating with life, cash, and sometimes even more titillating opportunities. By engaging in petty and illicit commerce—or just by living in the district and spending so much time on its streets—these people kept the place alive and full of possibilities. It was on those crowded streets and behind the doors of those decrepit buildings that passersby could stumble across unexpected deals. By mid-1980, everything from meat and coffee to other "luxury" goods such as toilet paper and soap could be found only on the black market. The Old Town continued to be a commercial hub, only that instead of going into the official shops with their shelves almost empty, people would search for things being sold around the corners, under the desk, directly from a warehouse, or other more hidden places. Pictures taken by a Hungarian photographer in the late 1980s captured a sad but populated Lipscani Street with omnipresent queues.

Fig. 3.6. Lipscani Street. Photo: Fortepan/Urbán Tamás, 1986.

Fig. 3.7. A food queue on Lipscani Street. Photo: Fortepan/Urbán Tamás, 1986.

Paradoxically, the Old Town maintained its economic power despite—or, in fact, due to—the increasingly crumbling socialist economy. People from all over Bucharest continued to come to the Old Town to shop because that is what others did, and what their parents and their grandparents used to do—proof that historically ingrained reflexes and symbolic geographies were mightier than the communist urban policies. The district continued to be a heterogeneous and dynamic mix of passersby, customers, and traders, including the sellers and buyers forming the district's thriving black market, and the tenants living in crowded old apartments. Often, those categories merged. Some of the poor state tenants made their living as petty sellers on the black market. Transgressors and bricoleurs themselves, these recent arrivals fit right in with the history of transgressions that made the Old Town a successful commercial district in the nineteenth century and the interwar years. Historically, the Old Town had been a magnet for transgressive lifestyles. Beginning especially in the 1980s, it became a well-known site for shady deals.

An acquaintance told me that when he was a student in the late 1980s, the Old Town was the place to go if you wanted a pair of jeans, music paraphernalia, or other things that were impossible to find in stores. He bought his first cassette deck in 1987, paying quite a bit of cash to a man he just met on the street. A friend had told him where to go and whom to look for. He thought that the man on the street matched the description, so he approached him and told him he wanted to buy a tape recorder. The man brought him into a narrow hallway of one of the old buildings on Lipscani, asked for the cash in advance, and told him to wait there as he went upstairs to get the merchandise. My interlocutor jokingly remembered that he waited anxiously, all the while thinking that the man might disappear with his money through a different door of the building. In the end, the man returned and handed him the cassette deck. Obviously, my friend never found out if the man lived in that building or just used it for his deals. However, it is likely that some of the tenants engaged in such deals, because, after all, they were the ones who knew best the buildings' multiple entrances and the convoluted narrow streets.

Conclusion

In the 1970s, the state had tried to symbolically capture the Old Town by making it into a "historic district": a tangible sign of a centralized past matching a centralized system of governance. Opposition of various kinds, and probably lack of resources, rendered this vision moot. In the 1980s, when the government channeled all of the resources toward building the new Civic Center, it actively abandoned the Old Town, hoping that the district would die a rapid death at the hands of its new residents, the poorest of the poor. Yet it was those residents who chipped away at the center through their everyday life on the margins.

Anthropologists Veena Das and Deborah Poole (2004) have prompted us to examine the processes of state making via a focus on the periphery. They pointed out that the "indeterminate character of margins [can] break open the solidity often attributed to the state" (20). This chapter has shown how the shabby and defiantly heteroclite environment of the Old Town and its equally defiant residents indirectly helped bring down the political center. Even if the Old Town of the late 1980s seemed to stand as a metonym for the Romanian society of that era—no time, no future, no alternative, no other place to go—it became a subversive margin at (literally) the very center of the city. It was the place of hobos, of bohemian artists painting and drinking vodka in the attics of the old houses on Lipscani Street.[60] It was also the place of black marketers offering hard-to-find cigarettes and coffee to those people who were willing to walk into dark hallways without knowing if they would receive their goods or would be tricked (Anghelescu et al. 2003, 201). It revealed the crumbling centralized economy while it paradoxically enabled the same system to sluggishly move forward, sustained by the thriving black market.

These people kept Old Town alive through the shoddy deals flourishing on its narrow streets—so much that one of these streets became known as Kent Street, by the name of the cigarettes sold there by the black marketers (Anghelescu et al. 2003, 201). They were the last element in a series that included accidental discoveries (the walls of the Old Court), finalized reconstructions (the Old Court Museum), and unrealized visions of architectural stylization (Joja's plans). The story of the Old Town's continuous oscillation, from being historically important to being politically irrelevant, shows that the state's attempts to define a socialist heritage were mired by fluctuation, indecision, and confusion. Such attempts were even further undermined by fierce competition among different professionals and institutional decision makers. And when the state eventually decided to abandon the Old Town, planning it for demolition, the place was rescued not only by time but also by its people and the houses they inhabited. The very heterogeneity of the place itself became a force that "pushed back" and challenged various forms of aesthetic and social regimentation (Herzfeld 1991).

Even though it eventually failed, the 1970 proposal to make the Old Town into a national architectural reserve revealed the state-sponsored strategies of producing or erasing value by justifying or denying the "heritage" quality to distinct objects (archaeological artifacts, old buildings, or entire districts). These strategies became pivotal mechanisms of capturing and consolidating power in the early postsocialist period (the 1990s and early 2000s). Despite the

official end of the former communist regime, key actors from the former political system would manage to amass vast economic and political resources under
postsocialism. They did so by drawing on insider knowledge about the assets of
the communist regime. More importantly, what truly mattered for those who
wanted to keep power was not only to know the location of these assets but
also how to play hide-and-seek with their value. Heritage making in socialism
had taught former party apparatchiks how to appeal to a nationalist rhetoric
to project value onto specific material forms while strategically neglecting others. The Old Town of the 1990s became a strategic terrain for postcommunist
politicians to erase their communist past and turn into the "entrepratchicks"
(Verdery 1996) of an allegedly new era.

Notes

1. AINMI, file 2159/1962–1970, 2–3, "Memoriu general."
2. "Memoriu general," 3.
3. Anton Golopenția and D. C. Georgescu, *Populația Republicii Populare Române la 25
ianuarie 1948*, Institutul Național de Statistică, București, accessed July 15, 2018, https://sas
.unibuc.ro/storage/downloads/analize-regionale-9/AG48a.RECENSAMANT48.pdf.
4. "Populația după etnie la recensămintele din perioada 1930–2011," Recensamantromania.
ro, table 1 (vol2_t1.xls), accessed July 15, 2018, http://www.recensamantromania.ro/noutati
/volumul-ii-populatia-stabila-rezidenta-structura-etnica-si-confesionala/.
5. "Mission to Romania" report, August 1989, 9, UNESCO archives, file 069: 7 (100)
A 218/101/8 (498), WNC—Correspondence with States not Parties—Romania. Part V
from 1.V.89.
6. The Romanian government promoted *sistematizare* as a territorial and administrative
reform whereby smaller settlements would be made more dependent on larger villages—
called agroindustrial centers and thus elevated to urban status. Those centers—rural
chameleons that had to look like towns—were to be endowed with residential buildings and
public amenities and thus function as the new nuclei for administrative clusters, offering
community services to other smaller villagers within a fifteen-to-twenty-kilometer radius.
The Romanian authorities separated the rural settlements into four categories: (1) 540
larger settlements that had already had some infrastructure, entitling them to be promoted
to the status of "towns," as agroindustrial centers; (2) around 1,800 larger villages, at that
moment administrative centers of the communes; (3) medium-sized villages that would be
maintained in the clusters around the "centers"; and (4) smaller or more isolated villages that
were seen as having "no prospects of development" and consequently would be abandoned—
in the words of the Romanian specialists, "let die a natural death." "Mission to Romania"
report, August 1989, 15.
7. "Decret nr. 92 din 19 aprilie 1950 pentru naționalizarea unor imobile," *Buletinul
Oficial*, nr. 36 din 20 aprilie 1950.
8. AINMI, file 2159/1962–1970, "Studiu de circulație si parcaje. Memoriu justificativ."
9. Information from "Oana," who grew up in the Old Town during the 1980s.
10. AINMI, file 2159/1962–1970, "Studiu de circulație si parcaje. Memoriu justificativ," 14.

11. AINMI, file 2159/1962–1970, "Memoriu General," Proiect no. 20737, signed by architect Nicolae Pruncu, not dated, citing a sociological survey conducted in the district in 1970. The report was written in 1988 because it responded to the urban remodeling plan (*planul de sistematizare*) that the Politburo ordered in 1987 and the Project Bucharest Institute was commissioned for in 1988, under contract number 20373.

12. As historian Mihai Chioveanu (2009) pointed out, the negative depictions of the Phanariots were meant to indirectly support the model of "Good Romanian," which began to dominate the historiography after the eighteenth century.

13. Joja's proposal in AINMI, file 2159/1962–1970.

14. Horia Sima, *Era Libertății: Statul Național-Legionar*, vol. 1, accessed June 19, 2018, https://archive.org/details/EraLibertatii-StatulNational-legionarVol.1.

15. For a detailed discussion of Joja's earlier involvement in the autochthonist discourse, represented by his participation in the 1940 competition for a Palace of Culture under the program "Legionnaire Works of Arts," and his winning project of the competition for the design of Odessa Cathedral in 1942, see Ioan (1996, 38–40).

16. Arşavir Acterian, "Gânduri în luna Bucureştilor şi despre urbanistica românească," in *Ideea Românească* 1, nos. 2–4 (June–August 1935), 133.

17. Those buildings were the Colţea water tower (demolished at the beginning of nineteenth century); the old Sf. Gheorghe church (Biserica Sf. Gheorghe veche); the Antim house, "reconstituted on the basis of documentation from the Brâncoveanu epoch [and] offering a very successful Romanian interpretation of Baroque"; and the house with four bow windows.

18. Acterian, "Gânduri," 1935, 133.

19. "Document. Scrisori către Constantin Joja," Fundaţia România Literară, accessed January 19, 2018, http://www.romlit.ro/index.pl/scrisori_ctre_constantin_joja (page no longer available).

20. Following the decision of the city council to assign the status of "historical heritage site" to the area circumscribed by the Old Court and Lipscani (with Joja as the project manager) and begin the "renovation" work (i.e., the stylization proposed by Joja), the president of the Office of Historic Monuments, Richard Bordenache, called on the help of Gustav Gusti, at that moment the vice president of the State Committee for Architecture. In late March 1968, Gusti issued a resolution approving the decision only on the condition that the transformation of the area would observe a set of prerequisites. Resolution 2410, August 24, 1967, of the People's Council of the city of Bucharest (Sfatul popular al orasului Bucureşti. Comitetul executiv). AINMI, file 2159/1962–1970.

21. See other letters in AINMI, file 2159/1962–1970.

22. Constantin Joja, "Punerea în valoare a unei vechi arhitecturi urbane rominești," in "Discuţii: Sistematizarea zonei 'Curtea Veche,' Bucureşti," *Arhitectura* 113, no. 4 (1968): 17.

23. Aurel Doicescu, "Arhitectura cu geamlîc: o improvizaţie minoră," *Arhitectura* 113, no. 4 (1968): 22.

24. Ion Dumitrescu, "Un alt punct de vedere asupra arhitecturii urbane bucureştene din sec. XIX," *Arhitectura* 113, no. 4 (1968): 24.

25. Doicescu (1968, 22).

26. Dumitrescu (1968, 24).

27. Nicolae Pruncu, "Aspecte urbanistice ale restaurării Palatului Domnesc," *Arhitectura* 113, no. 4 (1968): 25–27.

28. Radu Şerban and Marinela Şerban, "Integrarea imaginii urbane," *Arhitectura* 143, no. 4 (1973): 92.

29. Conversation, April 24, 2008.

30. "Ancheta revistei. Centrul actual al municipiului București, partea a II-a," *Arhitectura* 144, no. 5 (1973): 25.

31. "Ancheta revistei. Centrul actual al municipiului București, partea I," *Arhitectura* 143, no. 4 (1973):118.

32. Conversation, April 24, 2008.

33. The share of Romania's international trade with noncommunist countries rose from 20 percent in 1959 to 48 percent in 1967 and continued at around 45 percent throughout the early 1970s, thus making Romania the Eastern European country with the largest Western share of total trade. "Romania and the United States: The Command Economy Looks Further West," Central Intelligence Agency (CIA), Directorate of Intelligence, March 1972, https:// www.cia.gov/library/readingroom/docs/CIA-RDP85T00875R001700030035-9.pdf.

34. Starting in 1963, the Romanian communist government sought to establish stronger links with international organizations such as UNESCO and United Nations Development Programme (UNDP). In 1965, UNDP granted Romania $1,153,000 for an irrigation project in the Danube plain. In 1967, Romania sought further financial assistance from UNDP for economic, educational, and agricultural development. In the domain of culture and education, the National Commission of Romania at UNESCO launched a series of translations of European writers into Romanian and organized various international conferences bringing together scholars from Western and Eastern Europe (e.g., the conference of the international association for Balkan and South European studies, organized at Bucharest in 1967). "Brief on Special Fund Matters," and "Visite du directeur general en Roumanie (10–13 juillet 1966)," UNESCO archives, file X07.21 (498) A 562.

35. Letter from Ștefan Gane, head of the Association for the Protection of Romania's Historic Sites, to the General Secretary of UNESCO, March 26, 1985. UNESCO Archives, file 069: 72 (498) AMS. Sites and Monuments—Romania—P.P. and R.P.

36. The official response of UNESCO to such petitions was along the lines of the following: "The sites included in the list of the World Heritage sites benefit of a particular legal protection. However, UNESCO has no right to intervene in the plans that a member state has made about its own patrimony." Letter from Anne Raidl to Ștefan Gane, August 2, 1985. UNESCO Archives, file 069: 72 (498) AMS.

37. "Memoriu general," 2–3, in "Detaliu de sistematizare a zonei Lipscani—Curtea Veche," Proiect București, arh. N Pruncu, arh. Gh. Leahu, nr. 20737/1988. AINMI, file 2850/1988, 1–12.

38. "Memoriu," 3. File 2850/1988.

39. "Memoriu," 3. File 2850/1988.

40. "Memoriu general," 4. File 2850/1988.

41. "Memoriu general," 4. File 2850/1988.

42. "Directions given by Comrade Nicolae Ceaușescu," March 17, 1981; December 20, 1983, file 2850/1988.

43. "Directions given by Comrade Nicolae Ceaușescu," May 3, 1987; July 25, 1987. File 2850/1988.

44. "Memoriu general," 10. File 2850/1988.

45. "Notă," 1–2. Summary of the public debate about the area of the Old Town/Lipscani, organized at the Architects' Union on May 22, 1988. File 2850/1988.

46. "Notă," 2. File 2850/1988.

47. "Memoriu," 6. File 2850/1988.

48. "Notă," 2. File 2850/1988. The point about foreigners spending their money in the Old Town must be set in the broader context of the late 1980s, when the Romanian government viewed hard currency as gold. Romanians were not allowed to own Western currency, while special "shops" that accepted only American dollars and German marks were selling goods that no one dreamed of finding in the ordinary stores.

49. "Notă," 2. File 2850/1988.

50. Interview, April 18, 2009.

51. Gheorghe Sămărsan, "Locuințele construite fără autorizație și sistematizarea Bucureștiului," *Arhitectura* 143, no. 4 (1973): 129. For the sudden demographic explosion in the large cities, see Stoica (1997). See also chap. 1 for the debates about various ways to control the population growth and the migration to cities.

52. Sămărsan (1973).

53. Sămărsan (1973).

54. In 1971, the local authorities identified 11,500 illegal constructions built between 1958 and 1971, and they estimated that, in fact, the real number might have been twice that figure (Sămărsan 1973, 128).

55. Interview, April 19, 2008.

56. Interview, April 19, 2008.

57. Interview, April 19, 2008.

58. Interview, Bucharest, May 20, 2016.

59. Interview, Bucharest, May 20, 2016.

60. I thank Maria Bucur for this reference. Personal communication, March 26, 2016, Bloomington, Indiana.

4

LIPSTICK AND LINED POCKETS

Strategic Devaluation and Postsocialist Wealth

WHEN NICK FALK, A BRITISH URBAN PLANNER, VISITED Bucharest for the first time in January 1992, he was taken aback by its grayness. The only color he remembers seeing in the city was the red of the Coca-Cola umbrella outside some cheap pubs in the Old Town. Together with two other colleagues, Nick was in Bucharest at the invitation of a group of Romanian architects who wanted to save the Old Town from further degradation. Having worked in the field of urban renewal since the 1970s, Nick was one of the UK's best-known professionals. One of his most successful projects was the transformation of London's Covent Garden from a derelict and depopulated area into a thriving cultural site whose vibrant festivals, street performances, and dynamic night life have become a magnet for Londoners and tourists.

At the time of his visit, Nick was aware of Bucharest's recent history, especially the urban trauma produced by the construction of the Civic Center in the 1980s. He discovered a city "that had focused all of its resources on redeveloping only on one part of the city—the grand boulevard leading to [the House of the People]. The rest of the city had been largely neglected. So, even if you and I talk now about the Old Town, at that time [1992] it was not clear what it was. It was only the [Romanian] architects who saw any value in the heritage of Bucharest."[1] But when he and his colleagues walked around the Old Town, he came to agree with his Romanian hosts: "there was something of real value there." Nick believed that the first intervention should be to "turn the place around." His idea was to organize "[an urban] festival as a way of generating interest." This is how he justified his vision: "My idea was that until you could show that the place [has] some potential, that people see something valuable [in it], you would not get the investment that it needed in restoring the buildings. . . . It is nice to do things properly, but there will never be enough resources. You need to change attitudes first. . . . Like a woman putting on some lipstick—make the

Fig. 4.1. A street in the Old Town, 1990. Photo by Norihiro Haruta, 1990.

place look pretty. And then pretend that the area is going up, and of course, it will go up."[2]

Nick believed that before starting any repairs on the buildings, people should be enticed by the place. "Putting lipstick" on the Old Town meant adding an artificial value by making it look better than it was—a strategy to make people come to the district and encourage others to do the same. In contrast to earlier renovation attempts, such as Joja's plan to redesign the house facades according to a Romanian style, the British team's proposal emphasized the district's intense sociality and aimed to transform it into a social and touristic hub for people from all walks of life.

The British team's vision, however, went directly against the plans of the city officials. Although Nick's memories of his 1992 visit to Bucharest were already blurry when we spoke in 2016, he was able to recount one episode in detail:

> When we presented [our proposal] to the mayor, he was very cynical, very skeptical. We went into the great Ceauşescu palace [People's House in the Civic Center]. There was a big table around which sat a very large number of old men, whom I take to have been the councilors of Bucharest's mayor. There was a projector, but its electric cord did not fit into the socket. My Romanian assistant took out a pocket knife and fiddled with the socket until the cord fit, while all those people were waiting. At the end of our presentations, the mayor

said, "Thank you very much, but you are wasting your time because all of the buildings are going to fall down. The foundations are being eroded by the rising levels of Dâmbovița [River]."[3]

Recalling that encounter after almost twenty-five years, Nick sounded amused. Yet he seemed to be suggesting, in the way he set up his story, why his proposal for the Old Town never materialized. The details of the story pointed to the broader political context of the time, especially to the obvious continuities between the former communist system and the postcommunist structures of power, represented by the "old men" sitting at the table in Ceaușescu's former House of the People (which after 1989 became the Palace of the Parliament). The impossibility of a genuine dialogue was not just metaphorically captured by the projector that did not fit in the socket but especially by the mayor's blunt statement that the Old Town was already doomed. Although that assessment was not grounded in any evidence, it signaled something else: that city authorities actively rejected any attempt to "put some lipstick" on the Old Town.

This chapter argues that the strategic neglect of the Old Town represented a dual political and economic strategy. The elites of the 1990s had two reasons to dismiss proposals to bring new life to the Old Town. First, the new leaders aimed to use it as a spatial, tangible threshold that helped them deny their own communist past and present themselves as democratic politicians. Second, they wanted to keep the district invisible and thus artificially undervalued in order to exploit it as a source of cheap capital—and to transfer state-owned assets into their own pockets without giving too many explanations. Once again, the debates about the value and urban function of the Old Town during the 1990s offer a unique window into the broader power competition following the end of the communist regime. I use the tense negotiations among diverse actors— from foreign professionals, such as Nick and his colleagues, to local authorities, city officials, state politicians, and residents of the district—to argue that such negotiations were based on competing temporalities. The debates about the value of the Old Town were implicitly debates about the value of particular temporal frameworks—and revealed how the postcommunist state officials aimed to consolidate their power by controlling how such temporal boundaries were defined.

When Nick told the mayor and his team that he saw "some value" in the Old Town only to immediately be rebuked as merely talking gibberish, the two parties disputed what constituted "the past." Nick made a clear distinction between the pre-1945 past and the communist period; what he saw as valuable in the Old Town was an architectural eclecticism that mirrored the place's social diversity. He placed the value of that vibrant heterogeneity exclusively within the late nineteenth-century and early twentieth-century temporal framework, a time of modernity but one that preceded the communist era. I call this Past 1. As Nick confessed, he associated the communist past with an overwhelming "grayness," with a negative quality that he assumed local people wanted to forget. In his view, this particular past was quintessentially different from Past 1. I refer to the communist past he described as Past 2. To Nick, the only way to bring the Old Town back into the public life, to "put some lipstick" on it, as he put it, was to highlight its relation to Past 1, to emphasize its architectural uniqueness, and to make others see its value. His idea to do a street festival with people wearing nineteenth-century fashion as a way to revive the commercial life of the district was grounded precisely in a clear separation of the pre-1945 Past 1 and the communist Past 2. In short, for Nick, the Old Town could have regained value only if it reflected that clear separation. Past 1 could have had a future only via the erasure of Past 2.

By contrast, the local authorities strategically conflated the two temporal frameworks. They combined both the prewar period and the communist past into one totalizing framework of "the past," which they derided as being irrelevant and worthless. The mayor's comment that all of the Old Town's buildings were already doomed conveyed a view of the district as the epitome of the past—and an indirect dismissal of both the pre-1945 and the communist periods. By doing so, the new officials severed their own ties to the former political structures, detaching their current postcommunist identities from their former political lives as key actors in the communist apparatus. The state officials highlighted the Old Town's ruination with an eye to reinforcing the distance between their current and former selves. They used the district's run-down houses and its poor residents to portray the district as a place of the Other, both in temporal and social terms, while siphoning its valuable resources.

The chapter begins with an overview of the contrasts between the British specialists' vision and the local authorities' negative perception of the district. The second section situates these contrasts within a broader context of Romania of the 1990s in which the former communist nomenklatura maintained their power. Returning to the Old Town, the third part reveals the strategic devaluation of the district in the 1990s, while the fourth section explores the affective and sensorial maneuvering of that devaluation. In the last part, I argue that the construction of the Old Town as a place of the Other drew on a set of dichotomies informed by the communist times, such as "they" (the state) versus "us" (the people), only that they were imbued with new meaning. In the context of Romania of the 1990s, when the economy was on the verge of collapsing due to large-scale corruption while the net of social services and benefits was swiftly disappearing, "they" versus "us" became recoded in terms of class and ethnic hierarchies. Thus, the Roma and the poor—representing a large part of the Old Town's residents—became conflated in the same category and doubly marginalized as the "Other." The local officials exploited a rising xenophobia magnified by the financial crisis of the late 1990s. They made Roma and the poor into scapegoats, presenting them as the main culprits of economic and social disorder, thus diverting the public attention from the real origins of the large-scale corruption.

Contrasting Visions

The dire situation of Bucharest in the 1990s preoccupied many of its residents. In a 1991 public meeting, architects, historians, engineers, and other concerned citizens decried the city's dirty streets and the central neighborhoods that the former regime had planned to demolish and were now semiabandoned, occupied by squatters and stray dogs. They pointed to the skeletons of around a hundred thousand apartment buildings, waiting to be finalized while the government had other priorities, and that made the city look like an "unfinished pharaonic construction."[4] One of the professionals present at that meeting was architect Mariana Celac, whom I have already introduced in the previous chapter.

The British team's visit to Bucharest happened at her initiative. Just a few months after the fall of Ceaușescu's regime, finally able to rekindle the professional connections from which she had been cut off, architect Celac sought to mobilize interest, funds, and expertise for the Old Town's revival. She learned from a London-based architect of Romanian origins about a UK government grant that funded the transfer of British expertise abroad.[5] She applied for it and used it to bring the British team to the city.[6] At that time, she said, "the Old Town was entirely different. It was intact! The Gabroveni Inn was still standing, the Lipscani Street was undamaged, all of the houses were inhabited, all of the roofs in good condition."[7] Celac's account of the district was the polar opposite of what the mayor told Nick: that any intervention would be "hopeless."

As someone who deeply loved Bucharest and appreciated its eclectic style, Mariana Celac was not interested in a project that would focus on historic preservation per se. In fact, she had no qualms about openly criticizing the project that Romanian architects had launched in the late 1980s. Despite the latter's claims that their plans saved the historic district from demolition, she viewed their solution as one that lacked imagination, informed by an urban vision in which all of the houses were more or less similar elements in a homogeneous urban assembly—as if, she put it, someone rolled out a carpet on the street, decorating only the facades, and ignoring the rest. In her view, this approach did not make the Old Town much different from the newly built Civic Center, with Victory of Socialism Boulevard framed by a series of perfect replicas of monumental buildings. In short, she was fully aware of the limitations of the local professionals who already worked on the Old Town, so she searched elsewhere for alternatives.

She described the encounter with the British team as a breakthrough moment. She drew a strong contrast between the British proposal that highlighted the social dimension of a place and the Romanian architects' exclusive focus on the Old Town's houses, and not its residents and their needs. She said,

> To me, it was a moment of illumination because I saw a new philosophy of the relationship between society and space, between the contemporary society and the history of that place: [an approach that was] much softer, extremely aware of the scale of the area, extremely sensitive to what [public and private domains] mean in contemporary and dense urban space. . . . There was also a different approach to urban aesthetics. The British were not interested in an accurate reconstitution of all of facades. Instead, they focused on the eclecticism of urban expression in Bucharest and on the intrinsic value of this aesthetic for the memory of the city. It was a reading and a perception [of urban space] of a group of people who came from a highly liberal context and who favored individual cases, small initiative, small craftsmen workshops, and family businesses over [top-down] centralization.[8]

In our conversation, Nick confirmed this interpretation, noting that he has never been a proponent of historic preservation, which he called an antiquarian approach, adopted by people who "would like to restore things the ways they were 150 years ago." Instead, he favored what he viewed as an entrepreneurial approach, which "starts where it is easier, where the buildings are not falling down." Quoting Shakespeare—"There is a tide in the affairs of men, which, taken at the flood, leads on to fortune"—he explained, "Opportunities come along. You get to catch the tide, or take the tide and catch the wind. You got to have projects ready for when there is suddenly some money, and then it collapses again. If you started by rebuilding the sewers or consolidating the buildings' foundations, you'd go nowhere. I believe in starting with superficials and dealing with the big problems later."[9] By "superficials," he meant that in order to spark a new interest in the district, they first needed to persuade people to return to the Old Town to watch street festivals, to buy computers, or fix their shoes in the small artisan shops. To Nick, an expensive and messy restoration of the buildings was purposeless if it made people avoid the area.

Even though his vision got no traction with Bucharest's authorities, Nick did not give up. He invited a team of professionals and officials from Bucharest city hall on "a study tour [in the UK] to see firsthand how British cities had coped with a lack of resources and how partnership can be made to work."[10] Instead of getting Romanian officials to change their mind, however, that trip ended any prospect of collaboration. Architect Alexandru Beldiman was at that time the president of the Architects' Union and a strong proponent of the British project. This is how he described the reaction of the Romanian authorities: "The officials pretended to be interested in the project until they got themselves invited to London. That was the end of it. There was no political will [to continue it], and, in that period, nothing could have been accomplished without that political will. It wasn't that they didn't have the resources. They had other interests."[11] In 1995, Mariana Celac phoned Nick and invited him back to Bucharest. She had managed to find some resources, and the street festival was taking place after all. Nick had fond memories of that second visit but also remembered "the great contempt" for the Roma that he witnessed: "One of the events [in the festival] was a seminar (workshop) held by street children to describe what it was to live on the street. . . . It was possibly the first time—and maybe the only time—when the Gypsies and the other people coexisted without any conflict."[12]

Even though in our conversation in 2016 Nick highlighted the strong social dimension informing his vision of the Old Town's regeneration, the original text of the proposal tells a different story. In 1992, the British architects presented their initiative as a pilot project that would bring together "the private and the public sectors." Arguing that "the Old Town [could] not afford to wait until all of the laws and the systems of a free market economy [were] working properly," they recommended three lines of intervention: (1) "improving the environment of the main [commercial] routes, [which would] raise people's spirits, build confidence, and support activities that bring in foreign earnings such as tourism"; (2) "relocating the most inappropriate uses, to enable the banks to expand into some of their original property"; and (3) "revive the 'Old Town' as a major centre for creative small enterprises and . . . space for showrooms and trade."[13] Their solution was to make the district more visible, with an eye to eventually attracting more investors. But that was to happen also via an intervention in the social structure of the district, including the relocation of "many of the current occupants," who were "too poor to afford a better environment."[14]

In sum, even though the image of a festival was meant to symbolize an inclusive conviviality, the original proposal had favored a more intense commercialization of the place. Its success depended on multiple changes that favored exclusivity: in order for banks to expand by purchasing more real estate, public space had to shrink; for new traders to come in, others had to leave. In the case of the Old Town at that time, those marked for displacement were many of the 4,500 residents deemed to be too poor to "afford" better housing.[15] The British team sought to bring a new visibility to the Old Town, but that visibility automatically put the local poor in the shadow or even excluded them altogether.

Only by reading the original proposal against Nick's memories could we understand why Bucharest's authorities refused to engage in any way with the British team. It was not just a street festival that they rejected; they refused transforming the district into an economic resource because they did not want to share that resource with anyone else. In fact, the postcommunist officials seemed to be following the same strategy of "planned urban decay" that the communist authorities had pursued in the Old Town in the 1980s (see chap. 4). The state bureaucrats did so not only by rejecting proposals to enhance the district's social life but also by refusing to invest even in the buildings that used to be considered part of the national patrimony.

Such a neglected site was Manuk Inn, the seventeenth-century building that had been restored by Constantin Joja in the early 1970s, and transformed into a period hotel and restaurant targeting foreign tourists and their dollars. In 1991, its manager complained to a journalist that the place had seen no renovation since 1971 but that the state authorities were also not willing to sell it to foreign entrepreneurs: "Bulgarians, Serbs, Libyans, Italians, Greeks—they would have made the inn into a jewel. [City hall] did not want to do it. We don't have the funds to hire a security guard or make repairs. I don't count how many times someone came in to steal. There is water up to a meter in the basement. We live from one day to another, and Manuk Inn dies away."[16]

Behind local politicians' dismissal of the British team and their refusal to invest in the preservation of historic buildings such as Manuk Inn, we must read a long-term strategy of reinforcing invisibility. The local authorities pursued an active antiheritage agenda as a way to control (i.e., to postpone and marginalize) the restitution of many buildings that the communist state had confiscated during the 1948 nationalization. City hall's strategic attempt to keep the Old Town under the radar must be placed in the context of the fierce struggles over property restitution that were at the forefront of Romanian politics throughout the 1990s. The officials rejected proposals for the district's revitalization because they wanted to maintain the semidecrepit condition of many of the buildings. By doing so, they could keep in the shadow a terrain whose value grew exponentially from one year to another.

The mayor's comment to Nick—that the district was "hopeless" and that he was "wasting his time"—implied that, in the eyes of state officials, a law for property restitution was moot, because those old buildings had already lost any value and therefore should be left to die their own death. This type of justification relied on a circular logic in which the authorities' depiction of the Old Town as a moral and legal quagmire allowed them to postpone or dismiss any claims for property regulation. While criticizing the Old Town for the lack of (moral and economic) order it allegedly represented, the authorities exploited the legal haziness hovering over the district to create hidden clusters of capital.

The meeting between the British team and Bucharest's officials took place in early 1992. It took a few more years until the Social Democratic government passed a law in 1995 that allowed tenants living in state-owned buildings to buy their homes (properties that the communist state had nationalized in 1948) at prices much lower than their market value (Gallagher 2005, 230; Stan 2006). In the Old Town, some of the state tenants relied on this law to buy their apartments, but many others could not because they did not have the money. They remained state tenants and thus less interested in investing in repairing their buildings. A survey conducted in 2001 in the Old Town estimated that around half of the residents lived as state tenants, with very few (2%) having the courage to declare their illegal residence. Also, half of the residents considered the condition of their buildings as being highly dilapidated, but only 20 percent of them were willing to pay for repairs because they believed that that was the state's responsibility.[17] Local authorities, however, used the uncertain legal status of those buildings and the possibility that their pre-1945 owners might reclaim them to postpone indefinitely any repairs. At the same time, the state refused to give in to claims for restitution. Instead, the central authorities used the leverage it had over the courts to keep such litigation on hold for years, while judges felt enormous political pressure to deny restitution claims.[18] Moreover, the same authorities relied on the squatters to further destroy the buildings and thus make the former owners less interested in pursuing restitution. The strategic devaluation of the Old Town in the 1990s must be understood as part of the broader processes of value making and unmaking following the end of communism.

Monetizing Socialism

The creation of the new political regimes in the former Soviet bloc was fraught with tensions, and the struggles over how to divide and reevaluate the collective property of the former communist regimes reflected and magnified such tensions. The "reconstitution" of private property in the former Soviet bloc relied on a teleological understanding of history that treated the socialist period as an accident (Burawoy and Verdery 1999; Stark and Bruszt 1998; Verdery

2003). Many of the Western experts designing privatization policies refused to acknowledge an entire social landscape shaped by the complex networks of favors and connections and the particular economic practices that people had forged as part of or in reaction to a centralized system. The privatization policies imposed by these international experts who fully embraced the mantra of the free market created a domino effect that split asunder these former social networks. While many of the employees of former state companies supported these companies' privatization because they thought that "free market" equates with "political freedom," they also expected that such enterprises would continue to provide the social services and economic stability that they had taken for granted under the paternalist communist state.

In Romania of the early 1990s, the political establishment exploited such confused expectations. They promised welfare and especially financial protection from the foreign investors, while monopolizing the division and redistribution of the assets of the former socialist state. In the violent days of December 1989, when people took over the streets in Romania's major cities, asking for freedom and not just bread, a group of political insiders used the popular uprising as a guise for an internal putsch. They were mostly party apparatchiks with long-standing communist loyalties but who had fallen out of Ceaușescu's grace during the 1970s and 1980s. Shocked about the scale of the uprising and scared for his life, Ceaușescu fled the party's headquarters on December 22, 1989. On the same day, these political insiders formed a committee, the National Salvation Front (henceforth the Front), meant to function as a provisional government. Their leader was Ion Iliescu, a former member of the Party's Central Committee who had openly opposed Ceaușescu and his dictatorial behavior but who remained a staunch communist. Even though their initial agenda was not to abolish the communist rule but to only dismantle Ceaușescu's dictatorship, these former Party elites eventually had to give in to the popular pressure to end communism and declare Romania a democratic country. However, as Tom Gallagher has noted, this group managed "to preserve and upgrade aspects of the communist system that [became] the basis of the ostensibly pluralist regime now in place."[19]

The Front's founders greatly benefited from leading the revolution from the television. They appeared day and night, giving messages of support to the Romanians who stayed glued to their TV sets, and presenting themselves as the representatives of those who were dying on the streets.[20] After gaining such visibility during December 1989, the National Salvation Front became a political party, winning the first elections in May 1990 by a sweeping majority. Soon afterward, the democratically elected government turned against the opposition. In January, February, June, and September 1990, at the request of the new president Ion Iliescu, miners kept coming to Bucharest to first threaten and then to violently try to stop the wide antigovernment street protests. This series of events led to four people dead and almost five hundred injured.[21] The violent silencing of the opposition made Western countries consider Romania a failed democracy (Gallagher 2005, 96) and led to the first major wave of emigration after 1989, with almost one hundred thousand people leaving Romania by the end of 1990 to settle abroad.[22]

However, the government remained impassive to criticism. Under the slogan "We won't sell our country!" the Front-controlled government sealed off Romania from potential foreign investors while shrewdly orchestrating a systematic and speedy devaluation and "disappearance" of the assets of the former centralized economy. This general liquidation of resources was a step toward their eventual reacquisition by those who had previously administered them, who ranged from managers of regional factories to central figures in the ministries managing large industrial plants. In her analysis of land restitution in Romania in the late 1990s, Katherine Verdery (2003, 23) pointed out that the "unmaking of the socialist property regime" relied on a "devaluation and re-evaluation" of the goods of the former centralized system. As she put it, the "central problems for many actors were to discover what was valuable now and how one could get it, what practices were relevant to the valuations newly emerging, and how one could escape from things whose value was now plunging or make such things into assets—what or whom did one have to know and what did one need to have, so as to find value in someone else's liability" (23).

The socialist-era elites managed to keep their power through the thick networks of obligations and reciprocity they had forged during the years of the former regime. But they also strengthened their political alliances through their in-depth knowledge of the assets they had administered as part of the centralized system. They knew better than anyone how to treat these goods (state enterprises, state farms, industrial plants, buildings, land) as jigsaw puzzles that could be rearranged according to the economic demands of the postcommunist context. This process is illustrated by the circular mechanism undergirding the Front's rapid expansion, through which its members' political visibility enabled them to acquire fortunes and thus further strengthen their political capital. Through its regional and local branches established across the country, the Front gained more and more power as others joined in, from members of the secret police (Securitate) who had controlled foreign trade before 1989, to managers of the state enterprises and former elites of the Communist Party (Gallagher 2005). The economic network around the Front thus closely reproduced and fortified the communist-era social networks, which meant that those who had already been in the first network smoothly transitioned into the second, keeping their privileges intact (Grama 2004).

The Old Town's artificial devaluation in the early 1990s must be understood as part of this broader strategy of devaluation and revaluation. The new authorities knew that the neighborhood had a special flavor, the flavor of easy money, but in order to make the most of it, they needed to keep not only the place under the radar but also their own misdeeds. Between 1990 and 1992, one of the largest national newspapers started investigating how some of the new politicians (senators, parliamentary deputies, or other officials connected to the Front) became millionaires almost overnight. What they discovered was a convoluted but well-oiled system of favors and inside transactions by which state resources were smoothly transferred into the pockets and bank accounts of powerful individuals. Among such assets, there were many state-owned stores, art galleries, and workshops located in the Old Town. Here are some examples.

In November 1990, M. V., the head of a local branch of the Front and one of its representatives in the parliament, petitioned Bucharest city hall to transfer under his name several shops, including an art gallery, located on Lipscani Street, along with their current merchandise. With a simple signature, the deputy became the owner of the shops and of their merchandise, including rugs, paintings, and arts and crafts objects totaling around 5,790,000 lei (the equivalent of approximately $165,000 at that time, when the average monthly salary was $100).[23] In addition to this transfer, the deputy had already gained ownership of four other retail centers elsewhere in the city.

F. B., one of the founding members of the Front and then of the first provisional government, simply went to talk to the manager of the state-owned company that administered all of the retail outlets in Bucharest.[24] He walked into the manager's office and requested no fewer than seven stores, all of them on Calea Victoriei (a major commercial avenue bordering the western side of the Old Town). There was no way to refuse him, as the manager confessed to the journalists: "Without much discussion, he asked me to dispense of seven shops. 'Mr. B.,' I dared to respond, 'these are the outlets that bring the highest revenues. What about their merchandise?' 'I take it all,' he said. 'And the personnel?' 'I take all of them.' Eventually, we met in the middle. I gave him three stores, all of them on Calea Victoriei. The mayor's office signed off right away."[25]

C. I. was the vice president of the first provisional government between 1990 and 1992, and after 1992 he was elected as a deputy of the Front in the parliament. His wife had petitioned city hall for a commercial space in Union

Square. She was first refused, but then C. I. went himself to the local authorities, and suddenly that space became available and was transferred to his wife. In addition, C. I. solicited another location, a restaurant. The mayor's office also approved his second request, and C. I's father became the restaurant's owner.[26]

This evidence proves that far from being "doomed," as the then mayor described the Old Town to the British team, the new elite viewed the district as an asset. A hierarchy of power emerged, mapped onto the geography of the district. The shops that were more visible and thus would have brought higher revenues were taken by key insiders, such as powerful members of the government. The shops on the smaller streets within the district became the property of a second-tier category, such as deputies or members of the local branches of the Front. The politicians' maneuvers with and around the Old Town illustrate how they employed urban space to consolidate their power, erase value, and cover up theft.

Here are some examples of large-scale corruption that directly involved various mayors of Bucharest. Between 1990 and 1994, city hall endowed approximately 460 state officials (members of the government, senators, deputies, employees of the presidency and other central state institutions) with protocol housing, residences that the tenants were then (illegally) allowed to buy at a price significantly lower than its appraisal in the real estate market.[27] Between 1992 and 1996, the Court of Audit of the Romanian state found that Crin Halaicu, Bucharest's mayor between 1992 and 1996, transferred 25 million lei (the equivalent of approximately $1,671,000) from the local budget into the funds of a private foundation.[28] While Halaicu rejected the British architects' proposal to revitalize the Old Town, during his term as mayor, entire apartment buildings and land parcels were distributed to private firms and investors at a preferential price. Between 1997 and 2000, under another mayor, Viorel Lis, city hall lost 500 billion lei from its budget (the equivalent of around $310,000). In addition, that mayor authorized the restitution of numerous buildings, villas, and parcels of land to false owners, people who forfeited property deeds or used names of deceased owners to illegally come into possession of those assets. The journalists investigating these cases noted that under Lis's mandate, city hall lost the largest part of its real estate patrimony.[29]

These are just a few examples of how Bucharest's local authorities used their official position to launch businesses, to exhort funds, to make state property "disappear" and then reappear in the form of private bank accounts and property deeds. But they did not just make straightforward demands for land, villas, or centrally located stores. Nor did they solely rely on middlemen who took advantage of their jobs in the central government's bureaucracy to launch lucrative businesses, by forging ministers' signatures on privatization deeds, and selling these documents to those who wanted top commercial estate in the city center.[30] These officials also exploited urban myths, using the ill-famed reputation of the Old Town to their own benefit. They kept talking about the poor and the Roma who lived in the district, often conflating the two categories and portraying these residents as being mainly thieves and black marketers (*bișnițari*) who allegedly did not want to work. In parallel, these officials adopted a strategic disregard about the place, an attitude that allowed them to keep an alleged distance while maneuvering the district's resources in the shadows.

Writing about colonial officers in nineteenth-century Dutch Indonesia, Ann Stoler (2009) coined the term *imperial disregard* to describe the affective posture such officers took to convey their care and concern for the people under their control, despite being fully aware of the violence at the core of the imperial project—violence that they directly replicated. For Stoler, "imperial disregard" was a performance of "inattention . . . located on the edges of awareness" (256). The term thus implies an active "refusal to take notice" (256), highlighting the structural duplicity informing the lives and deeds of colonial bureaucrats. It was this duplicitous disregard that also informed the contrast between how the state officials talked about the Old Town and how they used it to consolidate their power.

Strategic Disregard

In the 1990s, the Old Town appeared, felt, and smelled old. Its semidecrepit houses oozed neglect. Its streets were filled with shrewd peddlers who sold almost anything, from cigarettes, coffee, Turkish jeans, and leather jackets to Soviet assault rifles, which some people had received during the 1989 revolution but never returned.[31] In 1996, Helmuth Frauendorfer, a German writer originally from Transylvania, visited Bucharest for the first time after he had emigrated from communist Romania in the late 1980s. He described Bucharest as a city whose people still struggled with the trauma of having lived under a dictatorship.[32] Walking on Lipscani Street in the Old Town, he encountered a colorful, loud, and unruly bazaar of people and goods: "'Only those who play would win!' Someone lures you to see if you are lucky. A slot machine in the middle of the crowd. Nearby, a group of people bargain and fight over a pair of jeans of an unknown brand. Few blocks down the street, a vociferous seller advertises its merchandise: women's clothes and shoes. The loudest place, though, is the corner selling music on compact cassettes . . . Next to them, a man offers cotton candy, and a woman, sunflower seeds. People elbowing their way in and out, ruckus, screams."[33]

This visually dizzying portrayal of Lipscani presents it as an intensely commercial place, where ordinary people tried to find better goods at cheaper

Fig. 4.2. Lipscani, the main commercial street of the Old Town. Photo by Norihiro Haruta, 1990.

prices, even though they knew the risks. When Bogdan, a friend of mine from Bucharest, was a student in the early 1990s, he went to the Old Town to buy a pair of jeans that he desperately wanted (at the time, no one could find jeans in stores, but traders traveled to Turkey to buy them and then sell them on the black market).[34] A man approached him and told him that he could offer him anything he needed. Bogdan had on him his entire monthly allocation from his parents. The man asked Bogdan to put the money into an envelope, give it to him, and wait there for him to come back with the jeans. Bogdan did what he was told, but then he changed his mind and asked for his money back. The man gave him back the envelope and said goodbye. Bogdan thought that the jeans were too expensive and that he could not do that to his parents. He was glad that he got out in time. When he arrived at home, he opened the envelope. Instead of his money, he found sheets of toilet paper.[35]

Such experiences reinforced ordinary people's ambivalent dispositions toward the Old Town and only confirmed their perception of the district as an ill-famed place. Anyone who lived in the district and had aspiration for a higher living standard wanted to get away. Some managed to do so, but others could not. Oana moved to the Old Town in 1985, when she was ten years old. Her mother had decided to exchange their apartment in the periphery for a smaller one in a more central location that allowed Oana to go to a better school.[36] It was a time and place about which she does not have warm memories. She and her mother always had to buy coal for the stoves because they had no central heating. There were almost no grocery shops in the district but the central market—the largest farmers' market in the city—was just fifteen minutes away on foot. As soon as she turned eighteen, she left that apartment and never returned.

Like Oana, those who could leave the district did so as soon as they found an opportunity. But others were stuck there. Take, for instance, the desperate plea made by a woman who lived in the Old Town and who sent the following letter in January 1991 to a major newspaper:

> My name is A. B. I am a state employee and I live in Bucharest, on 2 Academiei St [within the Old Town's perimeter]. I write this letter out of desperation with the hope that the authorities would finally hear me. In February 1990, I petitioned Bucharest's [city hall] for social housing so I could live like a human being. I have received no answer to my request. In my petition, I was asking to be given [to rent] one of the three apartments in my building, apartments that had remained unoccupied for the last three years. I have just found out that the state authorities distributed them to others. At the present, five families, including mine, live in two communal rooms, without access to cold or hot water. I have solicited housing with decent living conditions because I have already had tuberculosis twice, and I worry that I will get it again.[37]

The letter captures the woman's sentiment of powerlessness about her condition and her anger with city hall's carelessness and corruption. It is not as if the local authorities were not aware of the abysmal living conditions in the district. As Crin Halaicu, one of the first mayors of postcommunist Bucharest, noted, few people could live under those conditions, but those who had no other alternative had to find ways to subsist.[38] In an interview from 2011, Halaicu declared, "The entire central district had no water for hours every day, especially at the peak hours. That neighborhood was inhabited, but there were no streets, only some large piles of dirt. The people [living there] had no heat, water, electricity or gas. I don't know how they could have lived like that."[39]

In the interview, the former mayor boasted about the new housing that he had built for the district residents during his term (1992–96), but the story of those apartment buildings and who ended up living there was much murkier. In fact, this story reveals the conflicts among different factions of the political elites of that era. Around that time, the governor of the National Bank, Mugur Isărescu, asked the then president of the Architects' Union, Alexandru Beldiman, to help him. Since 1990, the National Bank has been located on Lipscani, one of the main streets of the Old Town. According to Beldiman, the governor was aware that "he had a gorgeous house in a shabby neighborhood, where he was ashamed to bring his foreign colleagues."[40] The governor rallied the Architects' Union to establish a foundation for the regeneration of the district.

Among other objectives, the foundation petitioned Bucharest's city hall to build three apartment buildings to relocate some of the poor residents from Lipscani and to begin the restoration of the most decrepit buildings. But as soon as the new housing was done, the local authorities "forgot" about their promises, and they gave these apartments to other people. Recounting that episode, Beldiman could not help expressing his stupor about that case: "The entire project fell through. These are arrangements that a normal person cannot understand—and I consider myself a normal person. . . . There was a purpose, there was a foundation, there were state institutions such as the National Bank and city hall. Theoretically, they should have held each other accountable. How could these three apartment buildings be distributed to others?"[41]

No one could answer that question—not that he expected an answer. At the end of his term, Mayor Halaicu left city hall and the political scene. He became a real estate mogul and soon one of Bucharest's first millionaires.[42] The new mayor, elected in April 1996, made yet another attempt to do something about the Old Town and its rapidly degrading buildings. Beldiman was involved in this project as well. Once again, the National Bank's governor insisted that the new mayor find a way to relocate the poor. And, once again, all the talk led nowhere. This is how Beldiman remembered the episode:

> We had yet another impulse [to do something about the Old Town's residents]. We took a walk in the district to see what we can do. There were four of us: Ciorbea [the new mayor], Isărescu [the governor of the National Bank], Caramitru [the minister of culture], and myself. Obviously, people recognized them, because they were public persons, and started talking to us. They began telling us that there were huge rats in their rooms and other horror stories. I was able to take an ad hoc survey while we talked. Out of six buildings whose residents I chatted with, only those who lived in one of the modernist apartment buildings [with much higher living standards] did not want to move. All of the others wanted to relocate. But this initiative again went nowhere. After six months, Ciorbea [the mayor] left, and [a new mayor] came in. The latter was a catastrophe. No one showed any further interest in the Old Town.[43]

The several failed attempts in the 1990s to intervene in the Old Town mark key political moments in postcommunist Romania. The British team's visit in 1992 and the overt rejection they received from the then mayor, emblematize the first moment, a period when government officials viewed the state resources as their own property. The overwhelming grayness that Nick remembered from his trip to Bucharest in 1992 was not only a legacy of how the communist regime had neglected the city but also reflected how Bucharest continued to be starved of funds by the postcommunist officials. This was a city in which social polarization began to take material forms, shown by the contrast between the newly built villas and the rapidly decaying apartment buildings.

The second moment is captured by the story about the stroll Beldiman and the three public officials took through the Old Town. This impromptu survey of the area took place immediately after the 1996 local elections, when Victor Ciorbea, the representative of the opposition and a relatively unknown lawyer, managed to defeat the powerful candidate of the Social Democrats (the governing party). The local elections in Bucharest that brought the opposition into city hall foreshadowed the results of the national elections that took place six months later, when a coalition of opposition parties defeated the Social Democrats.

The 1996 elections were crucial because they appeared, initially at least, to signal a political reawakening of the Romanian electorate: its collective disenchantment with the empty promises of Iliescu and his clique and a new hope in the power of civil society to actively engage in building democracy. Ciorbea, who had been Bucharest's mayor for only six months before the national elections, was asked to step down as mayor and take up the role of prime minister in the new government. That government vowed to fight corruption, to restore the right to property (by restituting houses and other assets confiscated by the communist state), and to demonstrate a moral probity and incorruptibility unmatched by its predecessor. The new leaders also promised to "open up" the country to foreign investors by offering more advantageous conditions to develop businesses in Romania, which meant that the local communists-turned-entrepreneurs suddenly had to compete with more powerful economic external actors—international investors and corporations.

Yet the networks of reciprocity Romanian elites managed to strengthen during the early 1990s proved extremely resilient (Solomon 2010). Their corruption-ridden economic arrangements made it very difficult for external investors to pursue business opportunities in the country (Gallagher 2005). The coalition government, which led between 1996 and 2000, turned out to be a deep disappointment, as petty divisions among different parties and "a failure to agree on a proper plan for reform" (Gallagher 2005, 176) quickly began to erode it from within. Despite the Democratic Coalition's initial promises of reform, nothing really happened—neither in the Old Town nor in much of the rest of the country. No buildings were repaired, no poor tenants were relocated to better living conditions, no houses were given back to their former owners. It was not a question of a lack of funds; on the contrary, the local authorities used public funds to build apartment buildings allegedly for the poor, only to then redistribute those apartments to people "in the network." The open dismissal of the residents' needs and the refusal to repair the buildings signaled not just the limitations of the new government.

Fig. 4.3. Narrow passage in the Old Town, 1990. Photo by Norihiro Haruta, 1990.

It showed that the middlemen of city hall and their business allies reigned supreme and that they would not concede to pressure, even from powerful economic institutions like the National Bank.

The fate of the Old Town in the 1990s reveals how powerful political actors employed distinct material and spatial strategies to maintain a centralized system under the appearance of a fledgling democracy. By allowing poor residents and squatters to live in the area, they wanted to signal concern for the poor. However, their purpose might have been more instrumental. Ruxandra, an urban planner who had worked on several projects in the Old Town in the late 1990s, shared with me some rumors. During the "muddy 1990s," as Ruxandra put it, many of those who moved into the abandoned buildings in the Old Town were suddenly made "quasilegal" residents in exchange for their votes.[44] That is, politicians offered the squatters the chance to receive an official identity card, with the address of those apartments that they occupied illegally, on the condition that the squatters used their newly acquired IDs to vote only for the candidates of a specific party. As commentaries on the unseen workings of power, these rumors pointed to more obvious strategies employed by the political and economic elites of the 1990s.[45] The rumors revealed these elites' duplicity, as they pretended to see no value in the district while seeking to keep it undervalued precisely so they could extract all of its resources.

The Old Town's poor did not function only as cheap votes; their presence also had a symbolic and affective dimension. The city officials exploited the affective qualities projected by the old things and buildings—along with the hunger for change and novelty that the Romanians felt in the early 1990s—to create new temporalities and affective divides. These officials used the ruined buildings of the Old Town as a contrasting background. They projected against it the illusion of social and political change while whitewashing crucial continuities between the elites of communism and those of postcommunism. In these politicians' hands, the poor of the Old Town, alongside its shabby old buildings, became means to "spatialize time," as Svetlana Boym (2007, 15) put it, to create a clear, visible threshold between the recent past of the communist dictatorship and the allegedly more optimistic present of a fledging free market.

Boym used this expression to describe what she called restorative nostalgia. In her view, the main purpose of restorative nostalgia was to block time: to create the illusion of a possibility of going back in time and to offer that promise by trying to capture time in place—by spatializing it and thus giving it a material form (from a territory to a town or a building). In the case of the

Old Town, I see such an attempt to spatialize time not as a nostalgic performance but, on the contrary, as an attempt to create a form of anti-nostalgia that would induce a collective forgetting. This anti-nostalgia relied on new sentiments of rejection and even repulsion about the place, sentiments that the local authorities tried to instill in ordinary people. Their strategy was by no means unique.

Walking through the historic district of Lefkosa in the aftermath of the Turkish-Greek war in Cyprus, anthropologist Yael Navaro-Yashin (2012) saw debris everywhere. The district, once the center of the city glittering with life, became literally and symbolically the margin: the mental and material fence of the border between the Greek and Turkish partitions cut like a knife through abandoned homes and lives. Navaro-Yashin viewed this active spatialization of affect as a survival strategy, one that allowed people to take a distance from the memory of the war. Drawing on Mary Douglas's (1966, 35) concept of "dirt as matter out of place," Navaro-Yashin noticed the powerful quality of abjection as a form of action: to recognize something as abjected presupposes an active participation in its isolation, in its moral, social, or economic annihilation. Processes of debris- and order making are interconnected (Douglas 1966), and in the case of the old Lefkosa, debris became the affective border against which the Turkish Cypriots forced themselves to create a new life from the ruins of the civil war and a new sense of order and stability (Navaro-Yashin, 158–59).

Navaro-Yashin drew on a theory of abjection grounded in psychoanalytical theory, particularly on Julia Kristeva's conceptualization of abjection as a somatic and symbolic response to something that is perceived as threatening a sense of order or identity. Kristeva (1982, 4) writes, "It is thus not lack of cleanliness or health that causes abjection but what disturbs identity, system, order. What does not respect borders, positions, rules. The in-between, the ambiguous, the composite." However, there is an ambivalence at the core of this reaction, as the abject may as easily attract as well as repel. The reaction to the abject becomes a litmus test for self-knowledge and thus the formation of subjectivity. Kristeva (1997, 372) describes it as "an external menace from which one wants to keep oneself at a distance, but of which one has the impression that . . . it may menace us from the inside. So it is a desire for separation, for becoming autonomous and also the feeling of an impossibility of doing so—whence the element of crisis which the notion of abjection carries within it."

How is this approach relevant for a better understanding of the affective employment of the Old Town as space of abjection in the 1990s? To start with,

Fig. 4.4. The architectural heterogeneity of the Old Town. Photo by Norihiro Haruta, 1990.

despite many attempts to discipline it and subdue it, the Old Town had stubbornly kept its ambiguity, its vibrant street life and its defiant heterogeneity. Magda Cârneci, a Romanian writer and poet, offered a deeply sensorial portrait of Lipscani Street as a particular olfactive landscape that triggered strong visceral reactions among its visitors:

> To fall in the pail of witchy stenches of Lipscani on a July morning. It is almost like a rite of passage, as if you found yourself in the vicinity of a putrefying cadaver, and suddenly realizing that that cadaver is alive, that new, smaller living elements are breathing in and out, each full of their own shallow but vital biological scent. Scent of Romanians, of Turks, of Jews and Gypsies, old and new, mixed with the smell of old Byzantine walls, now fully decrepit and exuding an unforgiving forgetfulness. A miasma of old and new merchandise, of jeans, artificial leather, plastic-made paraphernalia, mixed with ancient odor of narrow and dark old shops, full of useless objects and dust. And above all, as an invisible net, the odor of trade and sweat, the odor of mixture, of fornication, of crossbreeding, as if you could witness, in the midst of the crowded streets, the live synthesis, out of the older races, of a new group, maybe vulgar for now, but full of vigor and well-anchored in the future. Its pungent and powerful smell [captures] the piquant mix of the refined and the barbarian, its undefinable uniqueness, its synthesis.[46]

This unflinching portrayal of the Old Town as a space of profound contrasts, of a vitality that nonetheless derived from what the writer saw as immoral transgressions and cross-breeding, echoed earlier descriptions of the place, as well as perpetuated well-entrenched stereotypes of the Old Town as a place of moral and social abjection. Such descriptions revealed that the intellectual elites of the 1990s continued to regard the district with a mix of stupor and fascination. At the same time, this perception enabled the local authorities to justify their assessment of the Old Town as socially dangerous and economically worthless.

In a manner similar to former elites, be it interwar urbanites whose criticism of the district's disorder was a veiled attack on its Jewish residents (see introduction) or communist officials who viewed the Old Town as the quintessence of bourgeois capitalism (see chap. 1), the postcommunist authorities focused on the aesthetic and social heterogeneity of the Old Town to make it into a space of disorder, dirt, and doom. They further associated it with the recent past, especially with the dire penury of the late communist regime. They exploited exactly the sentiment described by Kristeva (1982, 4) as an adverse reaction to "the in-between, the ambiguous, the composite." By emphatically rejecting the district's unique mix of architectural styles, its ruined neoclassic facades, the old pipes running beneath the streets, the rusty wrought iron balconies, or the houses' foundations allegedly damaged by the waters of the Dâmbovița (as the mayor told Nick), the local officials portrayed the Old Town as a representation of the old, of the unwanted, of everything that actively rejected the new.

The strategic disregard that the authorities adopted about the district was meant to enhance the negative qualities of the place and especially to erase its nonorthodox vibrancy and heterogeneity. By keeping the place as if "frozen in time," they wanted in fact to take it out of time, out of the present, and make it into a material representation of the past—more specifically, of the recent communist past. In Kristeva's terms, the district became a border against which people could form a new skin and a novel postcommunist subjectivity. These people—the local authorities and anyone else who could afford to leave their past behind—did so not only by taking distance from and signaling their disgust with the recent past but also by denying their own links to that past, their own direct or indirect collaboration with the former regime, their shame, duplicities, and lies. A space of abjection like the Old Town offered them a chance to start anew because they projected that abjection, that past that they wanted to erase, onto those who were already living on the margins—and many of them in the semidecrepit buildings of the Old Town.

That image was promoted and naturalized via the national mass media. Here is how a journalist described the black marketers in Bucharest of 1990, in one of the best-known national dailies:

> The moneylenders of the ghettos borrow money, exchange hard currency and tips, arrange beatings of the competitors, manipulate the naïve customers, divide the zones of control . . . during the night, [these] parasites live in one single room, one on the top of another, but during the day, they go to the most expensive restaurants. Everything that these dandies of periphery have is made through moneylending and theft. . . . Should the illegal commerce be the solution to the acute poverty of a part of the population? We have serious doubts. Cultivating the mores of the periphery, Bucharest risks to become contaminated, and to further contaminate the entire country. The parasites have taken over, the parasites are traveling by plane, the parasites rule on the streets, they spread their pestilential ideas, the parasites buy villas, women, shops.[47]

This stigmatizing portrayal of the black marketers as the "parasites" that could "contaminate" a city and then a country should also be understood as a veiled anti-Roma criticism, reflecting the anti-Roma sentiment on the rise in Romania of the 1990s. The Old Town played a pivotal role in the spatialization of this anti-Roma sentiment, as the district had already been inhabited by many poor Roma. As discussed in the previous chapter, the social composition of the district had changed especially during the 1980s, when under the threat of the imminent demolitions occurring in the proximity of the Old Town, many of the better-off state tenants tried to move away, and in their place came a much poorer population, many of them Roma, whom the state authorities allowed to stay as temporary dwellers until the demolitions would begin. However, the bulldozers never came into the Old Town, and these temporary dwellers remained in the district. Their presence, combined with what appeared as the authorities' lack of interest in the district, functioned as a magnet for more squatters to move into the run-down buildings.

In their analysis of the illegal housing in post-1990 Bucharest, sociologists Ioana Floarea and Mihail Dumitriu (2016, 200) have argued that the "central city presence [of the illegal dwellers] was still tolerated by the new authorities due to several conditions: property status for each building was different and still unclear, there was no public funding for renovation, and alternative solutions for the numerous poor households inhabiting the area were still missing." However, while these factors played a role in the local authorities' passivity about the poor of the Old Town, I would argue that they did not merely "tolerate" but rather strategically employed the presence of the poor to divert attention from the suspect connections between private investors and state officials that flourished in the 1990s.

Scapegoats: The Old Town as a Place of the Other

In May 2016, I went to the population records division of city hall to search for more data about the social structure of the district. I asked a secretary about such data, and she directed me to speak to the manager of the institution. He was outside the building on a cigarette break. He did not even bother to invite me into his office, telling me curtly that he had no such data. Instead, he said, "What is it that you wanna know? It used to be a Jewish quarter, and now it's a Roma quarter. There! You shouldn't need any more data" ("*Ce vrei să știi? A fost un cartier de jidani, și acum e cartier de țigani, și cu asta basta*").[48] This well-placed bureaucrat, paid by the state to centralize as well as share what should be public information, told me that he had no such records. His disdain was obvious, not just in his tone but also in his choice of words. Instead of reciprocating the plural second person, *Dumneavoastră*, which I used when I initiated the conversation, he talked to me with *tu*, the pronoun of the second person singular signaling familiarity, or, in his case, a condescending dismissal. But that was nothing in comparison to the derogatory words he chose to refer to the Old Town's residents. He seemed to have no qualms about using, in a public institution, the most degrading terms for both groups: *jiidan* for Jewish and *țigan* for Roma.

This monolithic depiction of the Old Town as a place of the Other, formerly a Jewish district and currently inhabited by poor Roma, was an assumption that many of my interlocutors in Bucharest shared. This particular image of the Old Town has had a deep history and to a certain extent reflected the highly dynamic development of the district. Throughout its history, the Old Town had been a site of permanent negotiation of social and ethnic boundaries among different groups.[49] Indeed, during the nineteenth and early twentieth century there were many Jewish traders in the Old Town, but other Armenian, Bulgarian, Greek, Romanian, and German traders were also living in the district (Iorga 1939). Moreover, by the end of the nineteenth century, when Romania became an independent state under a parliamentary monarchy, the infusion of foreign capital heightened the economic and social polarization of the district. Many of the 170 banks established in Romania between 1880 and 1910 built their headquarters within the perimeter of the Old Town (Ionescu 1938). During the communist period, those banks became state institutions, large stores, and office buildings, while the apartment buildings were nationalized and redistributed to state tenants.[50]

Some of the poorer tenants were Roma, but they came to live in some of the substandard buildings in the Old Town not because they were Roma but because they were poor and could not afford better accommodation. However, when the communist regime strategically stopped investing in the district during the 1980s as part of the "planned urban decay" I discussed in the previous chapter, the increasingly poor population of the district became increasingly associated with the Roma. The Old Town's poor residents came to be seen as Roma just because they lived there (and this despite the fact that some residents, such as Oana's mother, mentioned above, moved to the district because they chose its location—the city center—over better living standards in apartments at the periphery so that they could offer their children a chance to attend better schools).

The social and economic contrasts that became increasingly acute during the early 1990s, combined with the overtly racist rhetoric of extreme-right political factions such as the Great Romania Party, created an even stronger incentive to strengthen social exclusion by associating the Roma with the poor and vice versa. In 1994, a World Bank report estimated that 21.5 percent of Romania's population lived below the poverty line (calculated at $3.30 per day) (World Bank 1997). A survey conducted in Romania in 1993 revealed that 16 percent of the total population of Romania was below the subsistence level (one that was considerably lower than the poverty line set by the World Bank), but that nearly 63 percent of Romania's Roma lived below that level.[51] Even though in that same survey only 4.6 percent of the population self-identified as Roma, such estimations must be approached critically. As a Roma professional and activist has noted, because of overt discrimination, only a third of the Roma in Romania have identified as such.[52] In Romania as well as in other countries of Eastern Europe, self-identifying as Roma has entailed a high risk: a higher exposure to institutional and social marginalization, lower access to education and living standards, and an inability to find better jobs.

Due to worsening economic conditions in the mid- to late 1990s, the category of "Roma" became itself a particular boundary to create and naturalize new social hierarchies by portraying them as grounded in ethnic difference.[53] To be or to become Roma began to signify class rather than ethnicity.[54] Noticing the expansion of the Roma category after the end of communism, Gail Kligman (2002, 73–74, in Rughiniş and Fleck 2008, 8) argued that "categories of classification such as 'Roma' are not fixed or immutable; they may be expanded or contracted to include or exclude. Hence, many of today's poverty stricken [Romanians] have been metaphorically 'Roma-fied,' regardless of how they self-identify. . . . The local transformation of attributing 'Gypsy identity' to those

Fig. 4.5. Abandoned stores and broken sidewalks. The Old Town. Photo by Norihiro Haruta, 1990.

who claim not to have been so identified before the collapse of communism seems to be largely the consequence of two interrelated factors: worsening poverty levels and geographical segregation."

I would argue that spatial segregation was not, however, as effective in enforcing a distinct intolerance of Roma as its opposite: spatial clusters that were ethnically mixed and increasingly economically polarized. By the mid-1990s, the Old Town became such a space of intense social polarization. The poor residents who had moved there during the 1980s stayed put. However, another, radically different group moved into the area after the end of communism: the banks.

The buildings that had been initially built for nineteenth-century and early twentieth-century banks and were afterward occupied by central institutions of the communist state became once again bank headquarters after 1989. Suddenly, some of the most powerful financiers in the country found themselves sharing the neighborhood with some of the city's poorest people. However, with the exception of the governor of the National Bank, no other bank in the district was interested in "doing something" about the poor and the shabby-looking buildings. The bankers' indifference only reinforced the local authorities' disregard for the place. But this charged proximity became yet another means for the new oligarchy to deny their liability and to cover up wide-spread corruption. The powerful blamed the poor for the derelict aspect of the district, making them into the symbols of abjection when, in fact, the real abjection lay elsewhere.

In the late 1990s, Romania began to pay the price for the "mistakes"—the diversion of state funds—that the former communists and their oligarchy had made into a political priority under Iliescu's regime. It started with the 1997 collapse of Ponzi schemes such as Caritas that exploited the culture of trust and financial practices from the communist period to collect and liquidate people's meager savings and salaries (Verdery 1996). In parallel, the banking system began to unravel (Cernat 2004). Between 1995 and 2000, some of Romania's largest banks declared bankruptcy.[55] Bancorex was the most important. The successor of the former Bank for External Commerce of the communist state, Bancorex started with enormous amounts of capital, which the bank leadership soon distributed on a discretionary basis to politically connected entrepreneurs—many of whom had been members of the communist secret police—and to other powerful actors in the system (Gallagher 2005, 116–17, 220).[56] All of these unsecured, low-interest loans were devalued by galloping inflation. In addition, many of the credits (around 70%) were never paid back. Judges, prosecutors, and police officials were also bribed with free credit to not pursue any serious investigations. When the 1996 coalition government learned about the catastrophic situation, it chose to continue to subsidize Bancorex for another few years out of fear that the bank's collapse would lead to a full-blown financial crisis. In 1999, the government finally decided to close it down. Between 1992 and 2004, the Romanian state lost $4.1 billion in nonperforming loans out of which Bancorex accounted for $1.2 billion (Gallagher 2005, 117, 220). Who did eventually pay for these losses? The taxpayers, in other words, Romania's citizens.[57]

The rise and fall of Bancorex is also significant because of the bank's spatial proximity to the Old Town. In 1990, Bancorex established its first headquarters in an imposing art deco building located on Calea Victoriei, very close to Lipscani Street (the building was donated by the National Bank). The leaders of Bancorex, however, found the location "unsafe and inappropriate" and wanted to move.[58] In 1994, the bank formed a partnership with city hall to build a new headquarters in the form of the city's first skyscraper, on a four-thousand-square-meter plot right in the center of the city, also on Calea Victoriei, and just five minutes on foot from the first location. City hall charged Bancorex no rent for that plot on the condition that the bank would share the revenues from renting office space in the shiny new skyscraper. When Bancorex moved into their new offices, it nonetheless kept the building of their former headquarters. Instead of renting it out, though, the bank chose to abandon it. When

Fig. 4.6. The former headquarters of Bancorex. Photo by Alex Iacob, 2012.

the government eventually closed down Bancorex in 1999, declaring it bankrupt and transferring its former assets to a new bank, the art deco building still remained abandoned. For more than twenty years now, its large entrance, framed by massive marble columns, has become a place that pedestrians on Calea Victoriei avoid or pass by very quickly, trying to ignore the dirt and the pungent smell surrounding the main entrance.

This building has become a ghost of a recent past for which no one was held responsible. Although in the early 1990s all of the largest transactions in the country went through Bancorex, none of the powerful actors who had received enormous credits and never paid them back has ever been brought to court. The partnership between city hall and Bancorex points to the intricate connections among different actors in the economic, political, and legal system—because why would city hall have chosen to offer for free a plot of land abutting the Old Town that was estimated (in 1994) at $40 million, for a bank to build a skyscraper? Note that this was the same city hall that rejected the British team's proposal in 1992 on the justification that no building was worth being restored in the Old Town, because the place's proximity to the river purportedly made it unsafe.[59]

The erasure of responsibility and the convoluted relationships between various structures of power in the 1990s have left some traces, but time has made these traces much harder to follow. When I met him in summer 2016, Doru was in his early thirties and worked as an investigative journalist in Bucharest. He covered hundreds of cases of corruption, of failed property restitution, and was a walking encyclopedia of stories about the creative ways in which "insiders" maneuvered laws and played with the system. One of the stories he shared with me speaks directly about the silences that accompanied the rapid social polarization of the 1990s and the concentration of wealth in the hands of very few.[60] Doru's office is located on Calea Victoriei, the boulevard delimiting the Old Town on its west side. It is the same boulevard where the initial headquarters of Bancorex used to be in the early 1990s, before they moved into the new skyscraper. One summer evening in 2014, Doru, together with other two colleagues, had decided to take a break from writing and go on an adventure. They left their office, crossed the street, and through a secret door in a passage, they entered the abandoned building of Bancorex. They went up on the roof, admired the sunset, and then decided to explore the basement. When they got there, they found piles of papers on the ground. He picked up one document, which happened to be an invoice. It turned out that they had stumbled on the abandoned archives of Bancorex. Doru said, "These were invoices from the early 1990s, when there were the first decapitalizations, the first wave of devalorization. There were other documents, from the former bank of external commerce, of the [communist] Romanian state. There was a huge file about a coal mine in Zaire."[61]

Doru and his friends found the documents in pools of filth, covered in dust, mud, and rat feces. But they decided to take them nevertheless; they put them in large bags, square meters of papers, carried them out to their office and deposited them there. A few days later, some of their colleagues suddenly began to complain that their eyes were swollen. It turned out that the cause was the papers in the bags: they were full of mold. Doru decided to call up the National Archives. "I'm a journalist. I found important documents. We would like to donate them to the archives." The people at the archives said, "Absolutely. Do not touch them. We will send someone to look at them tomorrow." Doru thought, "Wow, they are interested! I better take as many photos as I can before they come to take the documents away." In the end, though, no one came.

He said, "[In these documents], there are files with names of entrepreneurs who are now politicians. We are talking about the first millions made in Romania of the early 1990s. We will do two or three investigations, but many of the names on the files will tell us nothing. Some of the stories are still relevant: this one is today a famous banker, another is state secretary. But most of the files are about shoddy deals of the 1990s [*golănii ale anilor 90*]. They are now history. No one would want to look at this pile now."[62] Two years later, in summer 2016, Doru still had the bags of documents and just wanted to have more time

Fig. 4.7. Interior of the former Bancorex building, currently abandoned. Photo by Alex Iacob, 2012.

to look through them. But these stories were no longer "news"; they became "history"—a history few cared about.

Doru's story reveals how much of this history was hidden, erased, and eventually forgotten. The material remnants of the financial scandals of the 1990s, such as the moldy and rotten papers retrieved from the basement of the Bancorex building, continue making people literally sick, but their political and juridical relevance in the present becomes increasingly blurry. If they had been found ten years earlier, at the peak of the scandals, they might have offered the judges crucial evidence, to be used to punish the guilty and reveal the truth. Now they are filthy papers of uncertain value. Archivists do not want them; journalists do not know how to use them. As Doru put it, they are now "a page of history": stories to be told over a cup of coffee, no longer in a court. Kept in large bags, hidden in yet another basement, these papers are among the few tangible traces of the political filth of the 1990s, when the very few stole from so many, the poor became even poorer, and the Old Town's buildings fell into deeper disrepair.

I want to return now to my earlier question: Why did city hall reject any attempt to repair the buildings, and why did they keep the poorest of the poor in the Old Town? I argue that the state officials used the district as a multilayered site of contrasts that played a crucial role in altering the symbolic geography of postcommunist Bucharest and its residents' perception of the past. In a similar way that the French bourgeoisie invoked the system of sewers running underneath Paris as a symbol of the underworld against which they sought to define their social and political propriety (Stallybrass and White 1986, 125–48), the Old Town of Bucharest became the abjected underbelly against which a new postcommunist upper class could define itself.

The authorities reduced the district solely to a symbol of various outcasts and outliers, while they denied any value to its architectural and social eclecticism. By exploiting and encouraging the anti-Roma sentiment, these officials conflated the ethnically diverse poor and the Roma living in the Old Town within one category, thus exploiting and reinforcing the image of the district as the place of the Other, as a site of transgressions and shoddy transactions. They used the district's questionable reputation and especially its poorer residents to highlight, criticize, and closely monitor the petty theft happening on its streets while covering up the large-scale theft that took place behind closed doors of banks and other state institutions.

This radical simplification, meant to accompany and justify the Old Town's politically maneuvered devaluation, occurred through a set of contrasts that were first discursively produced but then made "real" by being inscribed onto urban space. These contrasts were projected onto particular things and groups, such as the shiny skyscrapers and the shabby houses or the black marketers and the bankers. To show how this happened, I draw on an approach proposed by linguistic anthropologists Judith Irvine and Susan Gal (2000). They employed the mathematical form of a fractal to explain how multiple differences are conflated into series of pure opposites, which are then replicated at different scales. By doing so, the complex ways in which ethnicity, class, race, and other identity categories influence and continuously reshape one another could be reduced to a series of dichotomies. Gal and Irvine focused on processes of language ideologization to explore how people assign social and moral meaning to specific language units, such as accents, vocabulary choices, and other linguistic devices, and how, in turn, such devices reinforce social preferences, prejudices, or hierarchies by encoding them linguistically. This search for a clear way to distinguish and isolate language units and to attribute moral conditions to such units characterizes especially multilingual environments, where prolonged and intensive language contact is inevitable.

Gal and Irvine have identified three semiotic tools that social actors employ to make and sustain such separations. *Iconization* entails exclusively highlighting one distinct characteristic at the expense of others and making it representative for the group as a whole. *Erasure* divests meaning and makes invisible persons and practices inconsistent with the dominant ideology established through iconization. Finally, *fractal recursivity* involves "the projection of an opposition . . . onto some other level" (38) and operates by reducing complex, interrelated social processes to a multitier set of dichotomies. Gal and Irvine pointed out that these three processes do not happen separately but simultaneously.

They function as a three-gear semiotic apparatus in which if one gear does not work, the whole operation might not be fully completed. All three contribute to normalizing and essentializing dichotomies and naturalizing links between disparate practices and people. But despite their semiotic sharpness—actually, because of it—they become highly effective social and political devices in situations of complex crisis. These situations could take the form of a financial or political collapse that further triggers crisis of meaning, status, and identity, making people reflect on who they are, what they can and cannot do, and where and whether they belong. They also come in handy as powerful devices for collective scapegoating.

The production of the Old Town as a place of the Other occurred through these three semiotic processes. Iconization happened as poverty was racialized, as the poor were automatically assumed to be Roma, and vice versa, and thus became doubly ostracized. Whoever was caught up in this circular logic also became tarred with impropriety and immorality. This perception had its own history. Before and during the communist era, the urban elites perceived the Old Town as the seat of corruption, illegal or petty commerce, impropriety, and urban chaos. This perception only became heightened after the collapse of communism. A double marginality emerged due to the rapid social polarization triggered by the slow but steady influx of foreign capital into the city. Destitution and the Roma ethnicity reinforced each other and reified the border between the extremely poor, often portrayed as being responsible for their own dire lives, and the imagined normality of middle-class life.[63]

Fractal recursivity occurred as one set of oppositions was projected onto a different scale, creating a dichotomous social landscape, especially in conditions of shared space. In this case, a radical discrepancy between the old, decrepit residences of the poor and the monumental buildings of the banks (especially Bancorex's new skyscraper) represented a set of contrasts, which were then projected onto the inhabitants of these two spaces. Each of these groups imbued their own space with a moral connotation. If the poor were "Roma-fied" and thus seen as intrinsically immoral, then the bankers were also implicitly portrayed as the opposite: the epitome of financial sophistication and moral propriety. As in so many other cases, propriety and property reinforced each other and kept the marginal out.

Finally, erasure happened when anyone tried to ask more questions about the dubious banking practices of Romania's new capitalists. Within the logic set out by the accompanying processes of iconization and fractal recursivity, a sophisticated banker could not be a thief because the poor Roma were the thieves, and the bankers were neither poor nor Roma. The category of corrupt banker could not, therefore, exist because it did not match the other dichotomies. The large-scale embezzlement of funds thus "disappeared" from the public view, leaving the petty thieves and the black marketers to bear exclusively the blame for the ill-fame of the Old Town.

Gal and Irvine's approach offers a key insight into how cultural categorization can easily become a political tool of exclusion and erasure. They make us understand how the intrinsic complexity of social life could be easily reduced to a simplistic opposition of "us" versus "them." The making of the Old Town into a place of the Other functioned not only as a space of abjection that would create a dichotomous landscape between the (then) recent communist past and the postcommunist present and thereby make invisible the deep connections between the former and current political elites. It also played a key role in muting the links between the state, the emerging private sector, and a politically controlled financial system. The real abjection of the Old Town in the 1990s was not concentrated in the homes of the impoverished residents but somewhere else: in the basements of abandoned bank buildings, in the offices of the shops and art galleries that the local officials had "transferred" to well-connected politicians in the early 1990s, and especially in their heavily lined pockets.

Conclusion

The rapid degradation of the Old Town in the 1990s, alongside the booming privatization and the new banks, offer a poignant picture of the broader processes of value making and unmaking following the end of the communist regime. The political elites of the "wild and blurry" 1990s strategically used the shabbiness of the district to turn it, as much as possible, into an abjected space, denying its colorful history and its defiant sociality. No longer a heritage site for the socialist state, the district became portrayed as an allegedly ahistorical place, populated by two contrasting categories, squatters and bankers—people without history and people who wanted to erase their own history so that they could keep their tight hold on power.

In this chapter, I argued that the authorities employed the district as a multifaceted site to gain and consolidate political and economic power. First, by choosing to not repair the old buildings, the local authorities sought to keep the area undervalued and thus to discourage the pre-1945 owners from asking for the restitution of their former property in the district. Second, they kept the poor in the same semidecrepit houses, because their presence enhanced the perception of the Old Town as a site of abjection, a place from which "ordinary," middle-class people should have kept distance. More importantly, they placed the responsibility of the ill-fame of the place solely on the poor, thus diverting attention from the real site of abjection: the shoddy deals and embezzlement of funds happening behind the closed doors of the major banks located in the district. Third, the Old Town was made into a marginal space that enabled the political elites to pretend that they have no connection to the pre-1989 structures of power. By promoting the district as a negative space, the political actors of the 1990s attempted to create a tangible, spatial divide between the recent past of the late communist period and the postcommunist present.

Their attempt was successful partly because it matched the ordinary people's deep desire to excise that recent past from their memories: those of a time and history that had begun with grandiose promises of a new social order meant to give everyone a much better life but that ended in a dictatorship. Some of these people also wanted to forget their own individual duplicity, petty compromises, or even their direct collaboration with the secret police. The burden of this recent past was too heavy to be fixed with just some "lipstick," as Nick Falk put it—a street festival that would bring people together in the Old Town and make them enjoy each other's company. Both politicians and people needed time: the former, to silence the opposition, amass fortunes, and consolidate their power; the latter, to forget the recent past and to project hope onto the future. But by the end of the 1990s, time had run out. People were hungry for reform, tired of the widespread corruption, and profoundly disenchanted with the politicians that brought the country into a financial morass. Most importantly, they wanted to become Europeans and be acknowledged as such.

Notes

1. Skype conversation, January 25, 2016.
2. January 25, 2016.
3. January 25, 2016.
4. "Cum arată capitala noastră?" *Adevărul*, January 29, 1991.
5. The architect was Şerban Cantacuzino.
6. Interview with Mariana Celac, April 19, 2008. See also letter included in the documentation provided by Nick Falk.

7. Interview, April 19, 2008. Gabroveni Inn was later abandoned and remained a ruin until its 2016 reconstruction and rehabilitation as a cultural center.

8. April 19, 2008.

9. The quote is from *Julius Caesar* by Shakespeare (4.3.225). Interview Nick Falk, January 25, 2016.

10. "Regenerating the Old Town, Bucharest: A Strategic Plan," a report by Urbed and Terry Farrell and Company, with the Romanian Union of Architects, 1992, 4. I thank Nick Falk of Urbed for providing me with a copy of the report.

11. Interview, April 24, 2008.

12. Interview Nick Falk, January 25, 2016.

13. Urbed report, 4.

14. Urbed report, 3.

15. This figure appears in the 1992 Urbed report. One should, however, take it with a grain of salt, because it appears to be an estimate and not based on real statistical data (no sources were cited regarding this figure). As I discuss in the next chapter, the exact figure of how many people lived in the Old Town at that time remains a mystery. At the time when the British team drafted their proposal in 1992, the last social survey in the area had been conducted in 1970, more than twenty years earlier.

16. Adriana Vela, "Cine ucide Hanul lui Manuc?," *Adevărul*, April 5, 1991.

17. "Atlasul Centrului Istoric al oraşului Bucureşti. Asociaţii ale comunităţii din Curtea Veche, ATU, 2001," 33, 65. Courtesy of Vera Marin, ATU.

18. At one point, up to August 2016, the website of the General City Hall of Bucharest offered information about specific situations of the buildings; after the new elections, however, that portal is no longer available. In the Old Town, there are still many litigations regarding the restitution of some buildings that had been opened in the late 1990s and have not yet been solved (as of summer 2016). In principle, one could learn more about the situation of one building by typing in the full address and see the juridical status or the status of the litigation. However, the information is rarely accurate. A change of ownership status on several buildings, which I could notice because they advertised that the place was for sale, appeared on the city hall website as being still in litigation. Other buildings, such as the one where Carmen and her neighbors live, appear as being solved, but in fact, according to the tenants, it seems that the litigation is still open.

19. Tom Gallagher, "Romania and Europe: An Entrapped Decade," Open Democracy, March 22, 2010, https://www.opendemocracy.net/tom-gallagher/romania-and-europe -entrapped-decade.

20. Despite all of the shooting that took place in those tumultuous days of December 1989, leading to thousands of deaths, no alleged "terrorist" ever tried to attack the public television headquarters or find ways to shut down the live transmission.

21. Mihai Diac, "Mineriadele au arătat lumii o Românie sălbatică şi neguvernabilă," România Liberă, October 21, 2015, https://romanialibera.ro/special/documentare/mineriadele -au-aratat-lumii-o-romanie-salbatica-si-neguvernabila-397117.

22. In 1990, the number of Romanians who settled abroad was 99,919. In comparison, in 1994, only 18,148 Romanians emigrated; in 1996, 24,888; and in 1997, 21,635. "Migration and Asylum in Central and Eastern Europe. Romania," European Parliament, accessed January 20, 2017, http://www.europarl.europa.eu/workingpapers/libe/104/romania_en.htm #N137back.

23. Ion Marin and Gheorghe Ioniţă, "Deputatul de Covaci," *Adevărul*, January 24, 1991.

24. Florin Bădinici was among the members of the government who ordered the violent crush of the street protests in June 1990. "Rechizitoriul dosarului 'Mineriada'," Hotnews.ro, accessed July 13, 2017, https://www.hotnews.ro/stiri-esential-21822095-rechizitoriul-dosarului -mineriada-interventia-din-13-iunie-1990-vizat-capturarea-manifestantilor-nu-dispersarea -lor-pasnica.htm.

25. Ion Marin and Gheorghe Ioniță, "A început balul," *Adevărul*, January 25, 1991.

26. "Magazinele clanului domnului deputat Cazimir Ionescu," *Adevărul*, February 1, 1991.

27. "12 ani de hoții în Primăria Capitalei," *Adevărul*, January 14, 2002, 2.

28. "12 ani," *Adevărul*, January 14, 2002. To calculate the equivalent value in dollars, I used a historical currency converter, available at Fxtop.com, accessed September 13, 2017, http://fxtop.com/en/historical-exchange-rates.php.

29. "12 ani," *Adevărul*, January 14, 2002, 2.

30. For such an episode, see Ion Marin and Gheorghe Ioniță, " . . . De la ușa parlamentului," *Adevărul*, January 26, 1991, and "'Obligațiile' domnului Sichitiu," *Adevărul*, January 29, 1991.

31. Ziua News, December 3, 2013, http://m.ziuanews.ro/dezvaluiri-investigatii/piata -neagra-de-armament-din-romania-se-ridica-la-20-000-de-arme-de-foc-109314.

32. Helmuth Frauendorfer quoted in Axel Barner, "Imaginea Bucureștiului în literatura germană contemporană," *Revista Secolului 20* 385–87, nos. 4–6 (1997): 246.

33. Frauendorfer in Barner (1997, 246).

34. At that time, "doing Turkey" became equated with risky but profitable entrepreneurship. For many people, traveling back and forth to Istanbul's markets in the early 1990s was the first step toward launching a business.

35. Conversation and field notes, May 23, 2016, Bucharest.

36. I received this information about Oana indirectly from one of my friends in Bucharest. I asked N. whether she knew anyone who had lived in the Old Town in the 1980s, and she mentioned "Oana." She approached Oana and told her about my project, and Oana responded by telling N. about her childhood in the district. While she agreed with N. sharing this information with me, when I asked N. to introduce me to her, hoping that I would learn more, Oana refused to meet with me. She said that she did not enjoy talking about that time and had nothing else to tell me. Conversation with N., August 30, 2016.

37. "Scrisori față în față," *Adevărul*, January 26, 1991.

38. Crin Halaicu interviewed by Carmen Dragomir, "Ce-au fost și ce-au ajuns. Cum a făcut Crin Halaicu primul milion de dolari," *Jurnalul*, November 29, 2011, http://jurnalul .ro/special-jurnalul/ce-au-fost-si-ce-au-ajuns-cum-a-facut-crin-halaicu-primul-milion-de -dolari-597863.html.

39. Interview, April 24, 2008.

40. Interview, April 24, 2008.

41. Interview, April 24, 2008.

42. "Ce-au fost și ce-au ajuns," *Jurnalul*, November 29, 2011.

43. April 24, 2008.

44. Ruxandra's story was confirmed by Ovidiu, who did extensive research on the politics of housing in Bucharest. Fieldwork notes, May 20, 2016.

45. I thank Britt Halvorson for the phrasing "rumors as commentaries on the unseen workings of power." For a discussion about rumors as part of broader occult cosmologies that approach power as operating in two distinct but related realms, one invisible and another visible, see Sanders and West (2003, 6–7).

46. Magda Cârneci, "Bucureşti—O colecţie de mirosuri, " *Revista Secolului 20* 385–87, nos. 4–6 (1997): 136.

47. Al. Gavrilescu, "Bonnie and Clyde . . . toacă banii în Obor," *Adevărul*, January 30, 1991.

48. May 12, 2016, Oficiul de evidenţă populaţiei [The Office for Population Records], sector 3, Bucharest.

49. The deep interconnection between the sociality of space and the formation of ideas of groupness through space has been analyzed by many scholars, promoted by Frederik Barth's (1998) seminal approach to ethnic boundaries as being continuously produced and negotiated among groups. For an overview of the use of the boundary in social sciences, see Lamont and Molnár (2002).

50. For instance, only on Lipscani Street, the main commercial street of the Old Town, there were hundreds of apartments nationalized by the communist state. For a detailed list of the number of apartments, the street, and the names of the former owners, see "Decret nr. 92 din 19 aprilie 1950 pentru naţionalizarea unor immobile," in *Buletinul Oficial* 36, 20 aprilie 1950.

51. Living conditions among the Roma were worse than those of the rest of the population: only 44 percent had a gas stove, and only 20 percent owned a refrigerator. In their households, there were more than 3 persons per room in comparison to 1.3 persons per room in the entire population (World Bank 1997, 23).

52. Marian Sultănoiu, "Recensământ 2011. Două treimi dintre romi se declară români. 700.000, 2.000.000, 3.000.000 . . . câţi romi trăiesc în România?" *Gândul*, October 19, 2011, http://www.gandul.info/stiri/recensamant-2011-doua-treimi-dintre-romi-se-declara-romani -700-000-2-000-000-3-000-000-cati-romi-traiesc-in-romania-8883047.

53. In 1999, 41.2 percent of Romanians lived on or below the poverty line, in comparison to 25.3 percent in 1995. Those living in extreme poverty formed 16.6 percent of the population in 1999, more than double of the total of 8 percent in 1995. World Bank data in Gallagher (2005, 274).

54. Ciprian Necula interviewed by Marian Sultănoiu, "Recensământ 2011," October 19, 2011, *Gândul*.

55. In addition to the Ponzi schemes and the banks, the National Investment Fund (FNI) collapsed in 2000, one of the biggest financial scams of postcommunist Romania when millions of ordinary people lost all their savings. For a detailed analysis of the financial markets and social practices that led to the rise and demise of FNI, see Tulbure (2013).

56. See also "România fără vinovaţi," Jurnalul.ro, April 27, 2006, http://jurnalul.ro /campaniile-jurnalul/romania-fara-vinovati/faliment-bancherii-de-mucava-22713.html; and especially "Dosarul Bancorex," Iasi1.ro, accessed March 25, 2017, http://iasi1.ro/iasi1/dosarul -bancorex-devalizarea-bancorex-operatiunea-securistilor-cele-mai-mari-fraude-bancare -romanesti/. The sixty-page single-spaced report entitled "Bancorex File," drafted in 2006, reveals highly sensitive information, including the juridical decisions about the magnitude of the fraud as well as lists with tens of thousands of people with "connections" who benefited from credits that they never paid back, amounting to billions of dollars that the Romanian state has never managed to recuperate.

57. Ilie Şerbănescu, "Privatizarea BCR: să plângem, să ne bucurăm?!," *Revista* 22, January 10, 2006.

58. See the investigation about what happened with the patrimony of Bancorex after the government decided to no longer support it and declared it bankrupt. "România furată |

Clădirile şi terenurile Bancorex, date pe nimic," Digi24.ro, July 28, 2015, http://www.digi24.ro /special/campanii-digi24/romania-furata/romania-furata-cladirile-si-terenurile-bancorex -date-pe-nimic-421221.

59. Interview, Nick Falk, January 25, 2016.

60. Interview, May 27, 2016.

61. May 27, 2016.

62. May 27, 2016.

63. For conversations over the meaning of normal and its new association with conspicuous consumption in another postsocialist context, see Fehérváry (2013).

5

DISPLACEMENTS

Property, Privatization, and Precarity in a Europeanizing City

SHE CAME IN FROM THE STREET AS I was standing in the main hallway of a run-down building in the Old Town, eyeing the stairs. The uneven, squeaking wooden steps, not repaired in decades, did not look too appealing. A part of me did not want to go up, while the other part was thinking that my gut reaction was just ridiculous. She passed me, dragging a handcart, and started walking slowly up the staircase. I offered to help and took the handcart. I could not believe how heavy it was—it must have weighed at least fifty pounds. I asked what was in it. "Water," she said. She told me that she would buy big bottles of water every week and lug them to her apartment on the third floor. The tap water would sometimes be cut off, and even when it ran, it did not have enough pressure to get up to the top floor. She had moved into the building in 1978 when she got married. I helped her up to the second floor, but then she took the cart from my hand and said she was fine on her own. I asked her if I could visit her sometime. She said, "You could drop by on Tuesday, but I am not sure if I would be at home." Then she went up the narrow stairs to the third floor.

When I came back on Tuesday, no one answered her door. I did not know if she was away or at home and chose not to answer. I respected her wish and did not knock again. Her refusal to talk to me might have been just an annoyed response to a stranger who asked too many questions. But the more I tried to talk to other residents of the Old Town, the more I realized that their unwillingness to talk signaled something else. Their reluctance to reveal too much about themselves hid more powerful sentiments: shame about their current precarity, one that older people would not have envisioned after a life of work as responsible citizens; hopelessness that the local authorities would ever improve the living conditions in the Old Town's deteriorated buildings despite continuing to collect the rent; and fear that they would be evicted even from these buildings and that their lives would become even more uncertain.

Confronted with the carelessness of state authorities, who have invoked lack of funds and inflation to justify their unwillingness to consider the needs of the most vulnerable and poorest part of Bucharest's residents, the latter have relied on a combination of resignation and resilience as a strategy of survival. This attitude was also signaled by individual acts of defiance. They included a seventy-year-old woman carrying plastic bottles of water amounting to almost half of her own weight up three sets of stairs to compensate for the lack of running water in her studio; a family from the same building who profited from the traffic ban instituted by city hall in the Old Town to open an unofficial parking lot on their street and watch the cars for a few hours in exchange of the equivalent of a couple of dollars; and thousands of families who have kept submitting their application for social housing (Ghiță et al. 2016, 12, 14) despite being told that they would never get housing, or being treated with contempt, or learning that city hall employees had applied for and received social housing even though they had already owned a home.[1]

What has been happening in Bucharest in the last thirty years since the end of the communist regime is nothing new. The incorporation of the former Soviet bloc in global capitalism has triggered a rapid social polarization, an accumulation of new clusters of capital and power prompted by what Saskia Sassen (2017) called predatory formations: assemblies of elites, ranging from governmental and transnational actors to techy entrepreneurs, all firm believers in the privatization of almost anything, including the transfer of the state-sponsored welfare system, already shrinking to extreme, into the hands of private charities. In the case of some of the postcommunist countries, such predatory formations were dominated by "entrepratchicks," the former party elites who turned into entrepreneurs almost overnight (Verdery 1996). From this perspective, postcommunist Romania has represented an extreme case of social polarization, with wealth rapidly concentrating in the hands of a few while a quarter of the population has been living in abysmal levels of poverty. Between 2012 and 2015, one in four people living in Romania was officially considered to be poor—that is, their income was less than 60 percent of the average income for the total population, which meant that one person had to live on less than $172 per month in 2013 or $179 per month in 2014.[2]

The origins of this polarization are twofold. The first phase occurred in the early to mid-1990s, when the former communist nomenklatura retained strong control over the political and economic landscape. Their refusal to begin property restitution and the privatization of former state assets—allegedly because they did not want to "sell the country" to private investors—was a justification to further consolidate a closely guarded network of intermeshed political and financial interests. The second phase began with the negotiations and preparations for Romania's inclusion in the European Union (EU), launched in 1999. This is when billions of euros in the form of preaccession funds meant to smooth the economic transition, to help small businesses and alleviate poverty, ended up being diverted by the political insiders, thus further solidifying the gap between the rich and the poor.

This chapter focuses on the latter phase: the privatization of Bucharest launched by the local authorities in the early 2000s. It argues that this process enabled the state to redefine itself from one that promised relative protection to one that overtly discarded social responsibility. The first section discusses the negotiations over Romania's inclusion in the EU in the early 2000s. It zooms in to the particular context of Bucharest, where the election of a new mayor from the opposition not only intensified struggles for political power but also revealed distinct urban visions and approaches to "Europeanization" held by different political parties.

The second part explores the increasing social polarization resulting from these urban policies, which went hand in hand with the privatization of the city. It argues that the commodification of the services that used to be state owned and considered as basic rights by most people (access to water, electricity, and heat) became in the hands of the new municipality a strategy of implicit eviction of the poorest residents of Bucharest from the city. The struggles over property restitution—specifically, of the houses confiscated by the communist state in 1948—form the topic of the next section. Politicians across the political spectrum used property restitution to signal that they obeyed the EU's requirements while also exploiting the legal malleability and bureaucratic complexity of the restitution process to further consolidate clusters of capital.

The focus on the Old Town in the mid-2000s is relevant to understanding these struggles, because the new municipality assigned it a key role in their strategy to Europeanize the capital. The district was to stand as proof of Bucharest's European history, but for that, it needed newly paved streets and a refurbished infrastructure network. With funds from the EU, the city authorities launched projects of urban refurbishment allegedly meant to modernize the city. In fact, such projects enabled the officials to redefine the boundary between the public and private spaces, and ultimately to gain a tighter control over the public space. In the last section, I examine the ruination of the Old Town's buildings and its long-term social and political effects in a city whose citizens have been seeking alternative ways to keep or remake community.

A City Not for Everyone: Europeanization as Gentrification

In the 1990s, the Romanians' effusive enthusiasm about their newfound freedom was soon replaced by a pervasive sentiment of discontent and confusion. Instead of instituting mechanisms of social protection, the political elites exploited this confusion for their own benefit. The serial bank failures and the heightened social polarization of the late 1990s had mostly derived from the decisions and deeds of the ruling groups of the early 1990s, mostly grouped around the National Salvation Front, the party of the former nomenklatura. However, this group refused to take any responsibility for the ensuing financial crisis, blaming instead the Democratic Coalition, which ruled the country between 1996 and 2000. Meanwhile, Romania's ordinary citizens, those who suffered most from the deepening poverty, viewed the crisis as a direct product of an incompetent, weak government. Under increasing popular pressure and people's disenchantment with the internal struggles for power within the Democratic Coalition, the Coalition eventually dissolved (Sandu 1999, 43). These circumstances enabled the opposition—that is, the ruling elites of the early 1990s—to return to power by winning the 2000 presidential and parliamentary elections. Making promises to end the financial crisis and implement a better welfare system, the former nomenklatura resumed political control under the new label of Social Democrats.

However, in comparison to the early 1990s when they closed the country to foreign investment, by 2000 the Social Democratic government was no longer interested in an economic nationalism. On the contrary, they signaled their interest in pursuing EU integration, and that fit the EU actors' own agenda. Starting in 2000, the EU began to channel significant nonreimbursable credits to Romania, intended to prepare the state to restructure its policies and priorities to meet the EU's standards.[3] However, much of these funds ended being used by "corrupt power brokers" (Gallagher 2014, 185). Simultaneously, the same politicians exploited the Romanian population's increasing trust in transnational institutions such as the EU and NATO and their hope that they would be again viewed as "European" after fifty years of communism.[4] Actors across the political spectrum, from the Social Democrats dominating the 2000 government to the Democratic Party and other parties in opposition, promised that they would do all they could for Romania to be accepted into the EU. The rhetoric of "Europeanization," translated as a fight against corruption, and the transformation of Bucharest into a "European metropolis" was what brought a new mayor to city hall.[5]

In 2000, Traian Băsescu, the candidate of the Democratic Party, became Bucharest's general mayor. During the 1990s, he had built a reputation as a

strong-willed politician who had no qualms about speaking his mind, a reputation that likely helped him win the elections. As soon as he began his term,
Băsescu launched an open war with his political opponents, the Social Democrats. Given that the latter won the 2000 parliamentary and presidential elections, this battle between the Băsescu-led city hall and the Social Democratic
government became increasingly fierce, being fought with all possible weapons:
mutual accusations in the mass media, the government's blocking EU funds
secured by Bucharest's city hall, followed by the latter retaliating by opening
hundreds of litigations to dispute such intervention by state institutions into
the local affairs of the city.[6]

Despite these fierce struggles for power, the local administration under
Băsescu managed to launch one of their declared priorities: the privatization
of the main utilities. This was one of the conditions imposed by the EU in
their preinclusion requirements (the *acquis communautaire*), and the local
administration wanted to signal their willingness to "promote the principles
of market economy, and to prevent a situation of monopoly."[7] The EU pushed
for such a privatization on the assumption that to have such services owned
and administered by the state was implicitly a form of monopoly that did not
encourage market competition. In Romania, however, the government ended
up selling these services to large transnational corporations, whose special
agreements and negotiated tariffs enabled a situation of de facto monopoly.
Suddenly, ordinary consumers in Bucharest and across the country found
themselves facing bills for water, electricity, and gas that sometimes equaled
their monthly income. For instance, in the winter of 2005, just two years
after the utilities privatization, the monthly costs for electricity grew by
30 percent, those for gas by 60 percent, and those for water almost doubled.[8]
This led to paradoxical situations such as poorer consumers petitioning the
gas company *not* to turn on the central heating in their apartment buildings
until temperatures were below freezing so that they did not have to spend all
their monthly income on gas.[9]

The privatization of the utilities infrastructure led to new social displace-
ments. The rapid rise in utilities costs made the poorer residents of apartment
buildings seek alternatives. Some moved to the countryside; others chose to
take without paying. For instance, in December 2006, in one of the poorest
neighborhoods of Bucharest, around one hundred people—the residents of
five apartment buildings—went out on the street and set some cars on fire,
to which the police reacted violently and blasted them with water cannons.[10]
The street incidents had started a few days prior, when the electricity company
came into the district and disconnected the five apartment buildings from the
grid, claiming that some apartments had been stealing electricity. By that time,

Băsescu had exchanged his mayor's seat for that of Romania's president, having won the 2004 presidential elections. Commenting on the incident, he alluded to his former position: "I will say what I had already said when I was the mayor: Bucharest is not a city where everyone can afford to live."[11] This remark proved that from the very beginning, starting in 2000, the municipal administration used the rhetoric of Europeanization as a justification for a state-sponsored gentrification.[12]

Bucharest's case thus complicates views of gentrification as solely triggered by real estate market trends (Smith 2002); it reveals that the state and transnational institutions, such as the EU, could act as direct agents of gentrification. Viewed from this angle, the EU-sponsored process of Europeanization could be viewed as a form of gentrification at a continental scale: the constitution of a union of European states aimed to engender flows of capital, people, and goods has been accompanied by an intensification of border control and internal surveillance meant to identify those who do not have the right to move freely and evict them.

In Bucharest of the mid-2000s, eviction via the privatization of basic utilities also took place in a subtler way. It relied on some residents' bureaucratic illiteracy—their lack of knowledge about how to navigate the new policies, forms, and requirements. This bureaucratic invisibility implicitly led to an infrastructural invisibility. Once the major utilities had been privatized, most of the providers requested additional guarantees to validate the new contracts. For instance, the water company required of private consumers living in a building with a shared utilities network that they first form an association of apartment owners and that the contract be between the company and the association, not each of the consumers. In other words, in order to receive basic services such as tap water, gas, electricity, and so forth, apartment residents first had to show that they lived there legally as tenants or owners and to pay additional fees to the state to form such associations. That is, they had to institutionally and legally become a community, pay their shares, and act as one cohesive group if they wanted running water and central heating in the winter. It was rather ironic that such forms of forced community making emerged as an effect of the privatization of basic services. These new requirements particularly impacted the lives of anyone who inhabited a residence illegally.

Infrastructural Invisibility

Here, I would like to return to the Old Town and especially its poor population. In 2000, city hall launched the privatization of the city by attempting to eliminate street commerce and the homeless, to privatize basic services, and to resolve the uncertain property status of tens of thousands of residences. Also that year, a group of enthusiastic architects and sociologists who anticipated some of the social effects of these policies, began a social project in the Old Town. With the financial sponsorship of a grant from the United Nations Development Programme (UNDP), they established a nongovernmental organization (NGO) and reached out to everyone living there: small business owners, residents, squatters. The result was a "social atlas" of the district that provided a detailed assessment of its social and economic structure. It was the first detailed survey conducted in the district after 1989 (the previous such survey dated to 1970).[13] In 2000, they assessed the social structure of the Old Town as being the following: 46 percent were state tenants; 16 percent rented from private owners; 30 percent owned their residences; and 8 percent declared that they lived there illegally (it is likely that the percentage was higher, but other residents did not want to admit that they were squatters).[14] This survey thus challenges the description of the Old Town as being inhabited mostly by a very poor population, formed mostly by squatters and illegal residents—the ways in which local authorities began to describe the Old Town in interviews and mass media to justify their plans for eviction.

For the NGO team, the survey was just a means to reach their ultimate goal—they hoped that by getting to know the people and listening to their specific needs, they would find practical ways to "strengthen the community."[15] This is how the researchers described the situation of the Old Town:

> The population in the area is formed of state tenants, individual owners, and commercial locations (both rented and owned). [In addition, there are] people who live illegally in buildings owned by the state, or that have a private owner, but that have not yet been restituted or sold. Despite the advanced ghettoization, the people who live in [the district] do not form a community and less so an active community. In the absence of an organizational form that would enable the population to take part in the decision-making process [on issues] that directly impact their everyday life, those people find themselves in a precarious situation in relation to the local administration or investors [interested in buying property in the area].[16]

To spur the residents into action and made them form a genuine community, the NGO aimed to persuade the Old Town's residents to form a legally constituted association. Ruxandra, a founding member of the NGO, conducted a large part of the research in the district. When talking about the project in May 2016, she admitted to me that one of the more practical goals of the project was to teach the poor, less-educated Old Town residents about their civic rights. Learning the intricate bureaucratic procedures was vital for this population if they wanted to make the authorities consider their needs. One of the immediate strategies was learning how to form an association that would represent them and give them some leverage in dealing with city hall. As they put it in their project proposal, the NGO team hoped to identify "enthusiastic young people who [were] born and grew up [in the area] and [were] aware that they must and could have their own 'voice' to express their needs and concerns."[17] The association was to serve more practical purposes as well, such as to enable the residents to learn how to form other associations—for example, one of tenants, so they could then access basic services. Ruxandra said,

> No one [from city hall] gave two cents about helping the tenants form associations. Especially when [those people lived in] the old buildings where the state was in litigation with others, such as the former owners, or those who bought the property rights, because no one knows who would ultimately end up being the owner. It's entirely their business if they don't form an association. [But without an association,] they cannot obtain services. For instance, Apa Nova [the water provider] does not accept individual contracts. Apa Nova wants to deal only with an association of tenants as one entity. No one can request to be connected to the central water system for an individual account [unless they live in a one-family house]. If they do not know how to form an association, they are left without water.[18]

This comment points to how profoundly political rights were linked to access to infrastructure. The NGO's focus on community making—trying to endow the residents with legal and institutional knowledge that would make them more powerful and thus visible to the state—challenged local officials' intention. The privatization of utilities went hand in hand with the privatization of social services, enabling the authorities to disavow their responsibility toward the poorest citizens. Local officials sought to keep these illegal residents and their needs invisible by way of infrastructure—or lack thereof. By imposing this rule of dealing solely with associations, some of the private contractors cut the underclass out of the system—an underclass that had no ability to engage with or even possess knowledge of the new bureaucratic rules. The state relied on the privatization of utilities to keep this underclass out by making it harder for them to access basic services. The providers relied on the insider network formed by some of the state officials and the corporate sector to keep raising the prices. Take, for instance, the water provider, Apa Nova: in 2003, one cubic meter of water was around the equivalent of $0.27; in 2005, it was $0.5; in 2015, it rose to $1.62.[19] With both sectors reinforcing each other's regulations, the underclass became infrastructurally invisible.

As other scholars have noted, such an infrastructural invisibility has been a strategy for elites to subdue the needs of the poor while consolidating their power via a rhetoric of modernization. Writing about city settlers in Mumbai and their maneuvering of political connections to gain access to water, anthropologist Nikhil Anand (2011, 56) has coined the concept of "hydraulic citizenship" to describe the forms of belonging (and exclusion) enabled by "effective political and technical connections to the city's infrastructure of water supply." As Anand shows, for Muslim settlers in Mumbai, whom the city's Hindu majority have treated as second-class citizens, identifying alternative sources of water that were not tied to the municipal system became a (temporary) source of political defiance and economic independence. In comparison, some of the residents living in Bucharest's Old Town in the early 2000s seemed to have been less interested in becoming more visible. On the contrary, some of these residents preferred this infrastructural invisibility, because it allowed them to stay, or rather to hide, in their homes, while expecting to be evicted at any minute.

In our conversation in summer 2016, Ruxandra distinctly remembered the clash between what the foreign sponsors (UNDP) envisioned and what the residents wanted and needed. This is how she described the tension:

> [The UNDP coordinator] had the idea of organizing an association. He did not wonder for a second whether this might be impossible. But since he put that in the project [proposal], we had to form an association! So we found three people. They were not representative, had no education, but when they heard that we would pay for the [administrative] costs [to make] the association, they said, "Sure, why not?" They had no clue, [no awareness] of something like, "I understand that I represent the committee from the historic center." Nothing like that! This is how we found ourselves with them at city hall signing the documents for this association. The costs were included in the project budget. After that, the association died; they stopped answering our phone calls.[20]

The three young men, who remained unnamed in the story, seemed to have been initially persuaded but gave up when they realized that they would gain nothing from this business. Although Ruxandra did not mention it, it is likely that they did not want to engage with state authorities in the first place, knowing from the start that that was a lost cause. By refusing to follow up with the NGO team, these young men signaled that they saw no benefit in being too visible by means of an association. Instead, they embraced a "politics of resignation," a term anthropologists Peter Benson and Stuart Kirsch (2010) used to capture the attitude of hopelessness and discontent of ordinary people when dealing with behemoth capitalist entities such as corporations. In the case of the Old Town's residents, the entity they feared and were seeking to hide from was the state: that is, the local authorities—the same authorities who persuaded the EU to channel more money into Bucharest on the promise that they would develop more solid "mechanisms of social protection of the disadvantaged groups in the population."[21]

The Old Town's impoverished residents had no interest in engaging directly with these authorities. On the contrary, they wanted to keep their heads down as much as possible in order to stave off a potential eviction. They were caught in a catch-22 mechanism of invisibility: if they dared to defy the state by forming associations and ask for their rights, such as the right to state-sponsored social housing, they would expose their current illegal status in the Old Town and thus increase their vulnerability. If they kept themselves invisible, they could hope to prolong state authorities' tacit tolerance of their presence in the Old Town, but that meant sacrificing their access to basic necessities, such as running water or heating. But their hopes turned out to be short-lived.

Struggles over Property

By the early 2000s, the fight over Bucharest's territory and the local real estate market had intensified. In the 1990s, the officials had employed what I called a strategic disregard toward the nationalized property to keep it artificially undervalued and thus appropriate it more easily (see the previous chapter). By the early 2000s, things had dramatically changed. The real estate market had matured. Noting Romania's interest in joining the EU, foreign investors became more courageous about bringing capital into the city. City officials began to formally acknowledge the high value of the city as both an economic and political resource.

One of the conditions that the EU imposed on the Romanian government prior to accession was that they solve the property question. Throughout the 1990s, the restitution of nationalized property had been the most contentious point of negotiation between international political actors and the Romanian government. As discussed in the previous chapter, the Social Democrats had initially passed a law (112/1995) that denied property rights to the pre-1948 owners and favored the state tenants, allowing the latter to buy their houses and apartments from the state on a preferential price. However, this law was one of the forms of artificial devaluation that state officials had promoted during the 1990s. It was actually a gift for themselves, as it enabled many of the politicians who had lived in state-owned villas as protocol housing to buy them for peanuts directly from the state, dismissing any claims of the pre-1948 owners. Ion Iliescu, Romania's president at that time and the Social Democrats' leader, had declared that court decisions that rejected the state tenants' property claims were "outside the law" and asked that these decisions be ignored (SAR 2008, 4).

In 2001, following pressure from international actors such as the EU and the US government, the Social Democratic government, back in power, passed a new law (10/2001), which in principle aimed to amend the previous law

(112/1995) and restore the ownership rights of the pre-1948 owners. The Romanian government used the new law to signal their willingness to take the EU's requirements seriously and to embark on a path toward democratization. Practically, however, while welcomed by a part of the population, the passing of this law triggered a wave of discontent among those who viewed the law as a disenfranchisement of their own property rights—more specifically, the former state tenants who had benefited from law 112/1995. In 1990, there were around 67,000 state-owned residences that had been acquired through nationalization.[22] Following law 112/1995, 44,500 were purchased by their tenants. However, once the new law was passed in 2001, the juridical status of around 30,000 of these residences was challenged by the pre-1945 owners or their heirs.[23] The latter requested that the property deeds obtained by the former tenants in 1995 be annulled by the court and these former tenants be expropriated.

Although many of the pre-1948 owners invoked law 10/2001 to regain their former estates, state authorities pushed back. As political scientist Lavinia Stan (2006, 198) noted, "the law [10/2001] unnecessarily complicated the [restitution] process and seemed to deter owners from claiming back their properties." Almost as soon as parliament passed it, the Social Democratic government began to "quietly undermine" the law (197). Ion Iliescu, who again became Romania's president in 2000, said that the property question was "a trifling matter" (198). Adrian Năstase, the Social Democrat prime minister, scoffed at the attempts of former owners to challenge the decision of Romanian courts by appealing to the European Court of Human Rights, noting that the latter was "not a real estate agent" (198). In fact, highly placed officials, including members of the government, found ways to finagle the complications of the law to their benefit. Their maneuvers relied on tedious and intricate bureaucratic procedures, causing the least advantaged parties to give up on their restitution claims. Top officials especially targeted those who had hoped to gain the most from the implementation of the law: the heirs of the wealthiest families from pre-1945 Romania.

I heard about one such episode directly from the injured party.[24] As the only heir of an extremely wealthy aristocratic family in pre-1945 Romania, my interviewee had opened multiple lawsuits to win back his parents' estate, which included land and mansions in central areas of Bucharest and in the countryside, all nationalized under the communist regime. He confessed that in 2000, Prime Minister Năstase informed him candidly that he would never gain possession of all of the assets previously owned by his parents. The prime minister proposed a deal: the heir would receive a part of the assets on the condition that he waive the right to litigate for a historical mansion on a large estate in the best residential area of Bucharest. The heir had little choice but to accept.

That house was then sold to various people and eventually left abandoned for more than twenty-five years. As I am writing this (January 2017), it is just a ruin, and it will probably be left in this state until it collapses, making way for an expensive new villa.

This is just an example of how the post-2000 Social Democratic government employed the property law as yet another instrument to accumulate resources, while promoting it as a sign of democratization and of their willingness to abide by the EU's standards. The convoluted bureaucratic procedures that accompanied the implementation of the law made it increasingly difficult for ordinary people to pursue restitution. Instead, many chose to rely on a third group: real estate intermediaries who sought to buy the property rights from the former owners—especially from those who were unaware of the value of their inheritance.

These dealers became the new owners, more knowledgeable about the workings of the restitution process and more able to recover the houses and land. Often, such individuals worked directly with politicians and lawyers "within the system." Take, for instance, one of the hundreds of cases in which the heir of the former owners chose to sign over her property rights to real estate intermediaries. By the time Elena decided to sell her rights, she had already spent a decade knocking at the doors of various state institutions, from the national archives to city hall, to the court, and back to where she started.[25] It was all in vain; she failed to win back the house lot that used to belong to her parents before 1948. She was tired, she said, of "battling windmills"—though, in contrast to Don Quixote's story, these were real, powerful state institutions, not imaginary enemies. In the end, Elena decided to cede her property rights to a real estate agent for a sum that initially seemed high (€25,000, or $30,000, in 2006). As soon as she did, the local authorities immediately agreed with the restitution and even expedited the process. The real estate agents received the lot in less than two months. In 2010, less than four years after Elena had signed off her ownership rights, the real estate company sold it for €900,000—and the local authorities received their share.[26]

Real estate groups that engaged in such practices did not restrict themselves to only relatively poor owners. I have heard of situations in which the intermediaries continued to exert pressure on the former owners to sell their property rights, even when the latter rejected their offers, and instead hired their own lawyers to represent them in court.[27] Ruxandra mentioned to me the case of the brother of one of her friends, a lawyer living in Bucharest who was hired by some people abroad to begin, on their behalf, litigation for property restitution in Bucharest. Soon thereafter, he began receiving threats meant to force him to cease his relation with his clients so that the latter would eventually acquiesce in selling their property rights. The lawyer did not give up on his clients, but he had to hire a personal bodyguard for more than a year (presumably until the legal disputes were resolved in court).

Law 10/2001 launched a new form of privatization of the city. It allowed networks of public officials and private investors to exploit their public authority, capital, and convoluted legal procedures to gain control over large parts of Bucharest. They did so not only by directly intervening in the restitution process, such in Elena's case, but also by forging, hiding, or "disappearing" property deeds, data about state housing reserves, and other documents. Once Băsescu became Bucharest's general mayor in 2000, he promised he would solve the tens of thousands of property claims. Soon thereafter, a special office was established in city hall that dealt only with restitution claims—an institution meant to signal that the new mayor honored the electoral promises and attempted to expedite the restitution process. However, as Stan (2006, 198) noted, the Bucharest office processed the claim at a snail's pace: by mid-2001, the authorities received 210,000 claims but solved only 2 percent of them; by late 2003, they received 70,000 more claims and managed to solve fewer than 3,500 petitions. These data appeared in the national media, but they do not match the official numbers declared by city hall.[28] According to the latter, the total restitution claims received between 2001 and 2004 was only 40,897, out of which the authorities managed to solve a total of 3,116 in four years (between 2001 and the end of 2004).[29]

Such discrepancy in data signals not just the overall confusion about the restitution process and the frustration of all the parties involved. It also reveals a particular modus operandi of the state institutions that still relied on the practice of "strategic disregard" developed in the 1990s (discussed in chap. 4). This practice entailed a set of behaviors, from the naive carelessness with which the city employees handled important documents to cunning schemes, undeniable conflict of interests, and intentional corruption. The national dailies of the early to mid-2000s reported numerous cases documenting such situations. I present here just two of the most preposterous ones.

The first case shows how easily official files and irreplaceable property deeds could vanish into thin air—as did many of such documents from the state institutions, including seven property deeds for protocol villas in Primăverii quarter, the most-sought-after neighborhood of Bucharest. In April 2002, one journalist went to the Bucharest courthouse to solicit copies of some documents in a file related to a restitution case. To obtain the file, she filled out a form, which an employee of the institution read and approved without asking the journalist for any proof of identity. Then, she took the form to the national archives, and presented it to the archivist, who also did not ask her for an ID.

The archivist told her that she would bring the file to the copy room set up in the same building (but not controlled by the institution of the archives). There, the journalist found a small room with two photocopiers and two women frantically photocopying document after document, surrounded by piles of files full of confidential information, which seemed to be in the care of no one. As the archivist did not show up, the journalist asked one of the women whether archivists brought more files that day. The woman directed her to some files in a corner, once again not asking her for her ID. The journalist found her file in the pile and made the copies she needed. She could not help noticing that if she had wanted, she could have taken any other file; she could have copied it, or even put it her purse, because no one would have noticed or cared.[30]

The second case illustrates blatant conflicts of interests that state institutions did not seem to investigate unless they were forced to do so.[31] On a Friday night, the head of the Division of Public Finances of Bucharest, the governmental institution in charge with administering and collecting taxes, came upon an employee in an office where she should not have had access. When discovered, the woman started eating documents from the files right in front of her boss. It turned out that the files contained the taxes filed by some private businesses for which the same employee had worked as an accountant. In other words, if the employee had not been caught, she would have continued to work for both parties (the state institution and the private businesses).

The strategic disappearances of files and the discrepancies in figures reveal a complex system of data manipulation, erasure, and even ingurgitation, which enabled and propagated corruption at multiple levels within the state institutions—despite the official promises of institutional transparency and the respect of the rule of law that Romanian officials had made to the EU. Ironically, the political factions used the pretext of legal transparency to only intensify their infighting and mutual accusations, as shown by the conflict around the property restitution between the Băsescu-led city hall and the Social Democratic government. In January 2002, a few months after the property law was passed by parliament, a journalist pointed out to Băsescu that some of the restitutions made by city hall might not have been legal. Băsescu abruptly rejected such accusations, claiming that city hall was required to apply the law if the claims were accompanied by legal proof of prior ownership. There were many cases in which city hall denied restitution claims because it questioned the legal viability of such documents, but Băsescu declared that he "did not do any illegal restitution."[32] He said, "My goal is that [the restitutions] be done properly. Obviously . . . if in this circuit of collecting the documents we receive a falsified archival document, an inaccurate notary act, a fake ownership deed, we are not specialized in detecting the falsehood. We just look at the notary's stamp, we say 'It's good,' and we give the house to the person. If that claim is made with false documents, we run a major risk of making an incorrect restitution. But it is not our business to verify [notarial and archival] documents."[33]

Instead, Băsescu turned these accusations on their head and blamed the Social Democratic government for interfering in the work of city hall and harassing the civil servants who dealt with the restitution cases.[34] He said that such interventions were, in fact, a veiled "threat." It was "inadmissible," he said, for city hall employees to be punished and thrown in prison for making errors in handling restitution claims, because they were not supposed to know how to distinguish a genuine document from a forged one.[35] Thus, despite the extreme slow pace in which the restitution claims were solved, Băsescu's declarations made city hall appear totally innocent, while he pointed to the Social Democratic government as the only culprit for the slow pace of the restitutions.

Once again, the Old Town came in handy for Băsescu to emphasize the difference between his vision and that of his predecessors. In 2000, the local authorities seemed to suddenly rediscover the district. In their development strategy for the next decade (2000–10), they brought up the district's heritage value as proof of Bucharest's European history as well as a means to put the city back on the cultural map of Europe.[36] The report read: "The unique character of the historic center area derives from its architectural value. This value must be preserved and promoted [as a key element for the plan to develop] the city . . . as the future capital within the European Union."[37] According to Băsescu, this transformation was to occur via two interrelated pursuits: the restitution of the houses to the former owners (or to those who had bought the property rights) and the renewal of the district's antiquated infrastructure, including its sewers, electricity and gas networks, and paved surfaces. He made the two projects appear interconnected. He declared that the owners had told him, "Mister Mayor, we would put money into those houses, many of them on the list of historic monuments, but only on the condition that you first renovate the infrastructure, the sewers, the water, the gas conduits."[38]

Băsescu presented the modernization of the infrastructure of the Old Town, to be pursued with EU funds, both as an end in itself and a means to solve the property restitution question. The infrastructural overhaul was part of the broader renewal of the city's utilities network. At the same time, it would have compelled the house owners to "exercise their rights and obligations" instead of "looking on as the buildings continued to be inhabited illegally, while [the owners] continued to live in Canada, Israel, Germany, and France."[39] By "obligations," he implied that the owners had a legal responsibility to maintain their property at functioning standards and to restore the historic buildings. But Băsescu's comment also implicitly contained a warning. It signaled that the local administration's willingness to clarify the legal status of the houses in the Old Town and to restitute them to the former owners were conditioned by these owners' consent to become fully responsible for these houses and for the costly repairs they needed. It also revealed the local authorities' plans to intervene not only in the utilities infrastructure but also in the current social structure of the district by evicting those who were too poor to invest in repairs.

Eviction as Political Control

Băsescu's allusion to imminent evictions in the Old Town was not just an empty threat. Since 2000, in parallel with the privatization of basic utilities and public services, the authorities employed the discourse of Europeanization to justify a more authoritarian policy of urban governance. They used it to signal their power to redefine the border between public and private spaces, and to decide who had the right to live in the city and who should leave. Their pursuit of Europeanization was an implicit multilayered erasure, from the expulsion of the street sellers and the euthanizing of street dogs to the eviction of the illegal residents and the removal of the homeless from the city. Despite bitter infighting and mutual criticism on other topics, Băsescu's city hall and the Social Democratic government agreed that the only way to keep the city "clean" was to clear out both the homeless and the squatters, to keep them "off the streets and away from the center of the city" (O'Neill 2010, 254). A government-sponsored program called Back Home, launched in 2000, targeted the squatters in Bucharest and pursued their forceful expulsion from the city back to their places of origin.[40]

The Roma was the most targeted group. In spring and summer 2000, the authorities evicted more than four hundred Roma from illegally occupied buildings and escorted them out of the city—presumably to be dispersed in the countryside.[41] The local mayors also relied on other administrative procedures, such as the surveys conducted for the national census in spring 2002, in order to identify "the Roma and all who occupy illegally state property" and "send them back to where they came from."[42] In July 2002, the local authorities confiscated sixty carriages owned by the Roma to deter them from collecting and commercializing scrap iron—one of the few means available to them to make a living—and stop them from entering the city.[43]

In parallel, Bucharest's city hall also declared illegal and forcefully dismantled the small kiosks that used to line the main streets.[44] This form of commerce represented a key economic venue for small entrepreneurs, who mostly purchased street space through informal arrangements made with local authorities (before Băsescu became mayor). In July 2000, at the order of city hall, more than twenty thousand kiosks were dismantled almost

Fig. 5.1. A street in the Old Town during the infrastructural overhaul. Photo by author, April 2008.

overnight. It was a veiled dismissal of not only the small-time traders but also of lower-class consumers, who usually chose the products offered by these kiosks—"the mall of the poor"—over those sold in more expensive super-markets.[45] The mayor's decision to eradicate the kiosks conveyed the message that making Bucharest "lawful" entailed restricting it only to the needs and capital of the middle and upper-middle classes, transforming it into a city in which the buyers and sellers of cheap products no longer belonged. It also showed that city authorities viewed the public space as their own domain, one they would directly control and define according to their own agendas.

Such forceful intervention in the public space foreshadowed city hall's intervention in the Old Town a few years later. On a late-February morning in 2005, the residents of the Old Town woke up to an eerie silence: the usual noise of the cars and small trucks slowing down on the cobblestone streets to bring merchandise to the shops or just to cross the district was gone. It turned out that the city authorities had ordered most of the streets in the district to be blocked overnight. Residents were told that the traffic ban was needed for the imminent repair of the local utilities infrastructure.

But the repairs kept being postponed. Initially, the local authorities said the works would start in summer 2005.[46] Then they postponed until fall 2005, then again until fall 2006, and so on.[47] Only in December 2006 did the project begin and only after multiple rounds of negotiations between the authorities and the companies commissioned for the project.[48] Meanwhile, the social life of the district had been undergoing a slow death. City hall presented the traffic ban as a response to the earlier petitions of both the residents and business owners to keep some of the narrow streets exclusively for pedestrians. But no one had petitioned for closing down the traffic in the entire district. Suddenly, all the small shops, pubs, and other commercial venues could no longer rely on an easy, steady flow of merchandise. When someone tried to complain to the authorities that he would go bankrupt because he could no longer park near his shop, they responded that there was a parking lot next to a major department store located a mile away. That meant that he had to carry all of his merchandise by hand or in a small cart.[49] One of the entrepreneurs then living in the Old Town captured the economic and social effects of the traffic ban by noting that since its imposition, "the streets are empty; people who used to come for the 'authentic atmosphere' now stay away. Business is much reduced. Petty crime has grown, and there are more creeps around. Garbage is piling up."[50]

When I talked to a former resident of the district, Andrei, in summer 2016, he had bittersweet memories of the Old Town in the mid-2000s.[51] At that time, he had moved into an apartment in the district and opened several businesses together with some Dutch friends, including a bar that soon became famous in the city as a hub for bohemians and cool people, with live concerts and a unique atmosphere. Andrei called the traffic ban a "great hoax." The intervention had a political purpose, he said. It was part of a political war between the new authorities, linked to the politicians on the right, and the former officials on the left, who had controlled the state and local politics during the 1990s. "They needed the [commercial] space to be free, so they kicked out the small fry to bring in their own," he said, pointing out that the easiest way to do so was to first "kill the business" —and indeed, many of shop owners complained that the ban drastically brought down their revenues.[52] These traders had rented commercial spaces for peanuts in the 1990s, when the economic realm was under the control of the former nomenklatura (see chap. 4). By blocking access to cars, capital, and merchandise, the authorities aimed to make those traders go bankrupt. And most of them did so in a year or two, making room for the new "insiders," as Andrei put it.

Initially, Andrei tried to fight off the authorities. In early summer 2005, he formed an association together with other entrepreneurs from the Old Town and began a campaign against what they saw as a radical and unnecessary intervention. Under the rallying cry "Yes to revitalization; No to isolation!" they tried to make their voices heard. They published their protests against city hall in an English-language local magazine, organized meetings with other business owners in the district, and above all, they sought to capture the attention of the city's new mayor, Adrian Videanu, elected in 2004. This association was not the only group that protested city hall's attempt to control the Old Town. Pro Patrimonio, one of the first NGOs to begin projects of built heritage preservation in Romania, had also tried to persuade the authorities to seek smoother, less disruptive solutions for the district. They initially hoped that if they called on more prominent political actors, such the then US ambassador, they would gain the ear of city officials. But they hit a wall: no matter the financial or political support that they managed to coalesce, city authorities were simply not interested in talking to them. Commenting on general interactions with the local authorities, Pro Patrimonio's manager emphasized their inaccessibility: "When they are told about specific interdictions, they do not want to listen. When they hear about the European recommendations, they do not want to be present." She added, "Bucharest is an area where we could not move on any front. It is impossible to have a conversation with the local authorities, especially at the level of city hall. We offered them our support [in forms of both expertise and funds]. We organized a press conference, but Mayor Videanu disappeared from the very beginning so he did not find himself caught in a discussion that would have become too embarrassing for him."[53]

City hall's real intention behind the much-advertised plans for eviction was to signal control over the Old Town and over public space more generally. This intention is revealed in the authorities' contradictory declarations. In the press and on television, different representatives of city hall talked at length about the danger illegal residents represented for both the buildings and the district, but there was no clear agreement about what officials planned to do about these people nor about how many of them actually resided in the Old Town. In July 2005, the new mayor, Videanu, declared that five thousand families were living illegally in the Old Town and that thirty-seven of them had already been sent away. He made these declarations in front of a delegation from the EU, then adding that the entire project of revitalization of the district would cost €200 million but that city hall had only €50 million—with the implication that city hall would need even more funds from the EU to finalize their projects in the district.[54] A year later, in May 2006, city hall's chief architect noted that "over forty families had been evicted. It was done in a civilized manner and no uprising occurred. People understood that they could no longer live there." But the local mayor (of the third city sector, which includes the Old Town) admitted that "the eviction had not yet taken place. There are 162 families, approximately 200 people, whom we have to relocate." Moreover, one of the shop owners living in the district clarified that "a few families had been taken out, but they returned during the night, and they continue to live in the same state-owned houses."[55]

Architect Ileana Hapenciuc (2007, 149) questioned whether such evictions ever took place, noting that despite all the talk, no photos of real evictions were published in the newspapers, nor did other residents of the district witness such removals. If the authorities were to be believed that thousands of squatters lived in the district illegally, their forced expulsions would not have occurred in silence. Hapenciuc argued that the administration's incessant talk about evictions was just a way to signal that they were taking seriously their promise to "clean" the city of the squatters, while practically doing very little (149).

But the authorities also talked incessantly about this topic in order to acquire more housing, allegedly to be distributed to all of the people who would be evacuated from the Old Town. Initially, in October 2006, Mayor Videanu declared that city hall would acquire two hundred apartments.[56] A few months later, in January 2007, the local authorities declared that they would acquire as many apartments as they needed to relocate the evacuees.[57] Theoretically, this housing was to be distributed to all people who were evicted from their Old Town residences. These categories included not only squatters who occupied the abandoned houses but also the state tenants in buildings that had been won back by the former pre-1945 owners, as well as those residents who had bought their apartments via law 112/1995 but then lost them through the new restitution law (10/2001).

However, despite their public promises, the authorities were much less generous—not just to the people evicted from the Old Town but to many other poor people living in Bucharest who could not pay the high prices on the real estate market and petitioned city hall for social housing. As anthropologist and urban activist Miruna Tîrcă discovered, in 2008 Bucharest's city hall had registered 44,000 requests for social housing, but by 2012, the number of such requests dropped to 15,000; as Tîrcă noted, the remaining 29,000 housing petitions "magically disappeared, because they definitely had not been solved."[58] In the case of the Old Town, city hall formed a special commission to figure out the situation of those state tenants or owners who had been evicted via the application of law 10/2001 (the pre-1945 owners having regained their ownership in court). However, for some of these people, it took almost ten years between the time they had received the eviction order and the date when they received a house from city hall.[59] Moreover, by 2008, many more others (90 out of a total 105 families) received no housing because they could not provide all of the necessary documentation.[60]

The dire situation of many of these people is captured by an online comment titled, "The real estate mafia exists because the laws are made with an eye to not being implemented."[61] The comment read:

> If you are a state tenant, and you go to the housing office of the "Historic Center" to ask if the house has been reclaimed by the former owner, you are told: "We don't know." But if you have a "connection" [if you know somebody], you do find out if it has or not has been [reclaimed]. There are so many rumors, that they would move us out and then that they would no longer do so. We are thrown to the fates. . . . The mayors pretend they do not hear our complaints. If you go to ask for a hearing, they talk to you in a dismissive tone [*ţi se vorbeşte la mişto*], and anyway, the mayor would never grant you a hearing.

In sum, the authorities used the remaking of the district's infrastructure not only to assert their control over the public space but also to acquire more financial traction. City officials called on the Old Town's European history to transform it into the city's "historic center"—a justification to request more and more funds from the EU to make Bucharest into a European capital. They invoked the Old Town's heritage value to detach the place from its current people, especially the illegal residents, and thus justify their eviction while maintaining a stronghold on the houses whose property title was still uncertain. At the same time, they used the traffic ban and the infrastructural overhaul for two purposes. The first one was more obvious: The city officials signaled their power over public space by simultaneously launching construction works on multiple streets of the Old Town and by delaying the reparations by years. They transformed the Old Town into a massive construction site in the middle of the city, without taking into consideration its residents' needs and complaints. Between 2006 and 2010, the streets remained closed to traffic, with the pavements cracked wide open and left as such for months, waiting for workers to begin changing the pipes and electricity lines. Ongoing debates among the municipality and the contractors led to prolonged periods of stagnation. The long, deep crevasses of what used to be the streets started being used as impromptu garbage dumps.

The second purpose derived from the first: by having the entire district look like a war zone, with streets transformed for years into trenches, accumulating snow, water, and garbage, the real estate value of the houses on those streets plummeted. Even though the new law (10/2001) should have spurred the houses' former owners to sue the state and pursue their restitution, the dire conditions in the district made them less interested in doing so. Thus, some of these houses remained "public property"—that is, under the administration of city hall. Meanwhile, the same city hall used this situation to acquire even more real estate on the justification that they needed extra housing to provide for those families to be evicted from the Old Town—evictions that the city officials pursued only partially but about which they talked extensively in an attempt to signal that they were proponents of property restitutions.

City hall's privatization of the district by means of infrastructure overhaul had another goal as well: to lessen local authorities' responsibility not only toward the buildings but also toward the state tenants who continued to live in the district. While many of the buildings had been restituted to their pre-1945 owners or to those who bought out the original owners' property rights (*drepturile succesorale*), there were still some buildings that remained legally in limbo.[62] Yet city hall kept pretending that the restitution process had been completed, that the buildings of the district were exclusively privately owned, and therefore that the municipal authorities were no longer responsible for the deteriorated state of some of the buildings. City hall thus relied on a circular logic that made these poor residents more and more invisible: while they continued to charge these tenants (state-subsidized) rent, local authorities pretended that they no longer administered buildings in the district. But the marginalization of these people occurred not just through the tangible ruination of their homes. Their systematic erasure of their rights has occurred also through the erasure of data—specifically, data about the housing reserves and the social structure of the Old Town.

Data Erasure as Property Appropriation

Data about the Old Town—the exact number of residents, of the privately owned houses, and those that are still owned by the local administration—are almost impossible to find.[63] During my fieldwork in summer 2016, I knocked on doors of several city institutions and filed written requests to meet with city officials—requests that caused a stir in the public office of the main city hall, with civil servants telling me that they had no category in their database to register my request, because, they said, the functionaries in city hall that I would have liked to talk to did not offer public audiences. After multiple encounters—ranging from polite refusals to more obvious eye-rolling and raised voices such as from a civil servant who asked me, "Who do you think you are to ask for such information?"—I gave up.

Eventually, I was lucky enough to find some official quantitative data only courtesy of Ovidiu, an urban geographer who had managed to gain access to some internal information from the institution in charge of state-owned housing (Direcția Generală a Administrației Fondului Imobiliar, DGAFI). However, when I saw the data, I became even more confused. Here is the information about the number of residents before 1989 and the more recent data (received from Ovidiu) about households in the Old Town district:

	1970	2000	2000–2002	2004	2009
Housing units	1,310 families/ 2,980 residents	478 housing units	40 restituted + 438	438	631
Source	ANIM (1988)	DGAFI	DGAFI	DGAFI	DGAFI

The radical discrepancies between the years could signal two things: either that the housing units were far more crowded in 1970, with more than two families occupying one housing unit, or that those households had "disappeared" from the state housing fund's documentation before 2000 (and very likely after 1989). I especially could not figure out how, following this "disappearance," within five years two hundred more housing units suddenly "appeared" in the housing data. Ovidiu helped me understand the politics of this peculiar bureaucratic magic.

According to him, those in charge of the state housing reserves were "more powerful than the Romanian government."[64] Through his previous work, he could see the complex mechanisms through which politicians and their acolytes controlled the housing reserves still owned by the state. They exploited a legislative jungle in which various layers of legislation intermingled, and made "magic" happen. This is how Ovidiu explained the maneuvers behind the disappearance of a part of those reserves:

> On January 1, 2009, DGAFI Bucureşti [the public institution controlling the housing reserves owned by the state] had twelve thousand housing units. Some of them were units that could not be included in clear categories; they were neither low-income public housing nor accommodation for government personnel. They called them "second-movement" houses [*case la mişcarea a doua*]. These were a combination of formerly nationalized housing that had never been reclaimed by the former owners or their heirs, and other buildings whose tenants had died and that the state did not know what to do with. Those houses could be rented again but also could be kept as a hidden reserve because they did not have a specific category. Only those who have been in control [*cei care au fost la butoane*] for the last twenty years knew which were the "second-movement" houses: which ones had not been reclaimed, which were not rented, and which could be sold.
>
> So, say you're a boss in a political party and you want to buy a house— or two, or three—in a central area of Bucharest. You contact someone inside the system who knows which houses are neither occupied nor reclaimed. You move in first as a tenant paying rent to the state, and because law 85/1992 is still valid [the law regulating the selling of state-owned housing, which privileges the current tenant over other potential buyers], you can request to buy the property. It doesn't matter if you have another three houses in Bucharest and two in Paris; you can buy this house according to law 85/1992—that is, dirt cheap [at the prices that the house was evaluated at in 1992].[65] You can buy a

house in the city center for ten thousand euros, which in a few years you can sell for a million euros. . . .

What happened to those twelve thousand housing units from 2009? There are now [May 2016] only 4,231! They sold them. And when the government asked DGAFI to report on the current reserves, they answered that those are the "convenient housing"! They invented a category that means nothing. In other words, they said, "We respect the laws that we find convenient, whenever we find them convenient!"[66]

Ovidiu told me this story about the secret map of housing in Bucharest in response to my anecdote about my frustrated efforts to obtain data about the Old Town. His story was confirmed by a journalistic investigation, though the numbers do not match.[67] Still, the discrepancy of the numbers revealed that an apparent lack of logic was in fact the logic of the system: that erasure and confusion were part and parcel of the political mechanism of conserving power by denying access to knowledge. Ruxandra was the one who put me in contact with Ovidiu. She was also part of that conversation, and after Ovidiu finished his story, she could not help but chuckle at me: "And you show up out of nowhere and ask, 'Hey, city hall, where do you have your housing reserves and how many of them are occupied?' Ha, ha, ha!"

The invisibility of a portion of state housing—such as those in the "second-movement" category—was part of a broader phenomenon of condensing or stretching value according to distinct political agendas and accompanying economic interests. In her work on the restitution of agricultural land in post-1990 Transylvania, Katherine Verdery (2003) wrote about the "vanishing hectare," an amount of land that kept disappearing from the official lists even though villagers knew exactly where their former property lay before the communist state forcefully incorporated it into the collective farms. Such forms of vanishing or disappearance were the extreme cases in a process of the strategic devaluation of resources that could not be easily moved, such as housing and land. Through this process, the immense wealth of the former communist regime became devalued, only to be later partitioned and sold for peanuts to the former apparatchiks turned into the entrepreneurs of the transition.

Local authorities, powerful politicians, and real estate agents knew that the central location of the Old Town constituted wealth in the making because it could become much more profitable if used for new, higher buildings. Government officials playing hide-and-seek with state-owned housing in the area were not an exception. On the contrary, they were among the key players in a secret game available only to the chosen few in postcommunist Romania: the game of rendering value invisible as a means to retain it and eventually own it.

Ruination as Eroded Trust

Carmen was smoking a cigarette, looking away from me. She said, "Every time it rains, small pieces from the ceiling begin to fall off. Everything is old here!" She paused for a second, turned to me, and emphasized, "Too old!" She continued, "City hall kept telling us that they would move us somewhere else. But if they want to evict us, they should give us compensation, right? A year or so ago, there had been talk about some apartment buildings where the mayor planned to relocate us. Then I saw those apartment buildings on TV—they were selling them for €30,000 each!"

When does old become *too* old? Carmen hinted to a much broader gap; the gap between "old" and "too old" was a gap between an old house still valued as an architectural monument and a run-down building that was no longer safe for anyone to call it home. It was a radical threshold between beauty and doom, between life and death. When I talked to her on a sunny Saturday morning in May 2016, in front of her room in a dilapidated building in the Old Town, there was a calm detachment in Carmen's voice; she no longer believed that anyone would ever come to rescue this building and its tenants from imminent decay.[68]

I asked Carmen if I could talk to someone older who lived there, and she suggested that I try the building administrator on the second floor. I knocked on his door, but his wife told me that the administrator was out. She had no time for me and closed her door. In the narrow hallway, I saw a woman smoking a cigarette and I went to talk to her. She looked at me with suspicion and asked me if I was from a TV station or a newspaper. I told her I was doing research about the Old Town and asked her how long she had been living in the building. She answered indirectly, saying that her husband had been living there since he was seven—and when he appeared for a second in the door, he looked to be in his midforties. She did not want to tell me her name, but she shared her woes with me.

I noticed that the hallway near her door was painted in a different color than the rest of the corridor and asked her if she had done it herself. Yes, she said, she had painted it, but now she regretted it because no one cared. "You want to make your own home beautiful, but the hallway? Why would I invest in the hallway? Are we the owners? City hall is the owner, but they do nothing." And then she added, looking straight at me with angry intensity, "We work, too, you know. We work very hard!" (*"Muncim pe brânci!"*). She said that they paid a monthly rent of "one million for two rooms" (the equivalent of approximately $30). However, if they could not pay on time and found themselves three months behind in rent, they had to pay a month extra. I asked her if she had

Fig. 5.2. The debris of the building that collapsed in summer 2013. Photo by Alex Iacob, May 2013.

tried to ask the authorities to do repairs. She shrugged and said, "The business owners [of the bars in the district] fixed the facades so the ceiling would not fall on their customers. Our client, our patron! But here? Who do you think would come? No one. They will come only when we are all under the ground." She grew angry when she started talking about the state; the state ignored them, she said, even though they were legal tenants who tried to pay the rent on time. She was right to be angry: no repairs had been done in years. It is only when the tenants were "under the ground," as she put it, when the house would have fallen down and killed everyone that the authorities would bother to come to the site.

Carmen had already told me she often saw rats running across the court-yard from another house across the street. That house, she said, had collapsed a year or so ago. Fortunately, no one had died; the squatters who had been living there had been evicted a few months earlier. When I did an online search to find out more about that building's collapse, I learned that the incident had occurred in May 2013—three years before our talk.[69] Carmen's comment revealed how current the event still felt for her. The other house had also been owned by the state. But when it collapsed, the authorities did not hurry to clean up the site. Debris was left on the street for more than a month. This was not just a sign of the authorities' lack of concern. It was also a veiled warning, one that the other tenants in similarly decrepit buildings easily grasped: that the officials would neither protect them nor guarantee their safety.

In May 2016, the building where Carmen lived was home to thirty families, out of which around twenty-five were legal state tenants. In the neoliberal logic that measures the value of a person by how much she or he can afford to pay for their home, such people were as invisible to the state as their meager rent, which would barely pay for dinner in a chic restaurant a few blocks down on the same street. When Carmen retorted that she got nothing from the state, she raised a broader question: To what extent can a place that is no longer safe be called "home"? How, and for how long, can one live there and attempt to maintain a sense of dignity when, in exchange for their monthly rent, they receive uncertainty on a daily basis? These people were not squatters but legal tenants. In principle, the state, as the landlord, should guarantee them proper living conditions and, obviously, safety under their own roofs. But Carmen and the other tenants had given up the hope that the authorities would eventually improve their living conditions. In fact, the state has been actively ignoring their complaints in an attempt to pressure them, indirectly, to move out.

In the case of Carmen and her neighbors, the state has won half the battle; the other half is for local authorities to wait until the building becomes so degraded that people will truly begin to fear for their lives and will eventually seek shelter elsewhere. As Carmen said, "The owner [who continues to be in litigation with the state about the building] keeps sending letters from America, telling us that she does not guarantee for our lives. The state did not bother to even send such letters."[70] These people cannot afford life insurance, let alone have the means to launch costly litigation against the state if something happened to one or more of them. Once they move out, the state can then sell the property at a "special" price to a real estate investor who already won the favors of a well-placed politician, who will then intervene with the authorities to perfect the deal. Despite the special status of the historic district as a protected area, the investor will find a shrewd architect who knows how to circumvent the building standards and regulations of protected areas. In a few years, the ruined historic monument will be replaced with a new commercial building, where the monthly rent for one single apartment will be much higher than what all of the thirty families can afford to pay as tenants of social housing.[71]

Starting with late 2000s, the local officials have used the strategic ruination of the Old Town to promote and naturalize an implicit link between privatization and heritage in which heritage was associated only with privately owned buildings and presented as a privilege for those who could afford it. In the Old

Fig. 5.3. A semiruined building in the Old Town, whose legal status was uncertain in 2016 but which the state continued to exploit as subsidized housing for poor tenants. Photo by author, May 2016.

Town, heritage became the propriety of property, whereas ruination came to act as its counterpart; those who could not afford to own were implicitly seen as agents of ruination. However, while the poor were portrayed as those responsible for ruination, they were in fact its targets.

I approach ruination as a tangible political act meant to undermine what Lefebvre (1968) called the right to the city: the political recognition of one's ability to inhabit urban space and use it according to his or her particular needs. A focus on ruination offers us a unique perspective on state making and the appropriation of political power. Noting that imperial projects are "processes of ongoing ruination," Ann Stoler (2013, 11) has urged us to consider its multiple meanings: "Ruination is an ambiguous term, being an act of ruining, a condition of being ruined, and a cause of it. Ruination is an act perpetrated, a condition to which one is subject, and a cause of loss" (11). Stoler thus emphasizes that ruination encompasses both a passive state of affairs and a planned action, and that ambiguity could be further manipulated. She notes that some actors could actively engage in destruction while pretending that ruin is something that "just happens" or has already happened. In other words, by appearing to be a mere by-product of an already completed act, ruination can also conceal the perpetrator of an act of destruction. Ruination is then a prerogative of power. An entity (a corporation, a state group, or a powerful individual) engages in ruination not just to signal threat but to also present it in a positive manner: as a necessary act of change, usually as a prerequisite for a promised future of progress, social order, or wealth.

In the Old Town, the local authorities' efforts to catalyze the ruination of the historic buildings, such as the one inhabited by Carmen and her neighbors, were meant to split asunder the social structure of the district. They heightened residents' uncertainty about their homes, their legal status, and the safety of their own lives. They made ruination appear as a tangible sign and a direct consequence of an uncertain ownership status. Carmen and the other poor tenants have become second-class citizens whose lives were increasingly inconsequential for state officials while their homes have turned into dangerous places. Under these circumstances, the state promoted property ownership as a necessary condition for caring for the historic buildings and thus considering them heritage. The policies adopted by Bucharest's officials implicitly reinforced a view that only an owner could recognize and protect heritage and, by doing so, further signal that she or he could be viewed as a full citizen, someone completely immersed in society's networks of rights and obligations. Within this logic of patrimonialization-as-privatization, whoever could not own and assume responsibility for the heritage quality of an old building was no longer a full citizen and thus became inconsequential to the state.

Corruption as Destruction and Death

The dilapidated building where Carmen lives is not an isolated case in the Old Town. The authorities have been fully aware that the Old Town has the highest concentration of high-risk buildings. In June 2016, city hall made public the list of historic buildings in Bucharest that experts marked as being most likely to collapse during a more powerful earthquake. Out of 365 buildings included in this category, 181 of them were considered to be a "public threat," a source of major danger (one of these buildings was the house where Carmen and her neighbors lived).[72] In principle, all of these sites should be visibly marked with a red dot, but very few of the buildings display the sign. More than a third of these "public threat" buildings (a total of 53) are located in the relatively narrow perimeter of the Old Town, and a few cases include many adjacent buildings on the same street, thus making large portions of the street potentially threatening to pedestrians.[73] But many of the fun-seeking tourists and locals filling up the hundreds of clubs and cafés don't even know that they are walking on an architectural minefield. Up to early 2016, despite rising pressures from the public and even with the government allocating special funds for these buildings' consolidation, city hall continued to invoke excuses and postpone any repairs.[74] It took a collective tragedy for local officials to decide to do something—but even then, they did not accomplish much.

When I was in Bucharest in summer 2016, I encountered many signs on the walls of the older buildings in downtown Bucharest that read, "Caution! Falling plaster!" I did not know what to make of them. During the previous summer, in 2015, I had seen no such signs. When I asked my host, a real estate dealer, he told me that they were indeed new. They had appeared at the beginning of 2016 as part of a broader campaign launched by city hall to make the public aware of the potential danger of the "red dot" buildings. The campaign was, in fact, a response to a tragedy that had taken place in October 2015: firecrackers were set off during a rock concert in a small, enclosed space, a warehouse transformed into a club whose interior had been coated with highly inflammable plaster. The building was engulfed almost instantly in an enormous fire. The tragedy, now known as Colectiv after the name of the club, took the lives of sixty-four people and left another two hundred gravely injured. The fire killed and seriously injured more than two hundred people, but a year after the tragedy, thirteen others died not because of their burns but because they contracted infections in hospitals that were not properly sanitized.[75]

Colectiv only made more visible the depth of the corruption of Romania's political system. After Colectiv, the entire country reacted with an unprecedented mobilization to help the wounded by donating blood, money, and time.

Fig. 5.4. Urban contrasts. Derelict house covered by a canvas with nostalgic images of interwar Bucharest. The Old Town. Photo by author, May 2016.

Fig. 5.5. "Red dot" building in the center of Bucharest (not in the Old Town). Photo by author, May 2016.

But they did more than that; they turned to the streets to voice their collective rage and loathing against a state that proved to be murderous. It was this state that had indulged in and encouraged the widespread corruption that had led the club's owners—among so many others—to illegally use cheap, flammable construction materials. Until then, officials had suffered no legal consequences for their greed. But a few weeks after Colectiv, the massive protests that took place all across the country brought down the Social Democratic government.

As a result, Bucharest's authorities imposed stricter regulations on commercial spaces (each club, bar, and restaurant had to have several entries and fire escapes and were allowed to stay open only if they were in new or recently consolidated buildings). If such buildings were not structurally sound, they were no longer allowed to host commercial activities. The new laws caused many shops on some of the largest boulevards in Bucharest to close down and relocate. My host and his friends complained about how these new regulations directly hit many of the business owners, forcing them to go bankrupt.

A simple walk through the Old Town, however, showed that the situation was not so dire. It turned out that the clubs and pubs in the district had reopened just a few weeks after the new regulations. Less than a week after Colectiv, only

Fig. 5.6. Interior staircase with garbage. A courtyard in the Old Town. Photo by author, May 2016.

ten of a hundred and thirty clubs in the Old Town had completely or partially closed.[76] It would have been practically impossible for most of them to complete the necessary structural repairs on all of the "red dot" buildings in such a short time—given that fifty-three of the buildings considered to be "public hazards" are located in the district. In fact, in summer 2016, the Old Town's nightlife was as vibrant as ever; restaurant and pub patios were completely packed—and the colorful facades belied the structural dangers of the teetering old buildings still awaiting structural rehabilitation. Paradoxically, the tourists and the middle-class customers seemed to emulate the strategic disregard that the state itself has shown toward the buildings and their residents. Being either unaware of or disbelieving the precarious structural conditions of these buildings, this well-dressed clientele enjoyed each other's company and did not seem to give the slightest thought to a potential danger.

I would actually attempt to go even further and suggest that in the Old Town, ruination was not just a means to gentrification but was also a quintessential part of it. Ruination has, in fact, been commodified. The contrast between the run-down houses and the completely renovated ones has been the driving force behind the transformation of the district into what a major real estate retailer assessed as "the major entertainment area in Bucharest," a place that in 2016 has generated the second highest revenues in the entire city.[77] The ruination and abjection that authorities initially employed as a means to force the state tenants to move out of the district have been upended by the private investors. They started selling it—by naming their locales "Vintage," "La Ruine" (At the ruins), "Vintage Deco," "Sinners," and so on.

Writing about post-Katrina New Orleans, anthropologist Shannon Dawdy (2016) saw the city's patina as a lacquer of histories, genealogies, and connections captured by and distilled in the unique look of old objects. She approached patina as both an affective and a material sign and medium of connection, one that brought New Orleanians together despite class and racial hierarchies, helped them to forge new bonds based on their love of old things and buildings, and gave them a proud sense of place and belonging grounded in a cosmopolitan history. In Dawdy's view, the bonds forged by locals' love of patina have also signaled the defiance and resilience of a society that felt increasingly marginalized politically and economically (with Hurricane Katrina being only one in a series of waves of collapse and revival).

In Bucharest, only a relatively small group of people have shared any love for the run-down antique buildings: people who see historic preservation as a form of political and cultural dissent. Indeed, what initially emerged in the late 2000s as a local association bringing together people who cared about the preservation of Bucharest's historic buildings, has transformed by 2016 into a

Fig. 5.7. Ruins next to a chic boutique. The Old Town. Photo by author, May 2016.

political party.[78] Many other inhabitants of the city, however, have regarded the wrinkled facades of the same buildings as becoming ever more ominous. With their signs more or less visibly placed on the walls to notify passersby that plaster may be falling, the "red dot" buildings now rhyme with danger. They heighten a sense of uncertainty among city dwellers and generate a pervasive wariness about a political system that seems unable to control the situation or that simply does not care. Here is how a well-known actor described his view of contemporary Bucharest: "We are not well in this city. Attention, a basic human feature, is overwhelmed. Collaboration is vitiated. Conviviality is risked. The guiding principle becomes circumspection. What kind of life are we living in this city, when you step off one sidewalk without knowing whether you will make it safely to next one? When you have to breathe in dust pouring on you from everywhere? Does it not feel like a failure? I think it does" (Iureş 2016, 14).

Juxtaposed with luxurious boutiques and chic cafés, the Old Town's decrepit buildings and graffiti, and especially the fragments of barely standing walls, have a powerful sensorial effect. By appearing simultaneously as starkly new and profoundly ruined, the district's aesthetic zero-sum cancels out its temporality and its history. People come and go all the time in a place that has become a nonplace (Auge 1995), characterized by high traffic, a sense of urgency, and a continuous, intense mobility. Commenting on how the Old Town works today, a former entrepreneur and resident of the district said, "Businesses do not last long. [They] appear and disappear, more than half of them in less than six months. It is a continuous process of bankruptcy and failure."[79]

But this effect is not solely aesthetic or affective. These heightened contrasts—freshness coexisting with morbidity, and wealth being made, literally, right next to waste—have a more important political function. Ruins next to luxury induce a sort of visual instability that percolates not just other senses but also reason. These contrasts have become a tangible symbol of the cacophonous, haphazard ways in which the state institutions work (or rather do not work). At the same time, the same contrasts visually capture the profound split between the Romanian state and its people—the profound disenchantment of a growing part of the population with a state that has abandoned them.

Conclusion

The late 2000s transformation of the Old Town into the historic center of a European capital aimed to cater to the aesthetic sensibilities of a neoliberal middle class. It entailed a radical intervention into the ways the Old Town had previously functioned as a place; as a complex node of relations, as a lively entanglement of affective dispositions and rhythms of living and working. If city leaders began by changing the tangible infrastructure, in the form of sewers, pipes, and utility networks, their end goal was to intervene in the district's social infrastructure. They wanted to bring in wealthier residents, owners who would honor "their obligations," as Mayor Băsescu put it, real estate entrepreneurs who viewed the new infrastructure as a means for rapid enrichment. But for these people to come in, others had been removed—either by direct eviction, as with the squatters, or through bankruptcy, as with some of the owners of cafés, bookshops, repair shops, and other small businesses. The artificial "freezing" of the commercial and social life of the district during the infrastructural overhaul of the mid-2000s enabled the new municipal administration to gain control over not only the district's commercial spaces but also the houses whose legal status remained uncertain. Some of these houses were then further made "invisible" through shrewd manipulations of data, allowing people within the system to eventually buy them because no one else knew of their existence.

Fig. 5.8. Retired man selling secondhand books in the Old Town. The dignified way in which he tried to make ends meet, wearing a suit and selling books, contrasted with the widespread corruption of the place. Photo by author, May 2016.

The multiple forms of erasures discussed in this chapter reveal a state that has increasingly abandoned those citizens whom it deemed to be too poor to be "European." Anthropologists Jennifer Shaw and Darren Byler (2016) have argued that millennial capitalism has promoted "a political logic of radical individuality, self-responsibility, and independence." This logic, they note, has encouraged those enchanted by these ideals to "see precarity as a result of moral failures of individuals, masking the power relations and structural violence embedded in our global political economy." Writing about Bucharest's homeless and low-class residents in late 2000s, Bruce O'Neill (2017) has shown how boredom has emerged as an all-pervasive sentiment shared by those left on the margins of the neoliberal economy. As an unwelcome stillness of senses and a profound sense of lacking agency, O'Neill argues, boredom becomes a circular mechanism of fundamental inaction in which the city's most vulnerable population finds itself caught and thus rendered further invisible. The analysis that I have offered in this chapter complements O'Neill's arguments by showing how ruination has become an overt strategy of Romania's political apparatus (both the central and local authorities) to signal power—by furthering class divides, by rendering the poor invisible, and by promoting individualism as a new moral ideal. The ruined buildings have further ruined social relations—the fine fabric of trust that a functional polity should be able to weave and maintain among its subjects and institutions. The decaying buildings do not just signal but also deepen the already rampant individualism that both state institutions and corporations have already enabled.

In 2016, according to EU official statistics, more than one third of Romania's population (37.5%, or 7.5 million people) was considered to be at the risk of poverty or social exclusion.[80] Carmen and her neighbor talking bitterly about the state abandoning them, the old woman carrying fifty pounds of water up some ancient stairs are among these people. Beyond their promises of rapid privatization, state authorities sold off their responsibility, disparaging the social contract between them and their constituents, and erasing any sense of trust the public might have had in state institutions. The recent transformation of the Old Town into an "urban brand," a space of commerce and consumption, and less of a community and conviviality, thus becomes a magnifying glass onto the workings of a ruthless state.

This chapter thus explored the full gamut of erasures practiced by the twenty-first-century Romanian state—not only of houses but also of social relations, of empathy, of connection, and of community. The state's willful neglect of the Old Town's aging buildings has perpetuated and heightened the ruination of human connections and the crystallization of social difference. The privatization of the city, as revealed by the social and infrastructural overhaul of the Old Town, went hand in hand with a strategic ruination not only of the old buildings but also of their residents' sense of hope, safety, and ability to imagine a future.

Notes

1. "Anca," interview, June 1, 2016. The street on which Anca and Carmen live borders the area of the Old Town that is exclusively meant for pedestrian traffic.

2. "Setul naţional de indicatori de incluziune socială corespunzători pentru anul 2014," Ministerul Muncii, Familiei, Protecţiei Sociale şi Persoanelor Vârstnice, 2015, http://www .mmuncii.ro/j33/images/Documente/2014/2015-07-27_Indicatori_2014.pdf, p. 34.

3. Between 1990 and 2000, the nonreimbursable credits from the European Commission to Romania reached a total of €1.4 million. Starting in 2000, the financial aid went above €600 million per year. "Asistenţa financiară nerambursabilă acordată României de Uniunea Europeană prin programele Phare," Ministerul Integrării Europene, June 2001, http://www .cdep.ro/interpel/2001/r93A.pdf.

4. Report showing an increasing trend in valuing institutions such as the EU and NATO. "Valorile românilor," Institutul de Cercetare a Calităţii Vieţii, July 5, 2009, http://www.iccv .ro/valori/newsletter/NLVR_NO_5.pdf.

5. "Program de dezvoltare a municipiului Bucureşti, 2000–2008," 6–7.

6. The national dailies of that time (2000–2004) covered extensively the open fight between Traian Băsescu and Adrian Năstase, the then prime minister leading the Social Democratic government. Between 2000 and 2004, Bucharest's prefect, the local representative of the government, contested in court one hundred decisions of the general mayor (Băsescu). In turn, the Băsescu-led city hall opened two hundred litigations to challenge in court the decisions of the local council (dominated by local mayors loyal to the Social Democratic government). "Program de dezvoltare a municipiului Bucureşti, 2000–2008," 19.

7. "Program de dezvoltare," 7.

8. Elena Pârvu, "Factura la întreţinere, egală cu pensia," *Adevărul*, October 17, 2005, 1, 3.

9. Georgiana Baciu, "Peste 10% din bucureşteni nu vor căldură," *Adevărul*, October 17, 2005, 3.

10. "Locuitorii din Ferentari vor fi branşati la curent," *Adevărul*, November 16, 2006. Eventually, a Bucharest millionaire stepped in and promised on live TV to pay the electric bill of 13 billion lei (equivalent of $520,000), which he did. A day after the protests, the mayor of the fifth sector promised another €125,000 to pay for the reconnection of the five apartment buildings to the electric grid. I could not find more information about what happened afterward.

11. "Locuitorii," *Adevărul*, November 16, 2006.

12. Sociologist Ruth Glass (1964) coined the term *gentrification* to describe the move of the gentry (middle and upper class) into London's lower-class neighborhoods, which changed the local patterns of living and the real estate prices, making impossible for the original residents to keep their homes. Neil Smith (2002) captured the duality of this process when he defined *gentrification* as "discrete double-faced process combining the penetration of middle-class and upper-middle-class population to poorer-yet-exotic neighborhoods followed by the displacement of the original residents" (Smith in Monterescu 2015, 145).

This Janus-faced dimension of gentrification—its promise for betterment that hides the implicit exclusion of other groups—has informed a wealth of studies highlighting the mutual coproduction of space and class.

13. AINMI, file 2159/1962–1970.

14. "Atlasul Centrului Istoric al orașului București. Asociații ale comunității din Curtea Veche," 2001, 39. Courtesy of Asociația de tranziție urbană (ATU).

15. "Atlasul Centrului Istoric," 4.

16. "Atlasul Centrului Istoric," 4.

17. "Atlasul Centrului Istoric," 5.

18. Conversation, May 18, 2016.

19. Loredana Voiculescu, "Apa Nova a cerut și a primit," *Gândul*, October 7, 2015, https://www.gandul.info/financiar/apa-nova-a-cerut-si-a-primit-de-14-ori-ajustari-tarifare -extraordinare-cum-au-platit-bucurestenii-apa-mai-scumpa-pentru-refacerea-balantei -financiare-a-companiei-14802405.

20. Conversation, May 18, 2016.

21. "Program de dezvoltare a municipiului București, 2000–2008," 8.

22. "30,000 de familii ar putea fi aruncate in stradă," *Adevărul*, September 2, 2002.

23. "30,000 de familii," *Adevărul*, September 2, 2002.

24. Conversation with Radu Miclescu, Botoșani, April 2010.

25. Elena Damian is the real name of one of the victims of the real estate transactions that have involved public officials of Bucharest's city hall. Ionuț Stănescu, "Orașul subteran: profit de 8.600 %, din afaceri cu terenurile statului român," Rise Project, February 15, 2017, https://www.riseproject.ro/articol/profit-de-8-600-la-suta-din-afaceri-cu-terenurile-statului -roman/. (Rise Project is a group of freelance journalists with an active anticorruption agenda.)

26. Ionuț Stănescu, "Orașul subteran."

27. Interview, Ruxandra, May 18, 2016.

28. *Gardianul*, October 26, 2002 and *Evenimentul Zilei*, August 5 and 14, 2002, cited in Stan (2006, 205).

29. "Planul de dezvoltare al municipiului Bucuresti, 2000–2008," 19.

30. Gabriela Ștefan, "Debandada din Arhiva Tribunalului București," *Adevărul*, April 1, 2002.

31. Dan Cărbunariu, "O funcționară a Ministerului Finanțelor s-a apucat să ronțăie documente compromițătoare," *Adevărul*, February 26, 2002.

32. Băsescu interviewed by *Revista 22*, "Corupția poate fi stopată numai de șefii de partide," January 7, 2002, http://revista22online.ro/19/.html.

33. Băsescu interviewed by *Revista 22*, January 7, 2002.

34. A few months after it passed law 10/2001, the government modified the law with an executive order (59/2001). The new order extended by a year the time in which the former tenants could challenge restitution decisions in court. As Lavinia Stan (2006, 196) argued, this stipulation was perceived by the public as a further centralization of power.

35. Băsescu interviewed by *Revista 22*, January 7, 2002.

36. "Program de dezvoltare al municipiului Bucuresti, 2000–2008."

37. "Program de dezvoltare al municipiului Bucuresti, 2000–2008."

38. Băsescu interviewed by *Revista 22*, May 19, 2004.

39. Băsescu interviewed by *Revista 22*, May 19, 2004.

40. "Romania: Country Reports on Human Rights Practices," US State Department, March 4, 2002, https://www.state.gov/j/drl/rls/hrrpt/2001/eur/8327.htm.

41. "Romania," US State Department.

42. "Piedone vrea să evacueze rromii aciuați în sectorul 6," *Adevărul*, April 17, 2002.

43. "Atelajele romilor, confiscate de autoritățile locale," *România Liberă*, July 19, 2002.

44. "Traian Băsescu ridică chioşcurile fără autorizație," *Capital*, July 30, 2000.

45. Liana Ionescu, "Traian Băsescu decide eliminarea comercianților stradali din București," Radio Europa Liberă, July 21, 2010, http://www.europalibera.org/a/2105297.html.

46. "Reabilitarea centrului istoric va începe în această vară," *România Liberă*, May 17, 2005.

47. "Şantierul din centrul istoric va fi demarat în octombrie," *România Liberă*, September 8, 2006.

48. "Roboții au intrat pe țevile centrului istoric," *România Liberă*, January 10, 2007.

49. Architect Aurelian Trişcu, interview, April 14, 2008, Bucharest.

50. Trudy Boos, "Lipscani: 'Closed,'" *Vivid*, October 2005.

51. Interview, May 30, 2016, Bucharest.

52. "Comercianții de pe Lipscani," *Adevărul*, February 16, 2006.

53. Interview with Irina Prodan, Pro Patrimonio, Bucharest, October 12, 2007.

54. "Din 5,000 de familii care stau illegal, au fost evacuate 37," *Adevărul*, July 8, 2005.

55. Luminița Pârvu, "Pata neagră din centrul Bucureştiului," Hotnews.ro, May 7, 2006, http://www.hotnews.ro/stiri-arhiva-1179800-pata-neagra-din-centrul-bucurestiului.htm.

56. "Apartamente pentru evacuații din centrul istoric," *România Liberă*, October 12, 2006.

57. Cristina Boiangiu, "Locuințe pentru persoanele expropriate şi evacuate," *România Liberă*, January 22, 2007.

58. Miruna Tîrcă, "Realități urbane la un pas de noi," Laboratorul Urban, April 5, 2014, https://laboratorul-urban.blogspot.com/2014/04/.

59. A family of six had received the eviction notification in 1998, three other families in 2000, one in 2002, two in 2005, two in 2006, and two in 2008. All of them received social housing only in 2009. "Diagrama locuințelor sociale repartizate familiilor evacuate sau în curs de evacuare din imobilele retrocedate în natură foştilor proprietari, situate în Zona Pilot A din Centrul Istoric," Primăria Municipiului București, February 16, 2009, http://www.pmb .ro/institutii/primaria/directii/directia_patrimoniu/docs/2008/diagrama_locuinte_sociale .pdf.

60. "Situația privind dosarele transmise de Primăria sectorului 3, pentru persoanele evacuate sau în curs de evacuare din Zona Pilot a Centrului Istoric în vederea repartizării locuințelor sociale," Primăria Municipiului București, 2008, http://www.pmb.ro/institutii /primaria/directii/directia_patrimoniu/docs/2008/anexa1.pdf.

61. *Gândul*, February 21, 2008, http://www2.gandul.info/stiri/mafia-imobiliara-va-exista -atat-timp-cat-legile-sunt-facute-sa-nu-fie-aplicate-2405676.

62. In 2004, Băsescu ran for the second term as a general mayor—which he won, but then he also won the presidential elections a few months later. When asked by a journalist about the situation of the Old Town, he replied that "the majority of the buildings [in the historic district] had been restituted." However, in late 2003, only a few months before his declarations, the same city hall had received fifty thousand claims for restitution (for financial compensation), but it had solved fewer than four thousand. For Băsescu's declaration, see his interview in *Revista 22*, May 19, 2004. For statistics on the restitution petitions, see Stan (2006, 198).

63. As I already mentioned in chap. 4, when I visited the municipal Office of Population Records (Direcția de Evidență a Populației), the institution's director curtly told me that "the district was a Jewish district, and it is now a Roma district, and that is all I should need to know."

64. Interview, May 20, 2016.

65. Section 1 of law 85/1992 stipulates that the tenants renting state-owned housing can buy their homes. "LEGE nr.85 din 22 iulie 1992 privind vânzarea de locuințe și spații cu altă destinație construite din fondurile statului și din fondurile unităților economice sau bugetare de stat," *Monitorul Oficial* 180/1992, July 1992.

66. Interview, May 20, 2016.

67. Antoaneta Etves, "Se caută 4.000 de case, care ar fi dispărut din averea Primăriei Capitalei," *Evenimentul Zilei*, January 5, 2017, http://www.evz.ro/au-disparut-4000-de-case -din-averea-primariei-capitalei.html.

68. Bucharest, May 14, 2016.

69. Amalia Bălăbăneanu, "'Atenție, pericol de prăbușire!': Clădirile din Centrul Vechi se dărâmă bucată cu bucată," B365.ro, July 22, 2013, http://www.b365.ro/atentie-pericol-de -prabusire-cladirile-din-centrul-vechi-se-darama-bucata-cu-bucata_192458.html.

70. May 14, 2016.

71. As of June 2016, based on the prices I saw listed in the Old Town, the market for real estate rent for renovated buildings in the district was €100 per square meter.

72. "Listele imobilelor expertizate tehnic din punct de vedere al riscului seismic actualizate la 09.02.2016," Primăria Municipiului București, Direcția Generală Dezvoltare și Investiții. This document contains the list of all of the buildings in Bucharest considered unsafe in case of the case of a medium-size earthquake. The list was updated on February 9, 2016, and was made public on the site of Bucharest's city hall, www.pmb.ro, in June 2016. However, as of August 2018, the list is no longer available.

73. After a low-scale earthquake occurred on an evening of December 2016, city hall immediately dispatched police officers to the Old Town to check on the buildings. "Cutremur cu magnitudinea de 5,3 în zona Vrancea, resimțit în Capitală și în județele din Sud-Est," Mediafax.ro, December 28, 2016, http://www.mediafax.ro/social/video-cutremur-cu -magnitudinea-de-5-3-in-zona-vrancea-resimtit-in-capitala-si-in-judetele-din-sud-est- seismul-a-fost-resimtit-si-in-ucraina-republica-moldova-bulgaria-si-vestul-turciei-16041416.

74. Claudia Pîrvoiu and Catiușa Ivanov, "Niciun imobil cu bulină roșie din București, din cele prevăzute în programul pe 2015, nu a fost consolidate," Hotnews.ro, January 20, 2016, http://www.hotnews.ro/stiri-esential-20740324-niciun-imobil-bulina-rosie-din-bucuresti -nu-fost-consolidat-2015-plus-studiu-caz.htm.

75. "Alianța medicilor reacționează," *Revista 22*, April 28, 2016, http://revista22online .ro/70253544/alianta-medicilor-reactioneaza-coruptie-ucide-si-nu-doar-in-colectiv-ci-zi -de-zi.html. This open letter of the largest association of Romanian physicians followed the public exposure of an appalling case of corruption. A company selling disinfectants to more than three hundred hospitals in Romania for years turned out to have drastically diluted its products, leading patients to contract deadly antibiotic-resistant infections while in hospitals. See also "Death of an Antiseptic Salesman. Romania's Latest Scandal Features Watered- Down Disinfectant in Hospitals," *Economist*, June 4, 2016.

76. "Riscul colectiv din Centrul Vechi al capitalei," Rise Project, November 10, 2015, http://www.riseproject.ro/riscul-colectiv-din-centrul-vechi-al-capitalei/.

77. Interview with Elena, an investigative journalist from Bucharest, May 30, 2016, Bucharest. In July 2013, the estimated revenues of the Old Town were around €150–200 million. Cristina Roșca, "Centrul vechi al Capitalei a intrat în depresie," *Ziarul Financiar*, July 8, 2013, https://www.zf.ro/zf-24/centrul-vechi-al-capitalei-a-intrat-in-depresie-consumatorii -vin-si-trag-de-o-apa-toata-seara-11106457.

78. The Save Bucharest Association was formed in 2007 by a handful of people deeply concerned about the vast demolition of Bucharest's historic buildings—a demolition that the local officials allowed and even promoted. I took part in some of the earlier meetings of the association during 2007 and early 2008. The association continued to fight with the authorities to preserve historic Bucharest and opened numerous litigations against real estate companies and even state institutions (and won some of these cases). By 2016, some of the founding members established a new political party, Save Romania Union, that rapidly gained visibility and leverage on the national political scene.

79. Conversation with Andrei, May 30, 2016.

80. Eurostat, October 17, 2016.

CONCLUSION

A Past for a Socialist Modernity

During the twentieth century, the Old Town's value fluctuated constantly in an ebb and flow that captured broader political shifts. Under socialism, the negotiations about the significance of the district revealed the state authorities' rather lukewarm interest in the national history during the 1950s, followed by an increasingly unconcealed nationalism starting in the 1960s and 1970s, and culminating with the megalomaniac nationalism of the Ceaușescu era in the 1980s. After the end of the communist regime, the debates about the Old Town exposed new struggles for political and economic capital, continuities between the former and current political and economic elites, as well as increasing social divides and more subtle forms of political and social marginalization.

The case of the Old Town exposes the material forms that the postwar communist government employed to create a workers' state of "socialist nationalities" out of an ethnically diverse and culturally heterogeneous Romania. Architecture and urban planning, as technologies of redefining spatial and social relations, played a pivotal role in the political homogenization that the socialist regimes launched in the early 1950s under the direct influence of a Stalinist USSR. The Romanian state began its own modernization project as soon as the communist party came to power in 1947, only to soon realize that they needed a history that would ideologically match a socialist future. This book has shown how state authorities translated these two interconnected projects in material terms—how they aimed to transform Bucharest both into a socialist modern capital and a historical city of national importance.

The 1953 discovery of the ruined walls of the Old Court in the city center offered a unique opportunity for this pursuit. Suddenly, these ruined fragments that archaeologists had stumbled on turned out to be a pivotal vehicle for the new socialist state to create a new history. These walls became peculiar devices to make the body politic—to transform people of diverse social and ethnic backgrounds into socialist subjects and loyal citizens. The Old Court was rescued from beneath the ground and fully reconstructed as a medieval palace meant to symbolize a political independence of the Romanians several centuries before Romania became officially a nation-state. As a heritage site of the socialist state, it coaxed its visitors to become aware of their national identity. They were to associate such awareness with distinct affective disposi-tions, depending on who they knew they were (Romanian nationals, Roma-nian citizens from ethnic minorities officially recognized by the regime, such as Germans, Hungarians, or Jews, or Romanian citizens of Roma origins whom the state did not consider ethnically different but who were nonetheless socially marginalized).

However, the criteria of who belonged to a socialist body politic were not informed solely by ethnic/national identity. The state systematically pur-sued order in multiple forms, from acquiring a "politically proper" history, as shown by the debatable dating of the archaeological artifacts collected at the Old Court, to seeking a sense of control through urban planning and architec-tural style. In the 1970s, a group of architects initiated the transformation of the entire district of the Old Town into a historical architectural reserve meant to symbolize the Romanian nation via a particular architectural style. Although the authorities eventually decided to forgo the project, the attempt still revealed broader aesthetic visions mirroring the political priorities of the moment. The project signaled the increasing importance of the national ideology for a gov-ernment trying to maintain an authoritarian governance. It was an attempt to advertise and commodify both national history and communism, because the redesigned district was to become a unique touristic resource, one that would especially appeal to foreign tourists and their money. At the same time, the Old Town's transformation into a symbol of "Romanianness" through houses redecorated with closed verandas was a project of creating material borders between those who belonged and those who did not to the nation.

The plans for redecorating the house buildings with an eye to hiding the poorer residents must be understood in correlation to a broader change in patterns of urbanization. In the first two decades of communism, the govern-ment promoted a rapid urbanization, which they viewed as a precondition for a successful industrialization. However, beginning in 1970, the state sought to curtail the wide rural-to-urban migration triggered in part by the industrial development and in part by the forced collectivization of agriculture (Stoica 1997). But despite the state's measures to control these patterns of relocation, the internal migration continued (320). The most intensive wave of rural-to-urban migration occurred during the 1970s, with two of the poorest regions of the country providing the bulk of the migrants (319).

This migration's immediate effect was a profound alteration of the social fabric of the larger cities through the formation of a new underclass, composed of the former poor villagers who did not fully want to or could not adapt to city life. The result was a more visible and acute social polarization. This poor population was on the bottom of the list for social housing and other benefits, being often the ones who had to accept suboptimal living standards. They were among the first to be given repartitions to residences that offered them only basic facilities, such as many apartments in the Old Town's old buildings, and the last to be able to leave these houses for better conditions. Not having resources to relocate these residents but trying to put them out of the sight of foreign tourists and other visitors, the city authorities sought to make them symbolically disappear. The redesigned facades of the Old Town's houses were meant to hide the increasingly glaring social inequalities in a system that claimed that it had abolished all social differences. Even if such plans led nowhere, the initial interest that the local authorities had for such plans signal Romania's socialist regime viewed *both* nation and class as key political differentials.

My study of the Old Town during the 1970s thus shows how class in socialism did not just emerge as an effect of institutions and education that separated workers from the white-collar intelligentsia, as Konrád and Szelényi (1979) argued. In socialist Romania, class was also produced through concrete and mundane things such as redecorated old houses and closed balconies. Such balconies functioned as both material and symbolic boundaries: they kept the Old Town's poor residents from public view, while also denying them a place in the national history that such redecorations were meant to represent.

Politics of Place and Time

The changing meanings of the Old Town also signaled how time and place became political resources under communism—how political elites used interventions in place and spatial practices to alter perceptions of time and history at distinct moments. The socialist elites used heritage to transform and play with chronology as a malleable political resource. The politicization of time is revealed by how archaeologists used artifacts first to prove the Slavic migrations on Bucharest's territory at the peak of Stalinism, only to redate them a decade or so later to suit the new nationalist agenda of the early 1960s. It is also shown by the Old Town's houses that would have "traveled" back in time had the local authorities pursued the initial plans for architectural redesign. The government used the reconstruction of the Old Court as a way to "stretch" the socialist present back into a historical time, represented by the medieval period. The state commissioned archaeologists to provide the material proof of the city's medieval history. The making of socialist heritage thus entailed the elevation of some temporalities over other—such as the medieval times becoming more valuable and therefore worthy of a material representation, while the nineteenth century or the interwar periods had to visually disappear from the urban aesthetics of the new cities.

A critical focus on the politics of place making brings to light key connections between the communist and postcommunist regimes. By exploring how political actors have tried to intervene in the form and meaning of places (be they historical districts or buildings), we can better understand how they consolidated their power during and after socialism. On the collapse of the socialist system in 1989, the postcommunist elites held the Old Town in a strategic disregard. Any attempts to bring more visibility to the district, even if supported by foreign money and expertise, were rejected from the start. However, the local authorities' alleged disinterest belied their true intentions to financially exploit the undervalued shops and real estate.

But they also did so, I argued, with the intention of keeping the Old Town as a place out of time and a spatial symbol of the recent communist past. They denied the district and its poor residents what anthropologist Johannes Fabian (1983) called co-evalness—the quality of being contemporary with others and thereby of having and claiming political rights and visibility here and now. In the Old Town, time was made to stand still so that the gaze of the public would be diverted somewhere else: to the more colorful and commercially alive parts of the city, which became rapidly absorbed by the "time-space compression" of the capitalism (Harvey 1989) that had come to town. This aesthetic contrast elicited particular affective dispositions: a rejection of everything the Old Town represented, especially the grayness and poverty of late communism. The postcommunist political elites used this contrast with an eye to whitewashing their own communist past. Spatiotemporal inequalities enhanced the contrast between an allegedly democratic present and an authoritarian recent past.

Europeanization: Hopes and Disenchantments

During the 2000s, as the struggle for political power among different factions intensified, the Old Town, once again, became a battlefield. For the opposition that came to power in the mid-2000s, the transformation of the district into a "historic center" in a Europeanizing city became a justification for the new authorities to launch an intensive gentrification of the district and a broader privatization of the city. The book offers a new angle of analysis onto Europeanization as an institutional and cultural process, which I view as (1) the production of a new, transnational sentiment of belonging to Europe as a cultural space, and as (2) the bundle of legal regulations and financial obligations (*acquis communautaire*) that the European Union (EU) has asked Romania and other new member states to abide by. An ethnographic analysis of how Europeanization happens on the ground shows that it is a more unpredictable process than the optimistic scenarios coined in the EU headquarters. Sometimes, it even goes against such scenarios (Ganev 2013). For instance, in Bucharest of late 2000s, EU monies and expertise ended up only strengthening the agendas of the local politicians, leading to further centralization of political and economic capital and producing new forms of social exclusion.

The uneven negotiations among foreign experts, state authorities, private owners, and poor residents over the economic value and cultural significance of the Old Town after the end of communism illustrate this process. The international nongovernmental organizations and the European experts who have started visiting Romania since the fall of communism have aimed to kindle new forms of political participation in a postsocialist country still controlled by the former communist elites. Some of these experts believed that teaching "heritage" in a country that, in their view, had lost its heritage during socialism, would empower people and make them into democratic political subjects. By making people aware of the value of the houses they inhabited, specialists hoped to spur impoverished residents to become more politically visible. The British team who visited the district in the early 1990s focused on "urban renewal," seeking to make the Old Town more visibile by rekindling social relations and commercial activities. The project sponsored by the United Nations in early 2000s aimed to make the Old Town's residents more aware of their rights.

But often, these people could see that learning about heritage did not automatically entitle them to new rights. Poor residents of dilapidated buildings in Bucharest's Old Town viewed heritage with a jaundiced eye. To these people, a category that includes many of the poor residents of the Old Town, heritage was nothing else but an empty word, not to say a joke. "Heritage" for them was a byword for corruption and for city officials' blatant disregard for both the condition of the historic buildings and the poor who survive in them. In fact, the more they heard about heritage, the more they knew that this might mean eviction. People like Carmen and her neighbors, state tenants who lived in a semidecrepit building that the city officials had abandoned, wanted nothing to do with heritage because they knew that they were not entitled to have it in the first place. They were not interested in the past because, in the eyes of the state, their own precarity had already denied them both a place in history and a stable future.

The spatial changes and interventions in the Old Town—especially the overhaul of the district's infrastructure network carried out in late 2000s and funded by the EU—point to new understandings of the relationship between the state, the private sector, and the citizens. The infrastructural repairs, combined with the privatization of utility services, have led some of the poor tenants who continue to live in the Old Town's state-owned housing to lose access to water. As the utilities companies became privatized, they wanted to deal only with associations, not individual tenants; however, the state has not offered these tenants the bureaucratic support to form such associations. Such an infrastructural invisibility thus leads to further social invisibility. In this light, Europeanization reveals itself to be not just a search for the "unity in diversity," per the Council of Europe's rhetoric, but also a more subtle justification for the exclusion of those people who are too poor to be viewed as European.

Starting in the early 2000s, the state authorities also employed a rhetoric of heritage with an eye to signaling their willingness to promote property restitution—and thus convey to the EU that they would obey by the union's preconditions for Romania's inclusion. However, by promoting a view of heritage as private property, state officials reinforced an understanding that only those who could afford to own property could afford a heritage. By promoting this view of heritage as the *propriety of property* and claiming that "Bucharest was not a city where anyone would afford to live," as the then mayor put it, the city officials endorsed an increasing social polarization.

The privatization of the right to heritage also enabled state officials to deny their responsibility toward the semidecrepit houses of the Old Town, even though some of them remain state property. This strategic carelessness has only enabled further privatization—very likely an outcome that the city officials had foreseen. In the Old Town district, café and restaurant owners have exploited the shabbiness of the old buildings as an element of cultural uniqueness, echoing trends of urban design that emphasize "shabby chic" elements. Ruination itself became commodified as heritage. However, that very move—the attempt of club and restaurant owners to capitalize on the current decrepit state of the old buildings in the district—came under the criticism of investigative journalists and civic activists. These groups pointed to the ruined state of Bucharest's old buildings as the tangible representation of a corrupt political system. They have used it as a starting point to launch a broader social movement, aiming to rekindle a sense of community and collective trust in a country whose citizens have grown tired of empty talk about individualism and free market as justifications for precarity, corruption, and dispossession. By August 2018, this movement has grown into a full-blown revolt at the national level, with people all across Romania marching in the streets to protest against the current political and juridical chaos created by a corrupt government.

Heritage Regimes

Socialist Heritage brings together the politics of cultural heritage under two distinct political regimes, with the politics of supranational entities such as the

Soviet Union and the EU. Such a comparative perspective allows for a better understanding of the specific relationship between cultural and political capital endorsed in two distinct political periods. Under socialism, the Romanian state monopolized not only the distribution of resources but also definitions and categories. It closely controlled the uses and meanings of "heritage" and "history." In the postsocialist context, the field of cultural politicking became much more fragmented as the postsocialist state found itself in continual competition with other cultural brokers, notably transnational organizations such as the United Nations and the EU. I have analyzed the impact of socialism as heritage—as a particular set of material and social practices and affective dispositions—following the collapse of that system. I explored how the communist regime's strategies of assigning political and cultural meaning to things continued to inform the processes of formation and erasure of value during the early phase of postcommunism (1990s) and then during the Europeanization that preceded and followed Romania's 2007 inclusion into the EU.

In socialist Romania, history in a material form became itself political capital. The story of making the Old Court into a socialist heritage site allowed me to revisit previous arguments that approached the formation of value in socialist systems via an exclusive focus on economic centralization. Archaeological findings—particularly the Old Court portrayed as the historic center in the midst of a socialist capital—offered the state the opportunity to present a tangible representation of that center and justify a centralized system by creating its historic counterpart.

Expertise was another type of political capital. The new regime needed as much expertise as it could get—confronted with lack of resources and a limited pool of specialized labor, they had to leave aside concerns about the class background or even political convictions of some experts and commission them to join others in building socialism. At the same time, the centralized system created a particular struggle over resources. Professionals from various disciplinary domains vied for the attention of the state—that is, a relatively small group of politicians. They needed the latter's validation if they wanted to pursue research—and they had to prove that their research was politically useful. The fights among these specialists occurred not only across disciplinary areas but also within particular professional fields, as different groups attempted to validate and impose their own hierarchies of cultural capital. Thus, the debates over what kinds of things—be they buildings, walls, or areas in the center of the city—represented "cultural heritage" exposed the competing pursuits of different teams of specialists, who were striving to outdo each other in defining what interpretations would be the best vehicles for political ideology.

By inquiring into what was "heritage" and its political function at different moments during socialism and postsocialism, I have examined the shift from a view on heritage as a collection of objects to one set within millennial global capitalism—a much more dynamic and fluid environment. I have argued that the socialist regime endorsed a view of heritage as objects because it needed to rely on both national history and materiality to consolidate its own power—to make itself as a state. Such a view drastically encroached on the options of cultural producers. That is, within a centripetal political system that thrived on the accumulation of resources at its center, a perspective on heritage as objects allowed the center to limit the range of forms of legitimate cultural expression.

The socialist state was not interested in developing too fluid a cultural field but rather one that could be easily manipulated. A vision of heritage set within a material culture framework permitted greater control over cultural production. Controlling the movement of objects, such archaeological artifacts, ruined walls, or redesigned balconies, in and out of the "heritage" category was easier than supervising culture as an inherently processual, dynamic, and continuously self-redefining field. Moreover, such view of heritage as a (static) collection of objects was meant to erase the ways in which the state engaged in a process of rewriting history. A focus of heritage as an immutable domain implicitly negated a view of history as a contested process. Instead, such an approach to heritage as object reinforced a view of the state as a given rather than a political product with its own historicity and limitations.

After the end of communism, this model of heritage as a politically curated collection of objects clashed with the perspective on heritage as a much more fluid and contested category. This key shift from heritage as object to heritage as a political strategy must be understood also as an effect of the shift from a Fordist system focused on mass production and a regulated conformity, to a knowledge-oriented economy. The promoters of neoliberal, post-Fordist capitalism have tried to distinguish from the Fordist phase by highlighting the link between niche marketing and identity politics. However, behind the rhetoric of *uniqueness, innovation, niche creativity,* and the emphasis on the economic potential of cultural diversity, there is an even broader attempt at commodifying culture. Heritage continues to be a means of selecting and congealing particular cultural forms and practices, of clarifying and cutting down a more fluid cultural domain into separate pieces, to be then evaluated and administered by specific political actors (an ethnic group, a national state, or a transnational institution such as the EU). In other words, an ideology of "heritage" seems to only have furthered social polarization; it has reinforced the power of the powerful, because it has become the privilege of only those who possess knowledge and resources to endow objects, gestures, or words with the most persuasive meanings.

This book uses the political changes in postwar Romania—from its inclusion into the Soviet bloc to its current EU-led Europeanization—to examine how distinct heritage regimes reflected and reinforced distinct visions of political order on the long arc from the postwar years into the early 2000s. The postwar view of heritage—as a global commodity of universal value—was part and parcel of the 1950s development model. The cultural counterpart of the US-led global project of economic development, whose failure became increasingly visible by the late 1970s (Ferguson 1999), was a UNESCO-endorsed view of heritage as high culture (Merryman 1986, 2005).[1] This model of heritage closely mirrored Western aesthetic standards, centered on monumentality and materiality. It consequently discouraged non-Western states from defining their own heritage and relied only on the cultural mimicry of Eurocentric values (Prott 2005). In the post-Stalinist socialist bloc, however, this view of heritage offered the socialist states a chance to selectively mobilize their prewar European past to connect with the West culturally. A focus on how socialist Romania used national heritage to resist Soviet domination thus places the socialist states squarely among the global anticolonial movements and their pursuit of political independence through culture.

A shift from "heritage as development" to "heritage as cultural recognition" was marked by the rise of identity politics during the 1970s, with postcolonial, indigenous, and other marginalized subjects increasingly claiming cultural uniqueness as a path to political and economic visibility. In the field of international institutions, the view of heritage as cultural recognition was reinforced by the UNESCO's 1970 convention, the purpose of which was to ensure the protection of the cultural property of the states that signed the convention and deter the illicit international trade.[2] In contrast to a development model focusing exclusively on economic redistribution at the expense of cultural diversity, heritage as recognition emphasized cultural difference as a potential source of economic value. In the Soviet bloc, a view of heritage as a nationally owned domain gave the socialist states the impetus to openly favor their national interests over those of the Soviets. By bringing those broader arguments to bear on the Romanian case, I argue that the Romanian socialist state captured the impetus for heritage as recognition to advance a radical nationalist agenda during the 1980s.

A post–Cold War shift from "heritage as cultural recognition" to "heritage as regionalization" must be situated within the new regionalisms emerging at the global level. Invocations of cultural links and shared histories have accompanied international attempts to create zones of free trade and to justify economic cooperation and further investments. The expansion of the EU into Eastern Europe offers a unique context to better understand the role of culture for the incipient EU-led regionalization. If we pay close attention to how various elites employ the rhetoric of "heritage," we could distinguish a phenomenon of reterritorialization in which standardization and border policing paradoxically undergird the EU's discourse on the free flow of goods and people. While enticing the Eastern Europeans to believe that they had been born again as new Europeans after decades of communism, the rhetoric and practice of heritage has become a strategy for various political elites, from postsocialist actors to EU politicians, to keep some people in place by prompting them to rekindle their ties with their histories, while denying others a history altogether.

Notes

1. A UNESCO ambassador and French delegate to UNESCO, Jean Musitelli (2002) echoed the rhetoric of modernization theory in his description of the 1972 UNESCO Convention Concerning the Protection of Cultural and Natural World Heritage. Musitelli declared that "the convention of 1972 established itself fully in the prospect of *development* [my emphasis]. It is a tool to help poor countries confronted with huge disparities between the amplitude of the means necessary to safeguard their heritage and the lack of financial and technical resources. To that end, the economy of the convention settles on a mechanism of redistribution between the north and the south" (325).

2. Convention on the Means of Prohibiting and Preventing the Illicit Import, Export and Transfer of Ownership of Cultural Property 1970, UNESCO, accessed May 20, 2019, http://portal.unesco.org/en/ev.php-URL_ID=13039&URL_DO=DO_TOPIC&URL _SECTION=201.html.

BIBLIOGRAPHY

Abu El-Haj, Nadia. 2001. *Facts on the Ground: Archaeological Practice and Territorial Self-Fashioning in Israeli Society*. Chicago: University of Chicago Press.

Almaş, Dumitru, and Panait I. Panait. 1974. *Curtea veche din Bucureşti*. Bucharest: Editura pentru turism.

Anand, Nikhil. 2011. "Pressure: The PoliTechnics of Water Supply in Mumbai." *Cultural Anthropology* 26 (4): 542–64.

Ancel, Jean. 2005. "'The New Jewish Invasion': The Return of the Survivors from Transnistria." In *The Jews Are Coming Back: The Return of the Jews to Their Country of Origins after WWII*, edited by David Bankier, 231–56. Jerusalem: Berghahn Books/Yad Vashem.

Anghelescu, Şerban, Ioana Hodoiu, Cosmin Manolache, Anca Manolescu, Vlad Manoliu, Irina Nicolau, Ioana Popescu, Petre Popovăţ, Simina Radu-Bucurenci, and Ana Vinea, eds. 2003. *Mărturii orale: Anii '80 şi bucureştenii*. Bucharest: Paideia.

Anghelinu, Mircea. 2007. "Failed Revolution: Marxism and the Romanian Prehistoric Archaeology between 1945 and 1989." *Archaeologia Bulgarica* 11 (1): 1–36.

Appadurai, Arjun. 1986. "Introduction: Commodities and the Politics of Value." In *The Social Life of Things: Commodities in Cultural Perspective*, edited by Arjun Appadurai, 3–63. Cambridge, UK: Cambridge University Press.

Auge, Marc. 1995. *Non-Places: An Introduction to Supermodernity*. Translated by John Howe. London: Verso.

Bachman, Ronald D., ed. *Romania: A Country Study*. Washington, DC: GPO for the Library of Congress, 1989. Accessed July 20, 2017, via http://countrystudies.us/romania/.

Bailey, Douglas W. 1998. "Bulgarian Archaeology: Ideology, Sociopolitics and the Exotic." In *Archaeology under Fire: Nationalism, Politics and Heritage in the Eastern Mediterranean and Middle East*, edited by Lynn Meskell, 87–110. London: Routledge.

Ban, Cornel. 2012. "Sovereign Debt, Austerity, and Regime Change: The Case of Nicolae Ceausescu's Romania." *East European Politics and Societies* 26 (4): 743–76.

Barbu, Eugen. 1977. *Principele*. Bucharest: Editura Minerva.

Barth, Fredrik. 1969. Introduction to *Ethnic Groups and Boundaries: The Social Organization of Culture Difference*, edited by Fredrik Barth, 9–38. Boston: Little, Brown and Co.

Békés, Csaba, László Borhi, Peter Ruggenthaler, and Ottmar Traşcă, eds. 2015. *Soviet Occupation of Romania, Hungary, and Austria, 1944/45–1948/49*. Budapest: Central European University Press.

Bennett, Tony. 1995. *The Birth of the Museum*. London: Routledge.

Benson, Peter, and Stuart Kirsch. 2010. "Capitalism and the Politics of Resignation." *Current Anthropology* 51 (4): 459–86.

Berdahl, Daphne. 1999. *Where the World Ended: Re-unification and Identity in the German Borderland*. Berkeley: University of California Press.

Berdahl, Daphne, Matti Bunzl, and Martha Lampland, eds. 2000. *Altering States: Ethnographies of Transition in Eastern Europe and the Former Soviet Union*. Ann Arbor: University of Michigan Press.

Berliner, David. 2018. "Can Anything Become Heritage?" In *Sense and Essence: Heritage and the Cultural Production of the Real*, edited by Mattijs van de Port and Birgit Meyer, 299–305. New York: Berghahn.

Bosomitu, Stefan. 2015. *Miron Constantinescu. O Biografie.* Bucharest: Humanitas.

Bottoni, Stefano. 2017. *Long Awaited West: Eastern Europe since 1944.* Bloomington: Indiana University Press.

———. 2018. *Stalin's Legacy in Romania: The Hungarian Autonomous Region, 1952–1960.* Lanham, MD: Lexington Books.

Boym, Svetlana. 2007. "Nostalgia and Its Discontents." *Hedgehog Review* 9 (2): 7–18.

Breglia, Lisa. 2006. *Monumental Ambivalence: The Politics of Heritage.* Austin: University of Texas Press.

Brown, Elizabeth. 1974. "The Tyranny of a Construct: Feudalism and Historians of Medieval Europe." *American Historical Review* 79 (4): 1063–88.

Brown, Michael. 2004. "Heritage as Property." In *Property in Question: Value Transformation in the Global Economy*, edited by K. Verdery and C. Humphrey, 49–68. New York: Berg.

Bryant, Rebecca. 2014. "History's Remainders: On Time and Objects after Conflict in Cyprus." *American Ethnologist* 41 (4): 681–97.

Bucur, Maria. 2002. *Eugenics and Modernization in Interwar Romania.* Pittsburgh, PA: University of Pittsburgh Press.

———. 2003. "Gender and Fascism in Interwar Romania." In *Women, Gender and the Extreme Right in Europe*, edited by Kevin Passmore, 58–79. Manchester, UK: Manchester University Press.

Burawoy, Michael, and Katherine Verdery, eds. 1999. *Uncertain Transition: Ethnographies of Change in the Postsocialist World.* Lanham, MD: Rowman and Littlefield.

Burchell, Graham, Colin Gordon, and Peter Miller. 1991. *The Foucault Effect: Studies in Governmentality.* Chicago: University of Chicago Press.

Cantacuzino, Gheorghe. 1965. "O mare locuință feudală descoperită prin săpături arheologice în București." In *Cercetări arheologice în București*, vol. 2, 325–40. Bucharest: S. P. C. (Sfatul Popular al Capitalei) Muzeul de istorie a orașului București.

Caragiale, Mateiu. 2001. *Craii de Curtea-Veche.* Chișinău: Editura Eminescu. First published in 1929.

Cernat, Lucian. 2004. "The Politics of Banking in Romania: Soft Loans, Looting and Cardboard Billionaires." *Government and Opposition* 39 (3): 451–75.

Chelcea, Liviu. 2004. "State, Kinship and Urban Transformations during and after Housing Nationalization." PhD diss., University of Michigan.

Chioveanu, Mihai. 2009. "The Constitutive Other: Topical and Tropical Phanariot in Modern Romania." *Studia Politica* 9 (2): 213–27.

Choay, Françoise. 2001. *The Invention of the Historic Monument.* Translated by Lauren M. O'Connell. Cambridge, UK: Cambridge University Press.

Clark, Roland. 2015. *Holy Legionary Youth: Fascist Activism in Interwar Romania.* Ithaca, NY: Cornell University Press.

Collins, John. 2015. *Revolt of the Saints: Memory and Redemption in the Twilight of Brazilian Racial Democracy.* Durham, NC: Duke University Press.

Comaroff, Jean, and John Comaroff. 2006. "Beasts, Banknotes, and the Color of Money in Colonial South Africa." *Archaeological Dialogues* 12 (2): 107–32.

Comşa, Maria. 1959. "Contribuţii la cunoaşterea culturii străromâne în lumina săpăturilor de la Bucov." *Studii şi cercetări de istorie veche* 10 (1): 81–99.

———. 1968. "Sur l'origine et l'évolution de la civilisation de la population romane, et ensuite protoroumaine, aux Vie–Xe siècles sur le territoire de la Roumanie." *Dacia. Revue d'archéologie et d'histoire ancienne* 12:335–80.

Condurachi, Emil. 1962. Prefaţă in *Cercetări arheologice în Bucureşti*, 3–4. Bucharest: S. P. C. Muzeul de Istorie a Oraşului Bucureşti.

Coombe, Rosemary J. 1998. *The Cultural Life of Intellectual Properties: Authorship, Appropriation, and the Law*. Durham, NC: Duke University Press.

———. 2016. "The Knowledge Economy and Its Cultures: Neoliberal Technologies and Latin American Reterritorializations." *Hau: Journal of Ethnographic Theory* 6 (3): 247–75.

Coombe, Rosemary J., and Lindsay M. Weiss. 2015. "Neoliberalism, Heritage Regimes, and Cultural Rights." In *Global Heritage: A Reader*, edited by Lynn Meskell, 43–69. Oxford, UK: Wiley-Blackwell.

Curta, Florin. 1994. "The Changing Image of the Early Slavs in the Rumanian Historiography and Archaeological Literature: A Critical Survey." *Revue des études sud-est européennes* 32:129–42.

———. 2001a. *The Making of the Slavs: History and Archeology of the Lower Danube Region, c. 500–700*. Cambridge, UK: Cambridge University Press.

———. 2001b. "Pots, Slavs and 'Imagined Communities': Slavic Archaeology and the History of the Early Slavs." *European Journal of Archaeology* 4 (3): 367–84.

———. 2005. Introduction to *East Central and Eastern Europe in the Early Middle Ages*, edited by Florin Curta, 1–38. Ann Arbor: University of Michigan Press.

Das, Veena, and Deborah Poole. 2004. "State and Its Margins: Comparative Ethnographies." In *Anthropology in the Margins of the State*, edited by Veena Das and Deborah Poole, 3–34. Santa Fe, NM: School of American Research Press.

Dawdy, Shannon. 2016. *Patina: A Profane Anthropology*. Chicago: University of Chicago Press.

DeHaan, Heather. 2013. *Stalinist City Planning: Professionals, Performance, and Power*. Toronto: University of Toronto Press.

Diaconu, Petre. 1958. "Observaţii asupra ceramicii din secolele XII–XIII de pe teritoriul oraşului Bucureşti." *Studii şi cercetări de istorie veche* 9 (2): 451–59.

Dobre, Florica, Florian Banu, Luminiţa Banu, and Laura Stancu. 2011. *Acţiunea "Recuperarea": Securitatea şi emigrarea germanilor din România (1962–1989)*. Bucharest: Editura Enciclopedică.

Dobrescu, Dem. I. 1934. *Viitorul Bucureştilor*. Bucharest: Editura Tribuna Edilitară.

Dolukhanov, Pavel. 1993. "Archaeology in the Ex-USSR: Post-Perestroyka Problems." *Antiquity* 67 (254): 150–56.

Douglas, Mary. 1966. *Purity and Danger: An Analysis of Concepts of Pollution and Taboo*. New York: Praeger.

Dragoman, Alexandru, and Sorin Oanţă-Marghitu. 2006. "Archaeology in Communist and Post-Communist Romania." *Dacia* 50:57–76.

Elian, Alexandru. 1965. Introducere in *Oraşul Bucureşti. Volumul I (1395–1800)*, edited by Alexandru Elian, Constantin Bălan, Haralambie Chircă, and Olimpia Diaconescu, 11–44. Bucharest: Editura Academiei Republicii Socialiste România.

Eurostat. 2016. "The Share of Persons at Risk of Poverty or Social Exclusion in the EU Back to Its Pre-crisis Level: Contrasting Trends across Member States." Luxembourg: Eurostat.

Fabian, Johannes. 1983. *Time and the Other: How Anthropology Makes Its Object*. New York: Columbia University Press.

Fehérváry, Krisztina. 2013. *Politics in Color and Concrete: Materialities and the Middle-Class in Hungary*. Bloomington: Indiana University Press.

Ferguson, James. 1999. *Expectations of Modernity: Myths and Meanings of Urban Life on the Zambian Copperbelt*. Berkeley: University of California Press.

Ferguson, James, and Akhil Gupta. 2002. "Spatializing States: Toward an Ethnography of Neoliberal Governmentality." *American Ethnologist* 4 (29): 981–1002.

Fitzpatrick, Sheila. 1996. "Signals from Below: Soviet Letters of Denunciation of the 1930s." *Modern History* 68 (4): 831–66.

Florea, Ioana, and Mihail Dumitriu. 2016. "Living on the Edge: The Ambiguities of Squatting and Urban Development in Bucharest." In *Public Goods versus Economic Interests: Global Perspectives on the History of Squatting*, edited by Freia Anders and Alexander Sedlmaier, 188–210. London: Routledge.

Foucault, Michel. 1970. *The Order of Things: An Archaeology of the Human Sciences*. New York: Random House.

Franquesa, Jaume. 2013. "On Keeping and Selling: The Political Economy of Heritage Making in Contemporary Spain." *Current Anthropology* 54 (3): 346–69.

Freud, Sigmund. 2003. *The Uncanny*. London: Penguin Classics. First published in 1919.

Gallagher, Tom. 2005. *Theft of a Nation: Romania since Communism*. London: Hurst.

———. 2009. *Romania and the European Union: How the Weak Vanquished the Strong*. Manchester, UK: Manchester University Press.

Ganev, Venelin I. 2013. "Post-Accession Hooliganism: Democratic Governance in Bulgaria and Romania after 2007." *East European Politics and Societies and Cultures* 27 (1): 26–44.

Geismar, Haidy. 2013. *Treasured Possessions: Indigenous Interventions into Cultural and Intellectual Property*. Durham: Duke University Press.

Georgescu, Florian. 1962. Introduction to *Cercetări arheologice în București*, 5–11. Bucharest: Muzeul de Istorie a Orașului București.

Ghiță, Alexandru, Alexandru Damian, Alexandra Toderiță, Roxana Albișteanu, and Ruxandra Popescu. 2016. *Locuirea socială în București. Între lege și realitate*. Bucharest: Centrul pentru Dezvoltare Urbană și Teritorială.

Glass, Ruth. 1964. Introduction to *London: Aspects of change*. Issue 3 of Report of Centre for Urban Studies of University College, London. London: MacGibbon and Kee.

Goldman, Wendy. 2011. *Inventing the Enemy: Denunciation and Terror in Stalin's Russia*. Cambridge, UK: Cambridge University Press.

Grama, Emanuela. 2004. "Networking Texts and Persons: Politics of Plagiarism in Post-socialist Romania." *Romanian Journal of Society and Politics* 4 (2): 148–73.

———. 2019. "Arbiters of Value: The Nationalization of Art and the Politics of Expertise in Early Socialist Romania." First published online January 24, 2019. *East European Politics, Societies, and Cultures*.

Groys, Boris. 2003. "Utopian Mass Culture." In *Dream Factory Communism: The Visual Culture of the Stalin Era*, edited by B. Groys and M. Hollein, 20–37. Ostfildern-Ruit, Germany: Hatje Cantz Verlag.

Hapenciuc, Ileana Blum. 2007. "Régénération urbaine et renouvellement des pratiques d'urbanisation en Roumanie: Le cas du centre historique de Bucarest." PhD diss., L'Institut National des Sciences Appliquées de Lyon.

Harvey, David. 1989. *The Condition of Postmodernity: An Enquiry into the Origins of Cultural Change.* Oxford, UK: Blackwell.

———. 2008. "The Right to the City." *New Left Review* 53:23–40.

Harvey, David C. 2008. "The History of Heritage." In *The Ashgate Research Companion to Heritage and Identity,* edited by Brian Graham and Peter Howard, 19–36. Burlington, VT: Ashgate.

Heinen, Armin. 1999. *Legiunea "Arhanghelului Mihail."* Bucharest: Humanitas.

Herzfeld, Michael. 1991. *A Place in History: Social and Monumental Time in a Cretan Town.* Princeton, NJ: Princeton University Press.

———. 2009. *Evicted from Eternity: The Restructuring of Modern Rome.* Chicago: University of Chicago Press.

Hitchins, Keith. 1994. *Rumania: 1866–1947.* Oxford, UK: Oxford University Press.

Hodder, Ian. 2010. "Cultural Heritage Rights: From Ownership and Descent to Justice and Well-Being." *Anthropological Quarterly* 83 (4): 861–82.

Hull, Matthew. 2012. *Government of Paper: The Materiality of Bureaucracy in Urban Pakistan.* Berkeley: University of California Press.

Iacob, Bogdan Cristian. 2011. "Stalinism, Historians, and the Nation: History-Production under Communism in Romania (1955–1966)." PhD diss., Central European University, Budapest.

Ioan, Augustin. 1996. *Power, Play and National Identity: Politics of Modernization in Central and East-European Architecture: The Romanian File.* Bucharest: Romanian Cultural Foundation Publishing House.

Ionaşcu, I., Vlad Zirra, D. Berciu, and Margareta Tudor. 1954. "Săpăturile arheologice din sectorul Radu Vodă." In *Studii şi referate privind istoria Romîniei. Din lucrările secţiunii lărgite a secţiunii de ştiinţe istorice, filozofice şi economico-juridice (21–24 decembrie 1953),* 409–60. Bucureşti: Editura Academiei Republicii Populare Romîne.

Ionaşcu, Ion, ed. 1959. *Bucureştii de odinioară în lumina cercetărilor arheologice.* Bucharest: Editura Ştiinţifică.

Ionescu, Grigore. 1938. *Bucureşti—Ghid Istoric şi Artistic.* Bucharest.

Ionescu, Stefan Cristian. 2015. *Jewish Resistance to "Romanianization," 1940–44.* London: Palgrave Macmillan.

Ionescu-Gion, G. 1899. *Istoria Bucurescilor.* Bucharest: Stabilimentul Grafic I. V. Socecu.

Iorga, Nicolae. 1939. *Istoria Bucureştilor.* Bucharest: Ediţia Municipiului Bucureşti.

Irvine, Judith, and Susan Gal. 2000. "Language Ideology and Linguistic Differentiation." In *Regimes of Language: Ideologies, Polities, and Identities,* edited by Paul Kroskrity, 35–84. Santa Fe, NM: School of American Research Press.

Iureş, Marcel. 2016. "O conversaţie cu Marcel Iureş." In *Oraşul: Antologie de proză,* edited by Cristian Fulaş and Ovidiu Şimonca, 9–16. Bucharest: Gestalt Books.

Jokilehto, Jukka. 2012. "Human Rights and Cultural Heritage: Observations on the Recognition of Human Rights in the International Doctrine." *International Journal of Heritage Studies* 18 (3): 226–30.

Kaiser, Timothy. 1995. "Archeology and Ideology in Southeast Europe." In *Nationalism, Politics, and the Practice of Archaeology,* edited by Philip L. Kohl and Clare P. Fawcett, 99–119. Cambridge, UK: Cambridge University Press.

Klejn, Lev S. 2012. *Soviet Archaeology: Schools, Trends, and History.* Translated by Rosh Ireland and Kevin Windle. Oxford, UK: Oxford University Press.

Kligman, Gail. 2002. "On the Social Construction of 'Otherness': Identifying 'the Roma' in Postsocialist Communities." In *Poverty, Ethnicity, and Gender in Transitional Societies*, edited by Iván Szelényi, 61–78. Budapest: Akadé miai Kiadó.

Kligman, Gail, and Katherine Verdery. 2011. *Peasants under Siege: The Collectivization of Romanian Agriculture, 1949–1962.* Princeton, NJ: Princeton University Press.

Konrád, György, and Iván Szelényi. 1979. *The Intellectuals on the Road to Class Power.* New York: Harcourt Brace Jovanovich.

Kristeva, Julia. 1982. *Powers of Horror: An Essay on Abjection.* New York: Columbia University Press.

———. 1997. *The Portable Kristeva.* Edited by Kelly Oliver. New York: Columbia University Press.

Kulic, Vladimir, Monica Penick, and Timothy Parker, eds. 2014. *Sanctioning Modernism: Architecture and the Making of Postwar Identities.* Austin: University of Texas Press.

Lamont, Michèle, and Virág Molnár. 2002. "The Study of Boundaries in the Social Sciences." *Annual Review of Sociology* 28:167–95.

Lăzărescu-Ionescu, L., Dinu V. Rosetti, Gh. Ionescu, Gh. Astangăi, arh. Horia Teodoru, C. Căzănișteanu, and M. Sănpetru. 1954. "Șantierul Arheologic București." In *Studii și referate privind istoria Romîniei. Din lucrările secțiunii lărgite a secțiunii de științe istorice, filozofice și economico-juridice (21–24 decembrie 1953)*, 285–538. București: Editura Academiei Republicii Populare Romîne.

Lebow, Katherine. 2013. *Unfinished Utopia: Nowa Huta, Stalinism, and Polish Society, 1949–1956.* Ithaca, NY: Cornell University Press.

Lefebvre, Henri. 1968. *Le droit à la ville.* Paris: Anthropos.

———. 1991. *The Production of Space.* Translated by Donald Nicholson-Smith. Oxford, UK: Wiley-Blackwell.

Lehrer, Erica. 2013. *Jewish Poland Revisited: Heritage Tourism in Unquiet Places.* Bloomington: Indiana University Press.

LeNormand, Brigitte. 2014. *Designing Tito's Capital: Urban Planners, Modernism and Socialism.* Pittsburgh, PA: University of Pittsburgh Press.

Light, Duncan, and Daniela Dumbrăveanu-Andone. 1997. "Heritage and National Identity: Exploring the Relationship in Romania." *International Journal of Heritage Studies* 3 (1): 28–43.

Light, Duncan, and Craig Young. 2015. "Urban Space, Political Identity and the Unwanted Legacies of State Socialism: Bucharest's Problematic *Centru Civic* in the Post-Socialist Era." In *From Socialist to Post-Socialist Cities: Cultural Politics of Architecture, Urban Planning, and Identity in Eurasia*, edited by Alexander C. Diener and Joshua Hagen, 29–49. London: Routledge.

Livezeanu, Irina. 1995. *Cultural Politics in Greater Romania: Regionalism, Nation Building and Ethnic Struggle, 1918–1930.* Ithaca, NY: Cornell University Press.

Machedon, Luminița, and Ernie Scoffham. 1999. *Romanian Modernism: The Architecture of Bucharest, 1920–1940.* Cambridge, MA: MIT Press.

Maxim, Juliana. 2018. *The Socialist Life of Modern Architecture: Bucharest, 1949–1964.* London: Routledge.

Mëhilli, Elidor. 2017. *From Stalin to Mao: Albania and the Socialist World.* Ithaca, NY: Cornell University Press.

Merleau-Ponty, Maurice. 2012. *Phenomenology of Perception.* Translated by Donald Landes. Oxford, UK: Routledge.

Merryman, John Henry. 1986. "Two Ways of Thinking About Cultural Property." *American Journal of International Law* 80 (4): 831–53.

———. 2005. "Cultural Property Internationalism." *International Journal of Cultural Property* 12 (1):11–39.

Meskell, Lynn. 2010. "Human Rights and Heritage Ethics." *Anthropological Quarterly* 83 (4): 839–60.

———, ed. 2015. *Global Heritage: A Reader.* Oxford, UK: Wiley-Blackwell.

Molnár, Virág. 2013. *Building the State: Architecture, Politics, and State Formation in Postwar Central Europe.* Abingdon, UK: Routledge.

Monterescu, Daniel. 2015. *Jaffa Shared and Shattered: Contrived Coexistence in Israel/ Palestine.* Bloomington: Indiana University Press.

Moreland, John. 2001. *Archeology and Text.* London: Duckworth.

Mucenic, Cezara. 1997. *Bucureşti: un veac de arhitectură civilă: secolul al XIX-lea.* Bucharest: Silex.

Murgescu, Costin. 1987. *Mersul ideilor economice la români.* Bucharest: Editura ştiinţifică şi enciclopedică.

Musitelli, Jean. 2002. "World Heritage, between Universalism and Globalization." *International Journal of Cultural Property* 11 (2): 323–36.

Navaro-Yashin, Yael. 2012. *The Make-Believe Space: Affective Geography in a Postwar Polity.* Durham, NC: Duke University Press.

Nestor, Ion. 1958. "Contributions archéologiques au problème des Proto-Roumains. La civilisation de Dridu. Note préliminaire." *Dacia* 2 (2): 371–82.

———. 1964. "Le données archéologiques et le problème de la formation de peuple roumain." *Revue roumaine d'Histoire* 3 (3): 384–423.

Niculescu, Gheorghe Alexandru. 2004–5. "Archaeology, Nationalism and the 'History of the Romanians' (2001)." *Dacia* 48–49:99–124.

Oldenziel, Ruth, and Karin Zachmann. 2009. *Cold War Kitchen: Americanization, Technology, and European Users.* Cambridge, MA: MIT Press.

Olteanu, Mihai Marian. 2014. "Reconstrucţia industrială oraşului Bucureşti (1948–1952)." *Studii şi Materiale de Istorie Contemporană* 13:5–22.

O'Neill, Bruce. 2009. "The Political Agency of Cityscapes: Spatializing Governance in Ceauşescu's Bucharest." *Social Archaeology* 9 (1): 92–109.

———. 2010. "Down and Then Out in Bucharest: Urban Poverty, Governance, and the Politics of Place in the Postsocialist City." *Environment and Planning D: Society and Space* 28 (2): 254–69.

———. 2017. *The Space of Boredom: Homelessness in the Slowing Global Order.* Durham, NC: Duke University Press.

Panait, I. Panait. 1962. "Observaţii arheologice pe şantierele de construcţii din Capitală." In *Cercetări arheologice în Bucureşti,* 139–70. Bucharest: S. P. C. (Sfatul Popular al Capitalei) Muzeul de istorie a oraşului Bucureşti.

———. 1980. "Studiu introductiv." In *Curtea Veche,* edited by Ioan Negrea. Bucharest: Editura Sport-Turism.

Panaitescu, Alexandru. *De la Casa Scânteii la Casa Poporului. Patru decenii de arhitectură în Bucureşti. 1945–1989.* Bucharest: Simetria.

Paperny, Vladimir. 2002. *Architecture in the Age of Stalin: Culture Two.* Cambridge, UK: Cambridge University Press.

Patmore, Derek. 1939. *Invitation to Roumania.* New York: Macmillan.

Patrik, Linda. 1985. "Is There an Archaeological Record?" *Advances in Archaeological Method and Theory* 8:27–62.

Pavel, Sorin, Ion Nestor, and Petre Marcu-Balş. 1928. "Manifestul Crinului Alb." *Gândirea* 8 (8–9): 311–17.

Petrescu, Dragoş. 2009. "Building the Nation, Instrumentalizing Nationalism: Revisiting Romanian National-Communism, 1956–1989." *Nationalities Papers* 37 (4): 523–44.

Pop, Ioan Aurel, and Marius Porumb. 2004. *Patrimoniul cultural al României. Transilvania.* Cluj-Napoca: Centrul de Studii Transilvane.

Popa, Maria Raluca. 2004. "Restructuring and Envisioning Bucharest: The Socialist Project in the Context of Romanian Planning for a Capital, a Fast Changing City and an Inherited Urban Space, 1852–1989." PhD diss., Central European University.

———. 2007. "Understanding the Urban Past: The Transformation of Bucharest in the Late Socialist Period." In *Testimonies of the City: Identity, Community and Change in a Contemporary Urban World*, edited by Richard Rodger and Joanna Herbert, 159–86. Aldershot, UK: Ashgate.

Popescu, Carmen. 2004a. "A Denied Continuity: The Shift of 'Heritage' as Ideology in Romanian Socialist Architecture." *Blok* 3:11–31.

———. 2004b. *Le style national roumain: Construire une nation a travers l'architecture.* Rennes: Presses Universitaires de Rennes/Simetria.

———. 2009. "Looking West: Emulation and Limitation in Romanian Architectural Discourse." *Architecture* 14 (1): 109–28.

Poulantzas, Nicos. 1980. *State, Power, Socialism.* London: New Left Books.

Prott, Lyndel V. 2005. "The International Movement of Cultural Objects." *International Journal of Cultural Property* 12 (2): 225–48.

Rady, Martyn. 1995. "Nationalism and Nationality in Romania." In *Contemporary Nationalism in East Central Europe*, edited by P. Latiawski, 127–42. New York: St. Martin's.

Rogers, Douglas. 2004. *The Old Faith and the Russian Land: A Historical Ethnography of Ethics in the Urals.* Ithaca, NY: Cornell University Press.

Rosen, Avram. 1995. *Participarea evreilor la dezvoltarea industrială a Bucureştiului din a doua jumătate a secolului XIX pâna în anul 1938.* Bucharest: Hasefer.

Rosetti, Dinu V. 1932. *Câteva aşezări şi locuinţe preistorice din preajma Bucureştilor. Asupra tehnicei, tipologiei şi cronologiei lor.* Bucharest: Institutul de arte grafice "Bucovina."

———. 1959. "Curtea Veche." In *Bucureştii de odinioară în lumina cercetărilor arheologice*, edited by I. Ionaşcu, 147–65. Bucharest: Editura Ştiinţifică.

———. 1971. "Însemnări privind activitatea Muzeului Municipal (1931–1948)." *Muzeul de Istorie al Municipiului* 8:349–56.

Rotman, Liviu. 2004. *Evreii din România în perioada comunistă, 1944–1965.* Iaşi: Polirom.

Rowland, Michael. 2004. "Cultural Rights and Wrongs: Uses of the Concept of Property." In *Property in Question: Value Transformation in the Global Economy*, edited by Katherine Verdery and Caroline Humphrey, 207–27. New York: Berg.

Rubin, Eli. 2016. *Amnesiopolis: Modernity, Space, and Memory in East Germany.* Oxford, UK: Oxford University Press.

Rughiniş, Cosima, and Gabor Fleck. 2008. *Come Closer: Inclusion and Exclusion of Roma in Present-Day Romanian Society.* Bucharest: Human Dynamics.

Sampson, Steven. 1984. *National Integration through Socialist Planning: An Anthropological Study of a Romanian New Town.* New York: Columbia University Press.

Sanders, Todd, and Harry G. West. 2003. "Power Revealed and Concealed in the New World Order." In *Transparency and Conspiracy: Ethnographies of Suspicion in the New World Order*, edited by Harry G. West and Todd Sanders, 1–37. Durham, NC: Duke University Press.

Sandu, Dumitru. 1999. *Spațiul social al tranziției*. Iași: Polirom.

SAR (Societatea academică din România). 2008. *Restituirea proprietății: De ce a ieșit așa prost în România*. Online Policy Brief no. 34, September 2008, http://sar.org.ro/wp-content/uploads/2012/12/Restituirea-Proprietatii.pdf.

Schlögel, Karl. 2014. *Moscow, 1937*. Translated by Rodney Livingstone. Cambridge, UK: Polity.

Senkevitch, Anatole, Jr. 1978. "Art, Architecture, and Design: A Commentary." *Slavic Review* 37 (4): 587–94.

Sfințescu, Cincinat. 1932. *Pentru București; Noi studii urbanistice. Delimitări, zonificare, circulație, estetică*. Bucharest: Institutul de Arte Grafice "Bucovina."

Shaw, Jennifer, and Darren Byler. 2016. "Precarity." *Cultural Anthropology* 29 (1). https://culanth.org/curated_collections/21-precarity.

Silberman, Neil A. 2012. "Heritage Interpretation and Human Rights: Documenting Diversity, Expressing Identity, or Establishing Universal Principles?" *International Journal of Heritage Studies* 18 (3): 245–56.

Silverman, Helaine, and D. Fairchild Ruggles, eds. 2007. *Cultural Heritage and Human Rights*. New York: Springer.

Smith, Laurajane. 2006. *Uses of Heritage*. New York: Routledge.

Smith, Neil. 2002. "New Globalism, New Urbanism: Gentrification as Global Urban Strategy." *Antipode* 34 (3): 427–50.

Solomon, Alexandru, dir. 2010. *Kapitalism—Rețeta noastră secretă*. Bucharest: HI Film Productions. DVD.

Stallybrass, Peter, and Allon White. 1986. *The Politics and Poetics of Transgression*. Ithaca, NY: Cornell University Press.

Stamati, Iurie. 2015. "Two Chapters of the Sovietization of the Romanian Archaeology (from the Late 1940s to the Mid-1950s)." *Archaeologia Bulgarica* 19 (1): 81–95.

———. 2016. "'Long Live Romanian Soviet Friendship!' An Exploration of the Relationship between Archaeologists from USSR and the People's/Socialist Republic of Romania." *Ephemeris Napocensis* 26:235–52.

Stan, Lavinia. 2006. "The Roof over Our Heads: Property Restitution in Romania." *Communist Studies and Transition Politics* 22 (2): 180–205.

———. 2013. *Transitional Justice in Post-Communist Romania: The Politics of Memory*. Cambridge, UK: Cambridge University Press.

Stark, David, and Laszlo Bruszt. 1998. *Postsocialist Pathways: Transforming Politics and Property in East Central Europe*. Cambridge, UK: Cambridge University Press.

Stoica, Cătălin Augustin. 1997. "Communism as a Project for Modernization: The Romanian Case." *Polish Sociological Review* 120:313–31.

Stolcke, Verena. 1995. "Talking Culture: New Boundaries, New Rhetorics of Exclusion in Europe." *Current Anthropology* 36 (1): 1–24.

Stoler, Ann Laura. 2009. *Along the Archival Grain: Epistemic Anxieties and Colonial Common Sense*. Princeton, NJ: Princeton University Press.

———. 2013. Introduction to *Imperial Debris: On Ruins and Ruination*, edited by Ann Laura Stoler, 1–38. Durham, NC: Duke University Press.

Strathern, Marilyn. 1988. *The Gender of the Gift: Problems with Women and Problems with Society in Melanesia*. Berkeley: University of California Press.

———. 1999. *Property, Substance, and Effect: Anthropological Essays on Persons and Things*. London: Athlone.

Stroe, Miruna. 2015. *Locuirea între proiect și decizie politică: România 1954–1966*. Bucharest: Simetria.

Swenson, Astrid. 2013. *The Rise of Heritage: Preserving the Past in France, Germany and England, 1789–1914*. Cambridge, UK: Cambridge University Press.

Teodorescu, Victor. 1964. "Despre cultura Ipotești-Cîndești în lumina cercetărilor arheologice din nordul-estul Munteniei (regiunea Ploiești)." *Studii și cercetări de istorie veche* 15 (4): 485–503.

———. 1971. "La civilisation Ipotești-Cîndești (V–VII-e s.)." In *Actes du VII-e Congrès international des sciences préhistoriques et protohistoriques, 21–27 août 1966*, edited by J. Filip, 1041–44. Prague: Academia.

Theodorescu, Răzvan. 1974. *Bizanț, Balcani, Occident, la începuturile culturii medievale românești: secolele X–XIV*. Bucharest: Editura Academiei Republicii Socialiste România.

Tismăneanu, Vladimir. 1992. "Gheorghiu-Dej and the Romanian Workers' Party: From De-Sovietization to the Emergence of National Communism." Working paper no. 37, Woodrow Wilson Center.

———. 2003. *Stalinism for All Seasons*. Berkeley: University of California Press.

———. 2008. *Fantoma lui Gheorghiu Dej*. Bucharest: Humanitas.

Tismăneanu, Vladimir, et al. 2006. *Comisia Prezidențială pentru Analiza Dictaturii Comuniste din România: Raport Final*. Bucharest: n.p. https://www.wilsoncenter.org/sites/default/files/RAPORT%20FINAL_%20CADCR.pdf.

Trigger, Bruce G. 1990. *A History of Archaeological Thought*. Cambridge, UK: Cambridge University Press.

Trouillot, Michel-Rolph. 1995. *Silencing the Past: Power and the Production of History*. Boston: Beacon.

———. 2001. "The Anthropology of the State in the Age of Globalization: Close Encounters of the Deceptive Kind." *Cultural Anthropology* 42 (1): 125–33.

Tulbure, Narcis. 2013. "Chary Opportunists: Money, Values, and Change in Postsocialist Romania." PhD diss., University of Pittsburgh.

Vasile, Cristian, and Vladimir Tismăneanu. 2013. *Perfectul acrobat. Leonte Răutu, măștile răului*. Bucharest: Humanitas.

Vasile, Cristian, ed. 2017. *"Ne trebuie oameni!" Elite intelectuale și transformări istorice în România modernă și contemporană*. Târgoviște: Cetatea de Scaun.

Verdery, Katherine. 1991. *National Ideology under Socialism: Identity and Cultural Politics in Ceausescu's Romania*. Berkeley: University of California Press.

———. 1996. *What Was Socialism, and What Comes Next?* Princeton, NJ: Princeton University Press.

———. 2003. *The Vanishing Hectare: Property and Value in Postsocialist Transylvania*. Ithaca, NY: Cornell University Press.

Verdery, Katherine, and Caroline Humphrey, eds. 2004. *Property in Question: Value Transformation in the Global Economy*. New York: Berg.

Waldman, Felicia, and Anca Ciuciu. 2011. *Istorii și imagini din Bucureștiul evreiesc*. Bucharest: Noi Media Print.

Weber, Max. (1889) 2003. *The History of Commercial Partnerships in the Middle Ages.* Translated by Lutz Kaelber. Lanham, MD: Rowman and Littlefield.

Weiner, Annette B. 1992. *Inalienable Possessions: The Paradox of Keeping-while-Giving.* Berkeley: University of California Press.

World Bank. 1997. *Romania: Poverty and Social Policy. Volume 1: Main Report.* Washington, DC: World Bank.

Zarecor, Kimberly. 2011. *Manufacturing a Socialist Modernity: Housing in Czechoslovakia, 1945–1960.* Pittsburgh, PA: University of Pittsburgh Press.

INDEX

Numbers in italics refer to illustrations.

EMANUELA GRAMA is Associate Professor of Anthropology and History at Carnegie Mellon University.